Salesforce Platform Governance Method

A Guide to Governing Changes, Development, and Enhancements on the Salesforce Platform

Lee Harding
Lee Bayliss

Apress®

Salesforce Platform Governance Method: A Guide to Governing Changes,
Development, and Enhancements on the Salesforce Platform

Lee Harding
Clayton-le-Woods, UK

Lee Bayliss
Clifton, UK

ISBN-13 (pbk): 978-1-4842-7403-3
https://doi.org/10.1007/978-1-4842-7404-0

ISBN-13 (electronic): 978-1-4842-7404-0

Managing Director, Apress Media LLC: Welmoed Spahr
Acquisitions Editor: Susan McDermott
Development Editor: Laura Berendson
Coordinating Editor: Shrikant Vishwakarma
Copyeditor: April Rondeau

Cover designed by eStudioCalamar

Cover image designed by Pexels

Distributed to the book trade worldwide by Springer Science+Business Media LLC, 1 New York Plaza, Suite 4600, New York, NY 10004. Phone 1-800-SPRINGER, fax (201) 348-4505, email orders-ny@springer-sbm. com, or visit www.springeronline.com. Apress Media, LLC is a California LLC and the sole member (owner) is Springer Science+Business Media Finance Inc (SSBM Finance Inc). SSBM Finance Inc is a **Delaware** corporation.

For information on translations, please e-mail booktranslations@springernature.com; for reprint, paperback, or audio rights, please e-mail bookpermissions@springernature.com, or visit http://www.apress. com/rights-permissions.

Apress titles may be purchased in bulk for academic, corporate, or promotional use. eBook versions and licenses are also available for most titles. For more information, reference our Print and eBook Bulk Sales web page at http://www.apress.com/bulk-sales.

Any source code or other supplementary material referenced by the authors in this book is available to readers on GitHub via the book's product page, located at https://link.springer.com/book/10.1007/978-1-4842-7403-3.

Printed on acid-free paper

It takes more than the author(s) to write a book that tackles an IT subject area. Books are mainly about sharing your knowledge, which in turn is gained from the people you work with and those who influence you. It is these people who provide the balance of work and life and help you grow into the person you become. I would like to thank all those people who have helped me, taught me, influenced me, and challenged me on the path that has brought me to this moment.

—Lee Harding

Table of Contents

About the Authors

Lee Harding, formerly a senior program architect at Salesforce, is the technology director at Harwoods Group, a large automotive retail company in the United Kingdom. Harwoods uses Salesforce's technology at the heart of its digital transformation and considers it a key enabler for the Harwoods business in the future. Over his 35 years in IT, Lee has used his skills and experience to help both large and small enterprises deliver business transformations. Lee has handled big transformational programs involving tens of thousands of users, and has helped customers get the most out of their investment in Salesforce Cloud technologies. Using his experience with large-scale transformation projects, Lee has helped many businesses accelerate their implementations and see benefits sooner, rather than later. With his broad knowledge base and keen interest in technology and its governance, Lee has been able to help customers navigate the pros and cons of technology decisions, and he keeps an open mind as to how technology can benefit his customers at the earliest opportunity, while instilling the right processes to help his customers be successful.

Lee Bayliss, a senior program architect at Salesforce, has worked in the IT industry for over 25 years and has held various positions in operations, engineering, product design, technical leadership, and Lead Architect for large service providers, such as DXC (formerly EDS/HPES). During Lee's extensive career in IT, he has worked across many industry sectors, including manufacturing, oil exploration, financial services, and health life sciences. Working with myriad enterprise businesses, Lee has amassed a wealth of experience delivering IT solutions ranging from lightweight projects to large-scale business transformations. For the last three years, Lee has been working for Salesforce, a company that is diverse in nature and focused on customer success. Salesforce has created a huge ecosystem of products and services that can help propel SME (Small, Medium, Enterprise) businesses to become trailblazers in their field. At Salesforce, Lee finds himself in the unique position of providing guidance on all of the things that large (and small) organizations struggle with: how to implement the Salesforce platform and its components successfully, how to control all the moving parts, and how to drive value throughout the business in a world where digital transformation is a success imperative.

About the Technical Reviewer

 **Kal Chintala** is one of around 300 Salesforce Certified Technical Architects (CTA) worldwide. He is an executive-level strategic advisor and Salesforce expert who solves complex, large-scale challenges across the Salesforce platform to produce solutions that maximize the full potential of Salesforce. Kal works with key business and technical stakeholders on their program vision and articulates strategies that enable technologies to achieve that vision. Kal has 15 years of experience delivering Salesforce CRM and KM systems architecture, software design, and data modeling; executing agile delivery; managing technical risk and change; and performing software quality assurance for enterprise-wide transformations. Kal has managed the Salesforce architecture for 65,000 global users for a Fortune 500 financial services company, including achieving more than $1.2 million in operational efficiencies by consolidating services into a single Salesforce application. He achieves operational efficiencies through innovative applications of technology and business process enhancements. In his current role at Accenture, Kal acts as a Salesforce practice strategy advisor, technology lead, and SME for forming a roadmap for the delivery of complex, enterprise-wide Salesforce implementations across Accenture clients. From an education qualifications standpoint, Kal earned a Master of Technology from Latrobe University, Australia, and has a Bachelor of Technology from Madras University, India. Kal has more than 20 certifications, including multiple certifications in Salesforce and many others around agile, etc.

Acknowledgments

First and foremost, there are no words that can express my gratitude to my wife and family, who were very patient and supportive while I worked throughout the evenings and weekends to complete this book. I am sure they are now grateful for the break, and perhaps know far more about governing the Salesforce platform than they ever wanted to know.

I am also very grateful to the team at Apress, especially Susan McDermott, whom Lee and I initially contacted about the idea of the book and who gave us the support and encouragement to make it happen. Also, to Shrikant Vishwakarma, who tirelessly checked in with us to make sure we knew what needed to be done and was patient and supportive when we were a little late. A big thank you to Laura Berendson for helping us get the book through its final stages.

I would like to extend a very warm thank you to Kal Chintala for his feedback and comments, which have helped improve this book from its original draft.

Last but by no means least, I would like to extend our gratitude to the Salesforce community and ecosystem that gave me the inspiration to write this book.

—Lee Harding

When Lee (Harding) approached me with the idea of writing a book, I was at first skeptical and unsure if this was something that I could commit to, or if I could support Lee in this process. However, we discussed the concept, and as we developed our ideas and discussed the approach to governance that we would take, I decided that this was something I just had to be involved in. I'm so pleased that I decided to embark on this unbelievable journey with him. For me, this has been a cathartic exercise of discovery, giving me the chance to work closely with a valued colleague, friend, and fellow technologist, which has been an enjoyable, and at times stressful, but ultimately a fantastic experience.

My family has been amazing: my wife, Claire, and my three children have been very supportive and encouraging throughout. However, my middle son was relieved once I could get back outside to play football with him after the writing and research were complete.

ACKNOWLEDGMENTS

I would also like to thank the Apress team, with a special mention to Kal Chintala, Susan McDermott, and Shrikant Vishwakarma for their support and encouragement throughout this process. Kal's thought-provoking and constructive comments were a source of inspiration and were always appreciated.

And finally, I would like to thank all the Salesforce trailblazers out there who work tirelessly to reimagine how to run their businesses on possibly the greatest cloud platform available in the marketplace. I sincerely hope that this book helps you to continue to realize success and to support your business process as you achieve limitless business outcomes.

—Lee Bayliss

Introduction

Both of our careers have been spent entirely in the information technology arena, and we sometimes crossed paths as we worked on various projects in all manner of industries. We both arrived at Salesforce later in your overall entire careers you came across Salesforce and were PAs at that time. During our engagements as PAs, we noticed that companies were looking to implement the Salesforce platform without using the normal governance and controls that we would have expected from large IT projects, and it got us thinking as to why this was.

For some businesses, providing users access to the Salesforce platform as their customer relationship management (CRM) system was no different from providing Microsoft Office to users as their productivity suite. This led us to observe a number of instances in which the typical controls and governance that we would expect to see were just not there. This demonstrated to us that there was a gap in the understanding of not only the Salesforce platform, but also how important Salesforce has become as the cornerstone of so many successful businesses. It is fair to say that without the Salesforce platform, many businesses simply would not operate or be in a position to achieve the desired business outcomes demanded by customers in this modern age.

With our background in large IT project implementations and business transformations, we had always put governance and control at the forefront of the delivery process. Ultimately, we were delivering projects that would underpin a business going forward, so why wouldn't they deserve rigorous control and adherence to standards with stakeholder participation and support?

One thing that makes the Salesforce platform unique is its diversity of use. Mark Beneoff raised this exact challenge during a conference discussion. The Salesforce platform is used by every size and type of business, from corner shops to multi-billion-dollar enterprises. Therefore, there was a need for a governance method that really covered the diversity of Salesforce's platform implementations.

We are not suggesting that a corner shop needs a lot of governance and control, and it is quite possible that they could use the platform with little to no changes, but in our experience there are always changes made to the platform, and how these changes are managed and governed could ultimately dictate the impact that they have on a business and its success.

This led us to create the Salesforce Platform Governance Method. Our solution, designed over many years while working with numerous customers, helps companies to govern this platform that has such diverse usage. We have worked with all sizes and types of companies, and used the platform for all manner of reasons, in some cases moving away from the basic CRM concept.

Our governance method is designed to help everyone take the time to help themselves, to deliver changes on the platform and challenge themselves that those changes are as good as they can be. We are trying to help customers to reduce their technical debt, and to make technical decisions that aid the business while ensuring the solution does not become something they will later regret. This is by no means a simple task. The Salesforce platform is known for its ability to deliver rapid changes, which is an aspect Salesforce customers love. The declarative nature of the platform makes creating a change a simple process to execute. However, governance applies to all aspects of change; just because something is easy to implement does not mean you should do it without due care and attention—the premise of solution governance. This is the core message of this book: how to deliver change that enables the business to move forward and grow, while considering the concepts of good governance. The challenge was to come up with something that was as lightweight as we could make it, while covering the breadth of the Salesforce platform's features.

We hope we have done something that you will find helpful in achieving a comfortable level of control over your Salesforce platform instance. We have tried to make the method something that you can pick from, like a menu in a restaurant, rather than your having to take everything offered.

We suspect that this book is the start rather than the final thing. The Salesforce platform does not stand still. With three releases each year, it is likely that features will come and features will go, and as such this governance method will ebb and flow. You should consider this a journey of change, as it has to be with a platform that constantly changes. Take what we have created and tailor it to your needs.

We wish you all success and hope you enjoy this book.

—Lee & Lee

CHAPTER 1

Salesforce Platform Governance Method

The Salesforce Platform Governance Method is designed to help organizations meet their strategic and tactical goals for utilizing the Salesforce platform.

The Salesforce Platform Governance Method can support the full spectrum of development activity on the Salesforce platform and is suitable for everything from the needs of your company's development on the platform through to the needs of a service integrator (SI) that has large teams of developers.

The Salesforce Platform Governance Method provides an organization assurance that all development activity taking place on the Salesforce platform is done in a consistent manner and to a consistent set of standards. This is not to say every developer will produce exactly the same solution given a common set of requirements. It does, however, mean that there is consistency in the structure and usage of the platform so that the same "rules" apply to anyone using the platform to deliver business value.

This goal is important because over time, without a clear set of standards, developers will just follow their own rules. The more developers that create applications that way, the higher the degree of technical debt that will build up, to the point where an application may be deployed and no one really has a clear understanding of what it does and why.

Note   One of the main reasons companies engage Salesforce's advisory services, and specifically engage a program architect, is to unpick the mess they have allowed their Salesforce platform to become.

© Lee Harding and Lee Bayliss 2022
L. Harding and L. Bayliss, *Salesforce Platform Governance Method*,
https://doi.org/10.1007/978-1-4842-7404-0_1

Overview

The Salesforce Platform Governance Method is split into two parts: the method, which utilizes nine phases to provide coverage to govern the Salesforce platform; and the resource base, which provides best practices and lessons learned so as to provide an initial set of standards to govern by.

The Method

As previously mentioned, the method is split into phases. Each phase is consistent in its approach. As this is a method, it is possible to simply reference the phase directly that relates to the area that requires governance, rather than tackle each phase one at a time. The nine phases are detailed in Table 1-1.

Table 1-1. *The Salesforce Platform Governance Method Phases*

Phase	Description
A – Application Architecture	The objective of Phase A is to ensure that this evolution of the application has adhered to the technical standards and policies defined for the Salesforce platform. The areas that will be assessed are as follows: • General Architecture • Localization / Global Deployments • Workflow and Process • Formulas • Files and Social
B – Data Architecture & Management	The objective of Phase B is to ensure that this evolution of the application has adhered to the technical standards and policies defined for the Salesforce platform. The following areas will be assessed during this phase: • Design and Optimization • Data Movement

(continued)

Table 1-1. (*continued*)

Phase	Description
C – Identity & Access Management	The objective of Phase C is to ensure that this evolution of the application has adhered to the technical standards and policies defined for the Salesforce platform. The following areas will be assessed during this phase: • Single Sign-On • Identity Management
D – Sharing & Visibility	The objective of Phase D is to ensure that this evolution of the application has adhered to the technical standards and policies defined for the Salesforce platform. The areas that will be assessed during this phase are as follows: • Declarative Sharing • Programmatic Sharing • Performance • Data Security
E – Integration	The objective of Phase E is to ensure that this evolution of the application has adhered to the technical standards and policies defined for the Salesforce platform. The areas that will be assessed during this phase are as follows: • Technologies and Overall Integration Strategy • Integration Solution Tools • Security
F – Apex, Visualforce & Lightning	The objective of Phase F is to ensure that this evolution of the application has adhered to the technical standards and policies defined for the Salesforce platform. The following areas will be assessed during this phase: • Design and Functionality • Performance and Scalability • Maintainability and Reuse
G – Communities	The objective of Phase G is to ensure that this evolution of the application has adhered to the technical standards and policies defined for the Salesforce platform. The following areas will be assessed during this phase: • Design • Identity Management

(*continued*)

3

Table 1-1. (*continued*)

Phase	Description
H – Mobile Solutions Architecture	The objective of Phase H is to ensure that this evolution of the application has adhered to the technical standards and policies defined for the Salesforce platform. The areas that will be assessed during this phase are as follows: • Mobile Strategy and Design • Mobile Security
I – Development Lifecycle & Deployment	The objective of Phase I is to ensure that this evolution of the application has adhered to the technical standards and policies defined for the Salesforce platform. The following areas will be assessed during this phase: • Development Lifecycle • Deployment Techniques and Considerations

These phases relate almost exactly to the path taken by a Salesforce certified technical architect (CTA), providing synergy between the educational path to understanding the Salesforce platform and the ability to govern it.

As previously mentioned, the Salesforce Platform Governance Method is designed to be referenced directly at the phase level (i.e., the phase that is currently being governed), so in that respect there is consistency in the way each phase has been documented. Figure 1-1 provides an overview of that structure.

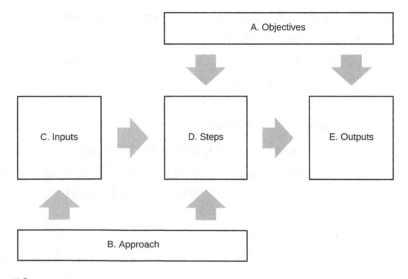

Figure 1-1. *Phase structure*

Table 1-2 provides a definition of the elements that define the phase structure.

Table 1-2. *Phase Structure Definitions*

Method Component	Description
A – Objectives	A specific result that the phase aims to achieve. In general, objectives are more specific and easier to measure than goals. Objectives are basic tools that underlie all planning and strategic activities.
B – Approach	A recommendation as to how the phase will be implemented and/or executed
C – Inputs	The artifacts that must be available before the phase can commence. Artifacts are key inputs into the phase steps.
D – Steps	The steps and sub-steps that should be completed for each phase to determine complete coverage of a project/product from a governance perspective
E – Outputs	The artifacts that will be produced by the phase and created during the steps

Although the phases clearly state what needs to be done to govern a solution on the Salesforce platform, it is the resource base that can be used as a starting point for the standards that governance should use to assess your projects' applications.

The Resource Base

The resource base is a set of resources—best practices, tooling ideas, guidelines, templates, checklists, and other detailed documents—that support each of the Salesforce Platform Governance Method phases. These resources can be used as is, tailored, or replaced to meet your requirements. The resources will underpin the Salesforce Platform Governance Method; therefore, it is critical that they work within the phases and support the inputs and outputs as detailed in the method.

Key Points

As a generic method, the Salesforce Platform Governance Method is intended to be used by enterprises in a wide variety of different geographies and applied in different vertical sectors and industry types. As such, it may be, but does not necessarily have to be, tailored to your specific needs. For example:

- It may be used in conjunction with the set of deliverables of another framework, where these have been deemed more appropriate for a specific organization.

- Some of the phases may be deemed as not required—for example, the mobile solutions architecture phase—if no requirement exists within the organization.

- The order of the phases is intentional, but not fixed. It may be that for certain organizations the order of the phases may change if early warnings are required for specific areas; for example, integration may be a key consideration that requires early assessment before any other phase is considered.

Basic Structure

The basic structure of the Salesforce Platform Governance Method is shown in its cycle. Throughout the cycle, there needs to be frequent validation of results against the original expectations, both those for the whole cycle and those for the phase of the method. Figure 1-2 shows the entirety of the cycle.

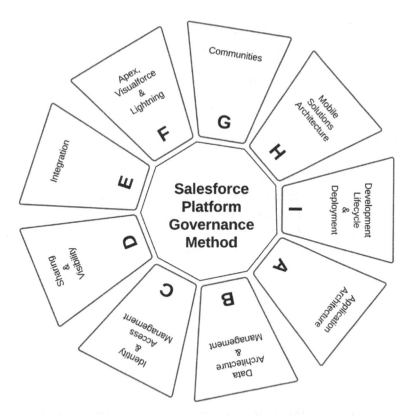

Figure 1-2. *Salesforce Platform Governance Method cycle*

Although your organization is at liberty to adjust the phases, there is a logical order to them. Each phase takes a more comprehensive and deeper technical view of your project's application.

Given that there is an order to the phases, it is envisaged that each phase provides the "gate" via which to proceed to the next phase. However, this should be a consideration during implementation of the Salesforce Platform Governance Method as you may prefer to assess the application in its entirety rather than phase by phase. The issue with not following the phased approach is that some phases may become unnecessary if an application fails prior phases (i.e., the phase will fail as a result of a prior failure).

The phases of the Salesforce Platform Governance Method cycle are further divided into subject areas, such as the ones depicted by the expansion of the Sharing & Visibility phase in Figure 1-3.

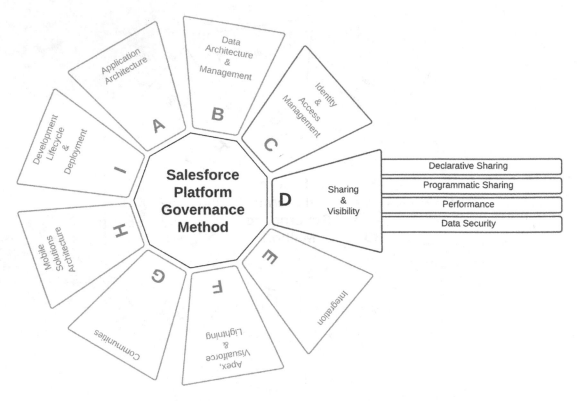

Figure 1-3. *Salesforce Platform Governance Method cycle, expanded*

The phases of the cycle are described in detail within the subsequent chapters. Note that outputs are generated throughout the process of using the method, and that the output in an early phase may be modified in a later phase; for example, the Identity & Access Management phase may have a bearing on the Communities phase.

Method Adaption

The Salesforce Platform Governance Method is a generic method for governing development on the Salesforce platform, and is designed to deal with most application and organizational requirements that use the Salesforce platform to either develop applications from scratch or enhance existing configurations or SaaS solutions (such as simply adding fields to SalesCloud or ServiceCloud objects).

Architecture Governance

The method, whether adapted by your organization or used as documented here, is a key artifact to be managed in the same manner as any other architecture artifacts in the Enterprise Continuum. The Architecture Board should be satisfied that the method is being applied correctly across all phases and iterations of application development. Compliance with the method is fundamental to the governance of the architecture, ensuring that all considerations are made and all required deliverables are produced.

Process Management

The management of all architecture artifacts, governance, and related processes should be supported by a managed environment. Typically, this would be based on one or more repositories supporting versioned object and process control and status.

The tailored method should be managed as with any other architecture artifact. The method will no doubt undergo a number of changes as refinement of the phases occurs. Additionally, the resource base is a key area that requires the artifacts that are used to implement the method be managed so that they are kept in line with the method itself.

Beyond version control, process management extends to the implementation of the process to support the method. Ideally, this process will control the governance gates that at a minimum control whether an application or project has passed or failed its governance.

Scoping the Application Governance Cycle

There are many reasons to want to limit the scope of the Salesforce Application Governance Method, most of which come down to the availability of people, financing, and other resources. The scope chosen for the architecture activity is normally directly dependent on available resources, and the final analysis is usually a question of feasibility.

Although the method's implementation is envisioned to be mainly software/tooling–driven with a goal of full automation, implementation of the full method may not be relevant if the organization has no appetite for such things, or if the amount of governance required is minimal based on simplistic applications.

Additionally, the target community should be considered when scoping the cycle. Citizen developers will more than likely develop less-sophisticated applications than a service integrator, whether due to level of expertise or to restrictions imposed on citizen developers.

Summary

The Salesforce Platform Governance Method defines a recommended sequence for the various phases and steps involved in governing the development of an application, but it cannot recommend a scope. This is determined by the organization or project.

Your governance team should review the method and determine what phases are relevant for your specific requirements and tailor it from there. It is, however, imagined that an organization of significant size wishing to encourage in-house development as well as large-scale project development undertaken by service integrators will almost certainly implement this method as-is, with a focus on tooling and processes.

CHAPTER 2

Application Architecture: Phase A

Phase A of the Salesforce Platform Governance Method tackles the application architecture aspects of your Salesforce solution. This is a more general view of the approach your team has taken to construct your solution.

Overview

The application architecture phase is shown in Figure 2-1. The architecture of your solution, if wrong, can create a lot of downstream technical debt. Getting the architecture correct early in the lifecycle of your solution will pay dividends in the future.

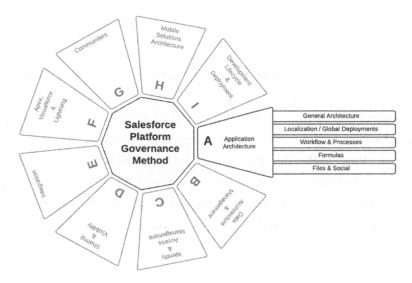

Figure 2-1. *The Salesforce Platform Governance Method, Phase A*

© Lee Harding and Lee Bayliss 2022
L. Harding and L. Bayliss, *Salesforce Platform Governance Method*,
https://doi.org/10.1007/978-1-4842-7404-0_2

Let's start by defining what we mean by application architecture, as it can have a few definitions. In the context of the Salesforce Platform Governance Method, we think the Gartner definition works well.

> *"Application architecture is the discipline that guides application design. Application architecture paradigms, such as service-oriented architecture (SOA), provide principles that influence design decisions and patterns that provide proven design solutions."*

—Gartner[1]

As the Salesforce platform already adheres to Salesforce's application architecture, Salesforce has already provided a technical framework of sorts in which you can construct your application. However, the technical options within that framework are quite extensive. This provides a significant level of flexibility in your project's application architecture, even though it effectively sits on top of the Salesforce platform's application architecture.

To put this into context, let's look at automation within the Salesforce platform. Automation can be accomplished using several technical options; for example:

- Flows

- Process Builder

- Workflows

- Apex

There are other options that might be considered less general and no doubt many more to come from Salesforce, but this highlights that, given the platform's technical options, the construction of your application can make use of any or all of these technical options for automation. Sometimes it is possible to achieve the same solution in any of those options (e.g., Process Builder and Flows, which at the metadata level are similar).

However, leveraging multiple options on the same object or area of your application can complicate your solution. If you have multiple developers or "app builders" using every and any automation solution provided by the platform, maintenance could become an issue.

---

[1] https://www.gartner.com/en/information-technology/glossary/application-architecture-aa#:~:text=Application%20architecture%20is%20the%20discipline,that%20provide%20proven%20design%20solutions

Our governance method does not dictate which technical options offered by the Salesforce platform you should use, as that is generally the responsibility of a technical policy in place within your organization, but rather shows how a project should govern the use of those technical options regardless.

It is desirable to standardize your governance, as tailoring the approach to governing an application's architecture in every instance of that application created within your organization would be too time consuming. Additionally, having varying governance within an organization just confuses people.

Further, how much governance you apply is something that your organization will need to decide and should be set at the organization level and not at the project level. Leave it to a project to set its own governance level and no governance will take place, or the project will fly through governance with everything "good to go."

In the context of governing a Salesforce platform application, application architecture encompasses the following broad areas that contain numerous technical options offered by the Salesforce platform:

- General Architecture (see Figure 2-2)

- Localization / Global Deployments

- Workflow and Process

- Formulas

- Files and Social

General Architecture

As shown in Figure 2-2, general architecture is the initial area in which to focus your governance activity.

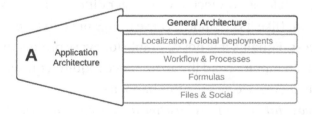

Figure 2-2. *Phase A: application architecture – general architecture*

When you are governing the general architecture of an application, your governing body looks to understand the construction of your application and whether it has considered a number of key points.

Has the project considered whether the application has been designed for optimal performance, scalability, usability, and ease of maintenance?

This is heavily context driven, as understanding the context in which your application will be used is important. There are big differences between constructing an application targeted for a few hundred concurrent users and doing so for tens of thousands of concurrent users (yes, the Salesforce platform can inherently scale from one extreme to the other). In general, the more users, the more processes are active, and the more data are created and consumed. These all play a part in the performance and scalability of your application.

If the application has an apex batch element to it, knowing whether you are going to process thousands of records or millions of records makes a big difference in how that aspect of the application should be constructed. Additionally, you want to govern the application in that context. If the application was only designed to be used by one hundred users, then it should be governed within that context. Equally, if the application was designed for a hundred thousand users, the governance should perhaps be a little more stringent. That is not to say the method of governance should be different.

Maintenance is a big issue. It can be very easy to create a mess in any platform, and Salesforce's platform is no different. When governing the application architecture, determining the maintainability of your application is key, not only in the context of maintaining the application in its own isolation, but also in its coexistence with other applications that reside within the same Salesforce org.

The ability to customize standard components within the Salesforce platform is second to none, but that customization becomes a bottleneck when several projects all try to modify those standard components. Take the Account object as a simple example. All too often, different projects try to trigger different processes based on things occurring to an account (like its creation). These things need to be considered during the governance process. Equally, it is not desirable for every project to invent its own Account object in an attempt to avoid the governance required on standard objects used across multiple projects (yes, we've seen this happen).

Govern the appropriate use of declarative and programmatic functionality.

This is key and often a difficult area to govern; after all, governance can be subjective. However, the main goal when governing declarative versus programmatic functionality should be to remind ourselves of what was just discussed: maintenance. If you have a

14

development team that has transitioned to the Salesforce platform from more traditional development technologies, then it would not be surprising to find a high number of programmatic solutions being used.

This is where the resources governing the organization's Salesforce solution really do need to know the platform. Understanding that a declarative solution could have been used rather than a programmatic solution is very important. Typically, programmatic solutions are more costly, simply because the resources needed to maintain them are more expensive, and working at the coding level is usually more of an art form. Therefore, reading other people's code is not always straightforward.

Note   One example of appropriate use of programmatic functionality was uncovered via a routine governance check during an engagement with a large enterprise. A solution integrator that was delivering projects on the Salesforce platform for the large enterprise had developed a piece of functionality, which took several weeks. The functionality was delivered mainly as code (Apex and Visualforce). Because of the large amount of bespoke code, the core governing body became engaged. On further investigation into the deliverable, it was determined that the same functionality could have been achieved with a mere few hours of declarative changes.

Of course, this scenario raised several questions, such as how you can determine the right route to take when creating customization on the Salesforce platform, and then, having discovered the work already undertaken, who should be paying for the unnecessary work that was done.

However, the damage was already done. The main lesson here is that the application architecture should have been governed before any major work was started. That would have highlighted the approach being taken and perhaps avoided the unnecessary work. This would have delivered a result for the business more quickly and cost the business a lot less.

This point cannot be stressed enough: having someone (or multiple people) within your organization who understands the capabilities of the Salesforce platform is paramount; otherwise, you run the risk of duplicating existing functionality, or going about building a solution in a less-than-platform-friendly and less-efficient manner. It's clear that duplicating existing functionality is time and money wasted.

Govern the considerations for a single-org or dedicated-org strategy.

Depending on the scale of your enterprise, there could be numerous applications being developed or in operation on a single Salesforce org at any one time. If this is the case, careful consideration must be given to the coexistence of these applications. This coexistence can take several forms.

Firstly, the use of standard objects. Have the record types been used appropriately, for example? If triggers exist on standard objects within your application, how will you manage them across projects and applications?

Secondly, the duplication of functionality should be minimized. In some cases, objects might be created at the project level, and over time they might become promoted to enterprise objects so that they can be reused by many applications spanning multiple projects. This could also apply to components and services. Recognizing that this scenario will occur, and in fact encouraging it, should be a key part of the governance process.

Thirdly, the consumption of the platform limits should be carefully considered. Governance should consider any platform-limit consumption in the overall landscape of your enterprise. Salesforce has several limits that may be impacted by the application's architecture, such as API calls or the number of custom objects. Projects that want to consume many specific platform limits may require further consideration in terms of the architecture.

Govern the usage of license types (capabilities and constraints).

Make sure the functionality and features used by your application are appropriately aligned to the licensing available, or have a plan to enhance the licensing as required. Licensing could be at the user level. In addition, the edition of the Salesforce platform that is being used will also carry limitations.

If multiple applications are being deployed by different projects, then some consideration around fairly distributing the licensing may be required so as to avoid one project's consuming the premium licenses, leaving nothing for the follow-up projects your organization has in the pipeline of work.

You will need to question your project's longevity, as well as consider how the application usage may change over time and whether that has been factored into the long-term maintainability of the application and associated costs.

Govern the data modeling concepts and implications of database design.

Your project's data model should be clearly defined and easily readable. Consider using a standard notation such that every submission to the governance body is generally documented in a standard way. You may also consider the use of different styles of data model, as follows, to help accelerate the understanding of the application under governance:

- Conceptual Data Model – Typically created by the business stakeholders and defines WHAT the application should contain

- Logical Data Model – Typically created by data architects or business analysts and defines HOW the application should be implemented, regardless of target platform

- Physical Data Model – Typically created by Salesforce developers and architects and describes HOW the application will be implemented on the platform

---

Note   The approach of using conceptual, logical, and physical data models was described by the American National Standards Institute (ANSI) in 1975 and is still relevant in the construction of applications today.

Standardizing your approach to documenting a data model will help accelerate governance and help your governance team to hone their skills in particular areas.

It is easy to create a poor data model within the Salesforce platform. A low-code approach can sometimes give people the false impression that this means low skills. That is not the case. To create a performant and maintainable application, your data model should be fit for the purpose.

Start by making sure you have named your objects in an informative way. Using nouns from the business domain can sometimes help you determine a good name for a custom object. Make sure you have applied the same principles down to the custom fields within your custom or standard objects. If you are supporting multiple projects that are working on the same Salesforce org (coexisting), you may want to enforce a name-spacing solution. See the resource base for more details on this.

Consider the search requirements of your data model. Salesforce by default allows you to search text fields on an object. Fields with a formula type are excluded from search.

Use record types within your custom or standard objects if you are using a single object to support multiple business requirements and processes. For example, you may have internal accounts and external accounts, which are treated differently. This could be modeled as two record types.

Select the correct data types and sizes for your custom fields. Although there is nothing stopping you from being over generous in sizing text fields within the constraints of the Salesforce platform, it is good practice to keep things sensible, remembering that Salesforce takes a broad 2K assumption of record sizes, except where rich text and file uploads are concerns. Additionally, the PersonAccount standard object is a mash-up of Account and Contact objects, and as such will consume 4K per record. However, the definition of "sensible" is beyond the scope of this book.

Note   An example of a badly sized field is perhaps the URL field type. This is limited to 255 characters (at the time of writing this book). Given the fact that URLs regularly exceed this size, what with today's popularity of cloud-based services, you could even consider that Salesforce doesn't always get it correct. However, as is commonplace, it is possible to overcome this limitation given URL compression tools.

Once you have a clear understanding of the objects and fields used, you will want to move into the relationships the objects have with one another. Again, you can lean on the business domain to get an understanding of the relationships between objects. What is important to remember from a governance perspective is the types of relationships, taking a longer-term view of how the application will work and the types of data that will be created.

Keep platform limits in mind; for example, an object can have up to two master–detail relationships and up to twenty-five total relationships. Look to best practices, such as limiting the number of child records in a master–detail relationship to 10,000 to avoid record skew. Most of all, create your own best practices based on what works from the experience within your organization. This is highlighted further in Phase B.

Take into account the testing required for the data model being governed. From a governance perspective, you should encourage your project to have testing taking place. As such, test data will be required to underpin that testing. Although not something the governance process should take a firm view on, it is important to make sure that it has been considered. As part of the governance checks and balances, a complex data model by its very nature creates complex testing requirements, and therefore a complex set of test data. So, as you'd expect your project to manage its code in a secure and structured manner, you would expect the project to do the same for test data. This is highlighted further in Phase I.

Lastly, consider the complexity of data access. Does your project require complex data visibility? This is highlighted further in Phase D.

Govern the usage of reports and analytics (platform considerations and trade-offs).

Leading on from the data model, reporting becomes an important aspect of your project. It is more than likely that your business will want some level of reporting and analytics back from all the hard work it has put into creating data via the application your project has built. A complex data model more than likely creates complexity in creating reports. A data model that is highly normalized might be difficult to report on.

Note   Normalization is the process of identifying objects by making sure that the object depicts one concept. For example, Case and Account are clearly different concepts and therefore could be considered objects (which they are in the Salesforce data model). It is important not to get carried away in this process, sometimes it is easy to spot concepts, such as Address, Name, and so on. Some people may argue that these could be objects in their own right, but that would create a very complex data model. As a rule of thumb, try to think of business-related concepts.

The more complex your data model, the slower reports will be to run and analytics will be to execute. Keep in mind the reporting strategy of your organization. Do you have standard tools that should be used in certain circumstances? Is the project introducing a new product (e.g., Tableau) that will need to be managed and governed? In the long term, who is responsible for creating reports?

Govern the usage of external applications (Salesforce AppExchange and application integration).

It is more common than not for a project to require the use of an external application. Such an application could be a pre-built component from the Salesforce AppExchange, or an existing system within your organization that contains important information or is part of your end-to-end business process.

When it comes to AppExchange components, from a governance perspective, you are going to look at a few areas.

Does the AppExchange component meet your security requirements? You may need to seek further clarification from your project regarding the due diligence they have performed in determining the security credentials of the component they want to use. Salesforce undertakes a significant number of checks for any component that is available within the AppExchange, but those may not be completely in line with your own security requirements.

Does the AppExchange component meet your commercial requirements? There may be support requirements that are needed by your business. If your application is required 24/7, and you provide in-house support to deliver this, you will need to make sure that any components you use within your application are aligned to these requirements.

The method will detail more areas you will want to govern to make sure you are happy that an AppExchange component is aligned with your organization and business requirements.

Integrating with external systems is a complex area. There are many tools on the market to help simplify this process (such as Salesforce's MuleSoft platform). However, as with the data model, integrating with external systems carries a number of complexities. In fact, the data model may extend into external systems, where data resides elsewhere in your organization's portfolio of systems. From an application architecture perspective, you are going to look at the relationship between those systems and the integration needed. As mentioned earlier with the application usage requirement of 24/7, you will need to make sure any integration with external systems is in alignment with your business requirements. If an external system only offers "near-time" integration, this may not be appropriate for a business process that has an end-user waiting.

Note   Near-time integration refers to data integration that occurs periodically, such as daily. Real-time integration refers to data integration that occurs on demand.

Overall, from a governance perspective, you are looking to understand the holistic application architecture. What systems are integrated to deliver your end-to-end business requirements?

Consider data ownership in the governing of any external system integrations. Understanding which system "owns" the data and is therefore considered the source of the most accurate version of that data will be an important consideration. In governing external system integration at the application architecture level, you will be mainly focusing on looking for discrepancies between requirements: the requirements of the project that you are governing and those that can be delivered by the external systems. In the main, these discrepancies are as follows:

- Does the external system align with the service level required of the project in question?

- Does the external system provide an integration solution that is aligned to meet the requirements of the project in question (such as near-time vs. real-time)?

- What system "owns" the data and therefore is the "source of truth"?

- How important is the accuracy of data to the business processes? Having an up-to-date name and address for your customer may be more important that having the most up-to-date name for one of your products displayed on the screen to the end user.

Phase E will go into more detail as to how to go about governing integration with external systems.

Localization / Global Deployments

As shown in Figure 2-3, localization and global deployments is the next area in which to focus your governance activity.

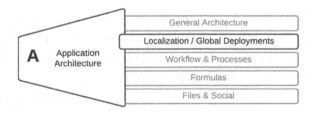

Figure 2-3. *Phase A: application architecture - localization / global deployments*

The Salesforce platform is designed to be used by any business, from a local corner shop through to a multi-national enterprise. As such, it offers many features to support its being used by people all over the world. These features include multiple currencies, translations, and multiple languages.

Fortunately, from an enterprise perspective, Salesforce has taken all the hard work out of deploying the solution to your organization, as they already have a globally accessible deployment of the platform. This leaves you to focus on the business of multiple users in varying countries getting the most out of the solutions you deploy on the platform.

Govern the usage of the platform's internationalization functionality (multiple currencies, translations, and languages).

From a governance perspective, you are focusing on the end-user community to whom the project is hoping to deliver its application. Given this, your governance should consider whether the project has covered the languages and currencies that are required for locations in which you do business.

Currency is one example. You need to make sure that the project has considered the implications of using multiple currencies, such as:

- Field-to-field filters in reports

- Existing records stamped with a default currency you provide

- Decimal places ignored in custom currency fields

These are just a few examples, so you must consider the implications to your Salesforce org when multiple currencies are enabled. Additionally, if you have multiple applications developed and delivered by many different projects, regression testing or some level of impact assessment should be made on those projects.

This may be complicated further if the original projects that created those applications have effectively shut down and are in maintenance mode only. The project that is instigating the multiple-currency change may have to provide support for testing and remediation on projects that are no longer actively in development.

There are two aspects to supporting multiple languages. Setting the language of the Salesforce user interface changes Salesforce to a supported language. This will change the language for any Salesforce-supported text and fields.

Projects that have created data labels for custom objects may introduce the need to use the Salesforce Translation Workbench. This tool allows the project to maintain translated values for metadata and data labels. This will drive another artifact to be potentially managed just like the source code for the application in question. Additionally, the project may be looking to import translation files, so testing and assurance may be required. Governance should look to the project to provide the correct assurances that they have assessed any risk associated with a change against any existing projects deployed within your Salesforce org.

Workflow & Processes

As shown in Figure 2-4, workflow and processes is the next area on which to focus your governance activity.

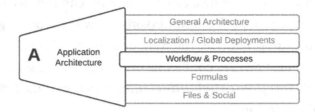

Figure 2-4. *Phase A: application architecture - workflow and processes*

As touched on previously, Salesforce offers a lot of workflow and process automation out-of-the-box tools. This can create some complexity for organizations that have multiple applications deployed by multiple projects. This is especially true for any sharing of standard enterprise objects.

Note   An enterprise object is an object that can be used by anyone within your organization. An example would be the Account object. You would not want each project to create its own custom Account object. This would create duplication of effort and completely break your single view of your customers (among several other good reasons to not do this). However, there comes some level of additional responsibility regarding the usage of enterprise objects.

It can become quite difficult to unpick a Salesforce org that has allowed projects to create automation across objects without any type of control in place. The classic scenario that everyone wants to avoid is the circular process, where a change triggers automation that then triggers other automation that then has a trigger that starts the whole thing over again.

Tip   Sometimes it is quite interesting to add some debug into automation because you can see how many times the automation does actually get called. This is especially easy to achieve if using Apex triggers.

From a governance perspective, you are looking at this in the entirety of the Salesforce org, especially if you have multiple projects that must coexist. At the project level, you want to make sure the appropriate automation solutions have been used. Keep in mind that multiple services on the Salesforce platform can achieve the same results.

It may be useful to create a policy around Workflow within your organization that provides guidance on appropriate use. You want to avoid building up a maintenance issue where several applications are conflicting over rules for the same objects.

Govern the use of Workflow capabilities (rules, tasks, emails, field updates, and approvals) within the solution.

When assessing the workflow, consider other automation that may have been introduced by earlier projects. Apex triggers could cause a conflict with a workflow rule. Equally, although Workflow only supports a single if/then statement, the same functionality could be achieved in Process Builder.

Govern the use of Flow by taking into account the limitations and considerations of a Flow solution.

Flow provides a declarative solution for complex automation tasks and as such can be used to develop very complex solutions, which can also include end-user interaction. As such, you should carefully consider the flows developed by a project and how these fit into your larger Salesforce platform usage.

With the complexity that can be achieved in Flow, it deserves the same attention from a governance perspective as perhaps Apex would.

Govern the capabilities and limitations of Salesforce actions.

Salesforce actions are a great way to add quick solutions for your end users. However, from a governance perspective, you want to make sure that any actions added to standard or enterprise objects are relevant for the end-user base. It may not be appropriate for all actions to be available for all end users.

Tip   Remember standard objects are those provided by Salesforce as part of the platform. Enterprise objects are your custom objects that have been promoted to allow any project to use them and are supported centrally.

As with making sure you have appropriate actions for the correct end-user base, you will want to determine whether the project has clearly defined the target end-user devices that are in scope for the actions.

Govern the use of Process Builder, taking into account the limitations.

In some ways, Process Builder is quickly replacing Workflow. It can do pretty much the same thing, but has many more features, though it is still more limited in functionality than Flow. However, Process Builder has some key capabilities that warrant more governance.

With Process Builder it is possible to invoke Apex or a flow. This adds complexity to the governance process in that you will need to determine whether the project is creating a challenge in the future. Set out guidelines regarding the use of Process Builder and perhaps limit what you will allow your projects to do. This will largely depend on what sort of organization you are building. If you have a single Salesforce org, with multiple business areas creating applications for that org, you will need to implement strong governance and controls so as to avoid conflicts between applications.

As Salesforce has no means of cleanly separating each application running on an org, any automation attached to standard or enterprise objects is subject to challenges later.

Formulas

As shown in Figure 2-5, formulas is the next area in which to focus your governance activity.

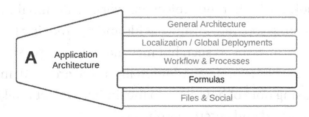

Figure 2-5. *Phase A: application architecture - formulas*

Govern the use of advanced formula features and check against limitations.

Some effort should be dedicated to making sure your projects' formulas are not exposing data that should not otherwise be seen by certain end users.

Cross-object formulas that reference a field on another object and display that formula in a page layout are visible to end users even if they do not have access to that object record. From a governance perspective, you must ensure that your security controls are not by-passed in any way by the formulas used by your projects (see Figure 2-5).

The project should assure the governing body that all possible efforts have been made to avoid having "#Error!" or "#Too Big!" displayed to the end user on failing formula fields. The project should clarify that it has

- checked that division by zero will not occur;

- checked that a formula is not calculating a value larger than the maximum value of the current type;

- checked that the formula handles negative numbers correctly; for example, calculating the square root of a negative number, or the LOG of a negative number;

- checked that they are not using the VALUE function with text that could contain special characters; and

- checked that the formula does not have HYPERLINK functions within a text function.

As part of governing the application, you will be looking to make sure the project has done everything possible to avoid these issues; for example, preventing division by zero by using an IF function that determines whether the value of a field is zero before proceeding.

You should consider the limits that are being reached during the governance of formula fields and look at whether the project has worked around limits, such as the character limit, by creating separate formula fields and referencing them in another formula field. This is not an issue as such but may indicate complexity that sets the scene for on-going governance of the project. Additionally, there are hard limits for cross-object formulas, so taking note of how close to the limit a project is taking an object is important for both standard and enterprise objects.

Govern the use of hierarchical custom settings in a declarative solution.

If the project is implementing hierarchical custom settings, you will need to make sure that the correct setting is returned for the users and profiles within your organization. The project will need to provide assurances that any settings implemented provide end users with the correct value given their profile.

Remember that hierarchical custom settings provide different values at the organization, profile, and user levels. The Salesforce platform provides values in a priority order of user, profile, and then organization level.

Files & Social

As shown in Figure 2-6, files and social is the next area in which your governance team should focus their efforts.

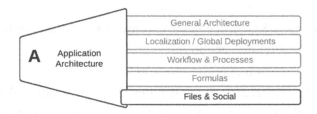

Figure 2-6. *Phase A: application architecture - files & social*

Govern the application's use of files and content, including Chatter files, attachments, content, and knowledge.

There are a number of key aspects to look at from a governance perspective when examining file and content usage (see Figure 2-6).

Storage capacity will be impacted. Ensure there is available capacity on the Salesforce platform initially, and also look at how that capacity will be consumed over the lifecycle of application usage. You should look for a capacity model from the project to detail the numbers and sizes of content being used. Depending on the way files and content are managed, a file could be as large as 2GB.

Given the capacity model, what if any archiving solution will the project have in place to age out old files or content as it becomes unused? How will that be achieved in the longer term, and who will own this responsibility?

Visibility of content and files—you will need to address this with the project to be assured that they have used the correct solution to achieve the content visibility desired.

Salesforce does not provide an anti-virus solution for content loaded onto the platform. It will be your organization's responsibility to ensure you are protected from any viruses. This might be an important consideration when dealing with files uploaded from your customers rather than internal files.

Govern the integration with social capabilities of the platform.

Salesforce offers a number of integrations with social media platforms. However, these seem to come and go. If your project is using links to social media from Contact, Account, and Lead objects, you may want to understand the business benefit and reliance on these integrations. As clearly stated by Salesforce:

> *"We can't guarantee availability of this feature or access to data that's currently provided."*

—Salesforce

Over the last few years, Salesforce has also removed a number of key social media platforms, such as LinkedIn and Facebook.

Additionally, Salesforce offers authentication to your customers by using their social media accounts to authenticate to your Salesforce site. You should take some time to assess the security implications and adherence to your own internal security policies to make sure your projects are aligned.

Method

This is the formal method for Phase A of the Salesforce Platform Governance Method. The objectives of this phase are to ensure that the evolution of the application being governed has adhered to the technical standards and policies defined for the Salesforce platform.

Broadly, the areas that will be assessed are as follows:

- General Architecture
- Localization / Global Deployments
- Workflow and Process
- Formulas
- Files and Social

Approach

To help accelerate an application's governance adherence assessment, a "whitelist" approach is taken, where specific attention is given to determine whether the application only contains certain characteristics so that an optimal approval route can be made through the governance process.

The exact content of the whitelist will be part of the resource base and of course should be tailored for your organization's requirements.

Fundamentally, this phase determines whether the application's architecture is within the parameters that the organization deems acceptable. Most organizations will have a technology policy, and therefore this phase should take that into account. For example, an organization may have a standard regarding integration with external applications, and thus this phase should determine whether that standard has been adhered to; for example, all integration must be done via an integration layer rather than peer-to-peer.

As the governance of the application uses the resource base to determine adherence to standards, the resource base should be a reference point for all development on the Salesforce platform. The resource base forms the basis in part or in whole for all standards used throughout the organization for development on the Salesforce platform.

This phase needs to be as objective as possible. There will be some cases where a subjective view will be unavoidable. In those cases, it should be a discussion point. Where this does occur, it could indicate a lack of clarity in the development standards and technical policies used.

The project team should present the application architecture covering the following suggested inputs to the governance team. This should be an interactive session to allow all parties to fully understand the solution being presented.

To avoid governance's being applied at the end of the construction of an application, Phase A should be used in an iterative manner. A project should present its initial view as to how they are going to construct their application and allow the governance team to highlight any areas of concern.

Inputs

For the governance process to be a success, the project must have a number of artifacts available to the governance team for review. Suggested artifacts for the governance team to review for Phase A of the Salesforce Platform Governance Method are as follows:

- Application data model

- Application configuration and source (or the repository in the example of using a configuration management tool)

- Application capacity plan
  - License requirements
  - User volumes
  - Data volumes
- Custom settings used / created
- External systems integrations
- AppExchange components and applications used

It is up to your organization to determine the formality of the artifacts just mentioned. Some organizations will look for formal notation to be used in the data model, while others will be happy with a high-level slide deck. This governance method should not force projects to undertake more work just for the sake of governance, but rather the governance process should utilize the standard artifacts your organization expects any project to produce.

Steps

At the application architecture level, the steps are specifically high level and attempt to cover the broadest aspects of the project team's application. The governance team is making sure the project team is heading in the right direction in terms of the construction of their application.

General Architecture

1. Has the project considered whether the application has been designed for optimal performance, scalability, usability, and ease of maintenance?

2. Govern the appropriate use of declarative and programmatic functionality used

3. Govern considerations for a single org or dedicated org strategy

4. Govern the usage of license types (capabilities and constraints)

5. Govern the data modeling concepts and implications of data model design

6. Govern the usage of reports and analytics (platform considerations and trade-offs)

7. Govern the usage of external applications (Salesforce AppExchange and application integration)

Localization & Global Deployments

1. Govern the usage of the platform's internationalization functionality (multiple currencies, translations, and languages)

Workflow & Processes

1. Govern the use of Workflow capabilities (rules, tasks, emails, field updates, and approvals) within the solution

2. Govern the use of Flow, taking into account the limitations and considerations of a Flow solution

3. Govern the capabilities and limitations of Salesforce actions

4. Govern the use of Process Builder, taking into account the limitations

Formulas

1. Govern the use of advanced formula features (VLOOPUP, roll-up summary, image, cross-object), check against limitations

2. Govern the use of hierarchical custom settings in a declarative solution

Files & Social

1. Govern the application's usage of files and content, including Chatter files, attachments, content, and knowledge

2. Govern the integration with social capabilities of the platform

Outputs

Once all the steps have been assessed, the outputs to Phase A are as follows:

> Not Applicable – Project team has no intention of utilizing platform feature.

> Fail – A failure to adhere to standards has been found, an explanation as to what was found versus what was expected will be provided.

> Pass – The input provided has passed this governance phase.

> Review – The input cannot be objectively measured and therefore a subjective view has been made, which will lead to a discussion with the development team to reach consensus. Although undesirable, this could be a consequence of unclear standards/policies.

Scenario

For this scenario and as an example, we are going to focus on the following step from the General Architecture group:

- Govern the usage of external applications (Salesforce AppExchange and application integration)

You will remember our fictitious company Bright Sound Guitars Ltd., introduced in Chapter 1. Kicking off their first project on the Salesforce platform, they are ready to review their application architecture.

The folks at Bright Sound Guitars want to make sure they start off on the right foot.

The project's architect, Hanna Snyder, has put together a high-level architecture view of the integration she expects to implement as part of her solution (Figure 2-7).

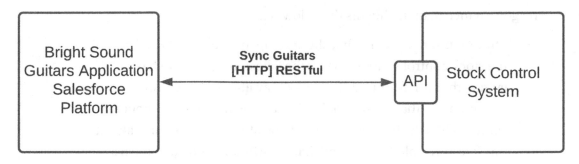

Figure 2-7. *Bright Sound Guitars integration architecture*

Hanna presents the architecture, trying to keep things as simple as possible to get her point across to the governance team. She explains that Bright Sound Guitars already has a stock control system, which stores the models and configurations of the guitars they make. Hanna thinks that it would help the business enormously if they could receive this information directly into Salesforce and then update it there.

Hanna mentions that she wants to take advantage of an API the stock systems offer that provides a list of all of the guitar models that are currently available. The API is pretty basic in that it only returns a list of guitar models and their configurations, but there is a "gotcha." The API paginates the guitars so that only twenty guitars are returned at a time. This means that the call to the API must specify which page of guitars is needed. What's more complicated is that the API does not provide the total number of pages or guitars until the first page is requested.

Hanna has spoken to her Salesforce development team, Ranveer Shah and Caitlyn Horton, and they think they can work with this API.

Given the complexity of the API because of its simplistic interface, Ranveer and Caitlyn both recommended Apex as the way to go. They feel that this would give them the flexibility they need to work with the pagination and the fact that the number of pages of data is unknown until the first page is requested.

The governance team likes the fact that Hanna has engaged her Salesforce developers, Ranveer and Caitlyn. They also commend Hanna on looking into more detail around the capabilities of the API offered by the stock control system. However, they have some concerns.

The governance team highlights the following:

- They mention to Hanna that she is going to take the data from the stock control systems so that the Salesforce platform has the guitars that Bright Sound Guitars sells available to use. However, they mention that Hanna spoke about a business requirement that sounded like the business expects to be able to update this data on the Salesforce platform. Given that the API only provided the list of models and their configuration, they wonder how this would be achieved.

- The governance team also raises some concerns around the nature of the API. They want to know what controls Hanna and her team are going to implement so that Apex limits are not breached. Given the unknown quantities of data, they recommended that a batch process be used to retrieve the guitar models. Using custom settings, the team could allow the size of the batch to be configured to allow fine-tuning in production if issues around timing and amount of data come up.

- The governance team also mentions that this API sounds like it will need to be scheduled, as they would not like to have this run manually every time the stock needs to be synced.

- Lastly, the governance team mentions that Hanna may have to consider an external ID to be used so that a record received from the stock system can be accurately paired with the correct Salesforce record.

Hanna takes the comments away to further investigate what Ranveer and Caitlyn can come up with. She recognizes that this API is less than perfect, but feels it is the right thing to do in terms of keeping the master data where it should be.

Hanna will talk to the business about the issue of updating the data received within the Salesforce platform, as these changes will be overwritten on the next batch of models received.

Also, Hanna likes the idea of keeping an external ID within the Salesforce platform so she can accurately relate records received from the stock control system with the same records stored on the Salesforce platform. This will at least allow updates to flow through so changes in models can be reflected on the Salesforce platform. She agrees that scheduling the Apex would be a great solution. The models do not change that often, may be once a week, so a schedule can be created around that.

Summary

Phase A tackles the governance of a project's application architecture by focusing on specific areas of that architecture. You have checked that fundamentally the architecture is good, and that your project has adhered to the security and technical standards and policies of your organization.

You have also highlighted for your project team any areas of concern within their architecture and are confident that the project will remediate any concerns you have.

CHAPTER 3

Data Architecture & Management: Phase B

This phase of the Salesforce Platform Governance Method tackles the data architecture and management aspects of your project's Salesforce solution.

This is a more detailed view of the approach your team has taken to construct its application rather than the high-level view taken in Phase A. As such, this phase of governance is more applicable to a project that is more mature in its solution, even if that solution has not yet been built.

Overview

Phase B focuses on the data aspects of your application. It should be governed by team members who specialize in Salesforce's data model and have an understanding of how data models can be integrated with the Salesforce platform and external systems.

As the governing team, you are looking to see whether the data aspects of the application being proposed by a project within your organization will be fit for the purpose at hand.

Understanding the pros and cons of design decisions at the data layer is not always easy to do, so you cannot assume your project teams understand all the implications of their decisions. As shown in Figure 3-1, this phase is broken down into two sub-phases for governance.

© Lee Harding and Lee Bayliss 2022
L. Harding and L. Bayliss, *Salesforce Platform Governance Method*,
https://doi.org/10.1007/978-1-4842-7404-0_3

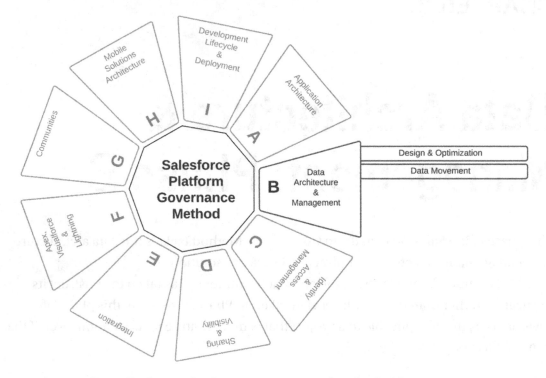

Figure 3-1. *The Salesforce Platform Governance Method: Phase B*

As with previous phases, let's first start by defining what we mean by data architecture and management, as the term can have several definitions; having a clear definition helps us understand the role of governance within this phase. For the context of the Salesforce Platform Governance Method, we will again use the Gartner definition:

> *"Data management (DM) consists of the practices, architectural techniques, and tools for achieving consistent access to and delivery of data across the spectrum of data subject areas and data structure types in the enterprise, to meet the data consumption requirements of all applications and business processes."*

> —Gartner[1]

As previously mentioned, dealing with data is complex. You need to understand the way the data is going to be used by your application so that the correct solution or

---

[1] https://www.gartner.com/en/information-technology/glossary/dmi-data-management-and-integration

solutions can be implemented to give your end users the best experience. Any end user sitting around waiting for reports to run or receiving errors that queries have timed out is not going to be satisfied.

It is therefore imperative that your data governance is not left to chance, and that you have properly challenged your projects to think not only about finding a solution to today's business challenge but also about longer-term challenges.

The Salesforce platform protects you from many potential issues that you might face if you were to develop an application using a traditional programming language and database, mainly by hiding the design burden on the database level, such as tuning, maintenance, and security. However, the platform can only do so much given it does not know how you are going to use the application within your business.

As the team responsible for protecting your company's Salesforce organization, you will need to explore as much as possible the data design and architecture of your project's application.

Design & Optimization

As shown in Figure 3-2, design and optimization is the first sub-phase of the data architecture and management phase.

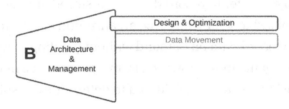

Figure 3-2. *Phase B: data architecture & management - design & optimization*

Governing the design and optimization of the data architecture is an important aspect of the governance process. Your team will be responsible for making sure that whatever a project produces will fit into the larger usage of the Salesforce platform. You need to be concerned with the overall performance of your Salesforce instance, but also the long-term maintenance and manageability of it.

Govern the data model, paying attention to modeling decisions made, such as the usage of lookup versus master–detail relationships.

Given that there are basically three types of relationship available within the data design space, you will be looking to understand whether the appropriate type has been used and assessing the impact of the choice. For example, an object can only have two master–detail relationships, so you will need to make sure that this relationship is absolutely necessary, especially for standard or enterprise objects.

Additionally, data visibility will need to be reviewed to ensure that the correct outcomes are reached in terms of data access controls. This is important if the child relationship must have different security and access than the parent object.

Recognizing custom objects as duplications of standard objects is important. It is easy to identify custom objects, especially when talking with the business stakeholders. Determining whether the custom object and support functionality could be delivered by a standard configuration on the Salesforce platform will reap numerous cost and maintenance benefits. Your main goal should be to deliver a business benefit as quickly as possible, while reducing the need to create bespoke configurations.

Where possible, avoid the duplication of data, especially important data that is only really useful if it is accurate. For example, a telephone number should be an attribute on an object it relates to, such as a customer, rather than on the order the customer places. That way, every order will refer to the same customer telephone number. These are simple examples, and it is not always easy to recognize these issues at the early design phases. Your governance board should be experienced in these types of issues.

Govern the use of external data (external objects).

External data or objects refer to record data that is stored outside your Salesforce organization and is exposed to your Salesforce organization as a form of custom object. This provides access to record data on demand without needing to have that data stored within your Salesforce organization. However, from a governance perspective, there are some limitations that will need to be considered to determine the suitability of using external data.

As an example, cross-org can be a great solution, sharing data from one Salesforce organization to another, but when using external objects, you should remember that each call-out counts toward the API usage limits of the Salesforce organization providing the data.

As with most limit considerations, if you are governing multiple projects with multiple applications, you will need to take a holistic view on consumption and fair distribution of resources.

Govern the use of picklist fields versus custom objects.

Careful consideration should be given to the complexity of the data model, especially the granularity of the objects created or the normalization. It is easy to become carried away in identifying objects, but the question should be whether a picklist field is more relevant than an object and its relationships.

Keep in mind the need to report on data and produce dashboards and analytics. These things become more complicated the more normalized the data model.

Govern the use of multiple data sources, focusing on clear decisions regarding system of record and single source of truth.

When data comes from multiple sources, it must be clear regarding the flow of change and where the master data resides. If this does not happen, you can become very confused as to what system has the most up-to-date view of a record.

As the governance body, you will want to know how data arrived in and goes out of your Salesforce organization. It will no doubt have security implications as well as functional issues if your data is out of date or keeps being overwritten.

Note   This is a common problem and has been encountered numerous times. There are so many organizations that do not know what system owns the source of truth when it comes to data.

You will need to make sure that transaction boundaries are adhered to. If a transaction fails within the Salesforce platform due to a validation rule or a trigger that fails, you will not want to update the external system. Keeping the integrity of data in this scenario is critical and should be explored by the governance team.

Given the complexities around data integrity, it may be wise to publish some design principles within your organization that detail what (as an organization) you are willing to accept projects doing. You may only allow one-way integrations with external data so that the system that owns the data will not allow incoming updates, therefore enforcing its position as a system of record.

Govern the use of custom metadata types versus custom settings.

As the governance body, you will need to look at how a project is aiming to store its configuration. There are pros and cons when comparing custom metadata with custom settings, some of which will really only be relevant in the context of your application. However, this might be a good candidate for having a design principle in place that can guide each project (and ultimately the applications being built) as to which way to go.

If hierarchical settings are required by your project, then custom settings might be the best way to go. However, custom settings are not deployable to sandboxes, unlike custom metadata. Again, if you are using custom settings to store web-service information, this may be a good idea as you will not want your production settings being copied to a sandbox.

However, custom metadata have many additional features and offer more flexibility from a permissions perspective.

Govern the usage of large data volumes, considering application performance, query, search, indexing, reporting, testing, sharing, and administrative functions.

Understanding the scale of your project's application is key so that a good picture can be built of the expected data values. Your project may already have accepted the need for large data volumes and be expecting to implement Salesforce's big objects. However, if this is not the case you need to know what to expect from a data generation perspective so that later issues are not uncovered and left to your administrators to resolve after your project team has disbanded.

Salesforce uses a relational database management system (**RDBMS**) at the infrastructure level, but due to the way in which Salesforce's multitenant architecture uses that database solution it is not possible for the RDBMS to effectively optimize any queries it receives from the Salesforce platform. Given this scenario, Salesforce has implemented its own query optimizer, which helps the RDBMS' optimizer produce effective query performance.

Where the capacity model provided by your project indicates a large data volume or where there is an initial data load requirement by your project you may want your project to provide evidence that any queries it has developed are efficient. Your project should provide evidence that it has understood the selectivity of any filter conditions used by its application with SOQL (Salesforce Object Query Language) queries, list views, or reports.

If your filter condition involves a custom field, you may have to work with Salesforce's customer support to create a custom index on the field your filter uses. Not all fields can have an index, such as non-deterministic formula fields.

Where your project is frequently querying the same fields and using the same joins in reports, for example, you may want your project to investigate the usage of skinny tables. Again, you will have to work with Salesforce's customer support teams to have this set up, but it may make a big difference in performance for reports.

Consider your project's use of indexes. It may be necessary to create a custom index, but bear in mind the types of field that can be indexed. Flagging a field as an external ID causes an index to be created on that field, but this can only be applied to certain field types, such as email, number, text, and auto number. For other field types, you will need to contact Salesforce's customer support.

If search is a big win for your business, then you may need your project to consider divisions. Divisions allow you to partition data—for example, by region. Again, this is a feature that must be discussed with Salesforce's customer support.

Given the complexity of using large data volumes and the impact it can have on performance and other areas, it is important to make sure the project you are governing takes time to think about the longer term. If you need to engage Salesforce's customer support for help, it will take time, so the earlier you understand any potential longer-term issues the better the outcome for your business.

Govern the application for performance, scalability, and maintainability of the data model.

As mentioned previously, there are a number of places where the scale of data can create a problem in the longer term, so plans must be in place to avoid disaster. As the team governing the applications that are targeted for the Salesforce platform, you may look to the project to provide evidence that first they have considered the scale at which the application will be used—the number of end users, for example.

The project team should then be able to create a model that gives some indication as to the data that those end users are expected to generate over a time period of twelve or twenty-four months, or even longer. Given that information, the project team should be able to create a test scenario that proves that their data model design works efficiently at the scales they expect to see in production.

Govern the use of AppExchange packages to maintain data quality.

As with all AppExchange packages, you will want to ensure they meet your organization's security and commercial policies. If those are met, then from a governance perspective you need to understand what is happening to the data and how confident the project team is that they have fully understood the third-party package.

The levels of governance you apply could be determined by the types of data and quantities that the AppExchange package will have access to. If the package is restricted to data that is only relevant to the project, it is an easy situation to deal with, as opposed to when the package is accessing data used by all applications within your organization.

However, it is commonplace to use a package to take care of duplication recognition. Even though the Salesforce platform offers some features in this area, there are other solutions that provide a broader set of functionalities.

Your role in governing this situation is to make sure at least the following are understood:

- Are any data changes well documented and clearly defined so that all projects understand why and how their data is changed by a third-party package?

- Data residency needs to be considered; does anything happen to the data that takes it off of the Salesforce platform temporarily?

- Can data changes be reversed if things go wrong, or if the business is unhappy with the changes made?

- Are there sufficient support arrangements in place for the third-party package?

The key here is that you are not trying to block the use of third-party packages to help increase benefits to your business and reduce the effort exerted by your project teams to deliver functionality, but rather are just double-checking that due diligence has taken place.

Data Movement

As shown in Figure 3-3, data movement is the next sub-phase for your governance team to focus on.

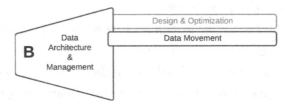

Figure 3-3. *Phase B: data architecture & management - data movement*

At some point during the lifecycle of an application, your project or support team will more than likely need to move data into or out of the Salesforce platform.

It is important that any data movement is governed to ensure that data remains secure throughout its lifecycle and that the business is clear regarding any data archiving policies that you may have within your organization.

There are numerous reasons why data will be moved into or out of the Salesforce platform. Here are some examples:

- Data migration. This is typically part of moving data from a legacy system into the Salesforce platform. This may happen during the early phases of a project because of the work involved in extracting, transforming, and loading the data into Salesforce and subsequent testing.

- Archiving. This is typically part of an information lifecycle management policy. Your organization may require data to be archived onto a separate platform after a predefined period has passed, or if the data in question has not been accessed for some time. All archiving solutions should also deliver a recovery solution so that the business can recover data from the archive in the future if required. Bear in mind when governing these types of solutions that the project will need to take into account data structure changes over time, which may invalidate the data structure in the archive.

- Data backup and recovery. Although the Salesforce platform is secure and robust, most organizations insist on a separate backup solution. Don't forget the restore solution too.

- Data insurance. Not all organizations want to feel tied into the Salesforce platform, and will therefore store their data on an alternative platform as well.

- Off-platform analytics and data mining. It is not unusual for the business to want to mine the data they have been capturing with the Salesforce platform. This generally leads to data's being extracted from the Salesforce platform and loaded into a separate database, sometimes referred to as a data lake.

Govern the usage for data movement (data loading).

From a governance perspective, the reasons behind moving data into or out of the Salesforce platform are down to the business requirements. However, it is your responsibility to ensure that the project has properly considered this area, because at some point it will rise to the surface, and more often than not it ends up being the problem of the platform support team.

Challenge the project team to be confident that they have considered the long-term requirements of data movement. Then discuss with the team the options they are going to use, as well as the tools, and make sure they understand the movement's impact, if any, on the performance of the Salesforce platform while the data movement is under way.

Remember, if making large changes to data that has a significant number of sharing rules, the Salesforce platform may require a significant period to revaluate the sharing.

Tip   If you are bulk-loading data, or making significant changes to a large data set, consider the impact on any sharing rules you have implemented.

Method

This is the formal method for Phase B of the Salesforce Platform Governance Method. The objectives of Phase B are to ensure that the data aspects of the application have adhered to the technical standards and policies defined for the Salesforce platform. The areas that will be assessed during this phase are as follows:

- Design and Optimization

- Data Movement

Approach

This phase focuses on the data arena and requires the data model that will have been produced by your project and will later be provided as an input into the subsequent phase. Additionally, data volumes will be needed, predictive or otherwise, as well as the configuration and code elements where used.

For the initial pass, the data volumes will be predictive. However, proof should be provided that the application has been tested to support the data volumes—where those volumes are in excess of 20 million records, for example. Subsequent passes through this phase can use actual figures from the production environment so the data volumes can create a prediction model for future volumes.

Any SOQL and SOSL should be reviewed with the aim of determining the use of appropriate indexing. You may want to investigate the use of automation tools such as static source code analysis and comparing the usage of fields in queries against the indexes created as part of the application's configuration.

Data movement requires the application owner to detail any requirements and the solution to moving data into and out of the Salesforce platform.

Inputs

For the governance process to be successful, the project must have a number of artifacts available to the governance team for review. Suggested artifacts for Phase B of the Salesforce Platform Governance Method are as follows:

- Application data model

- Performance & scale test exit reports

- Application configuration & source (or the repository in the example of using a configuration management tool)

- Custom settings used and created

- Data unload and load details

- Predictive or actual data volumes

It is up to your organization to determine the formality of the artifacts previously mentioned. Some organizations will look for formal notation to be used in the data model, while others will be happy with a high-level slide deck. This governance method should not force projects to undertake more work just for the sake of governance, but rather the governance process should utilize the standard artifacts your organization expects any project to produce.

Steps

The steps for governing the data architecture phase should help the project team understand how their application uses data and how that might affect the Salesforce platform overall. The governance team should feel confident that over the lifespan of the application, there should be no fundamental issues with the applications used.

Design and Optimization

1. Govern the data model, paying attention to modeling decisions, such as the usage of lookup versus master–detail relationships

2. Govern the use of external data (external objects)

3. Govern the use of picklist fields versus custom objects

4. Govern the use of multiple data sources, focusing on clear decisions regarding system of record and single source of truth

5. Govern the use of custom metadata types versus custom settings

6. Govern the usage of large data volumes, considering application performance, query, search, indexing, reporting, testing, sharing, and administrative functions

7. Govern the application for performance, scalability, and maintainability for the data model

8. Govern the use of AppExchange packages to maintain data quality

Data Movement

1. Govern data migration (data loading) strategy and solution

2. Govern the data archiving strategy and solution provided by the project, including

   a. tools selected, and

   b. archived data storage and retrieval solution.

Outputs

Once all the steps have been assessed, the outputs from Phase A are deemed one of the following:

- Not Applicable – Project team has no intention of utilizing platform feature.

- Remediate – The governance team requests that the project team remediates their design to accommodate the issues raised during the governance review.

- Pass – The input provided has passed this governance phase.

- Review – The input cannot be objectively measured, and therefore a subjective view has been made, which will lead to a discussion with the development team to reach consensus. Although undesirable, this could be a consequence of unclear standards/policies.

Scenario

For our scenario we are going to focus on two steps from the Design & Optimization group of the data architecture and management Phase B method. These steps are as follows:

- Govern the data model, paying attention to modeling decisions made, such as the usage of lookup versus master–detail relationships.

- Govern the use of picklist fields versus custom objects.

You will remember our fictitious company Bright Sound Guitars Ltd. introduced earlier. Having embarked on their first project for the Salesforce platform, they are ready to review their data architecture and management strategy.

The folks at Bright Sound Guitars understand that getting the data model right is important, as it's going to be the foundation of their application, and once it is in use, fundamentally changing it will be hard, time consuming, and expensive.

The project's architect, Hanna Snyder, has readied the data model; she is going to present three model types. First will be the conceptual data model. She feels that this will help the governance team to grasp quickly the business concepts she needs her data model to support. Then she's going to show her logical model to demonstrate to the governance team how she has clarified optional and mandatory relationships and added more detail regarding the types of data each entity will store. Lastly, she is going to show the physical model, which will demonstrate how her data model will be represented on the Salesforce platform.

First, Hanna presents her conceptual data model, which is shown in Figure 3-4.

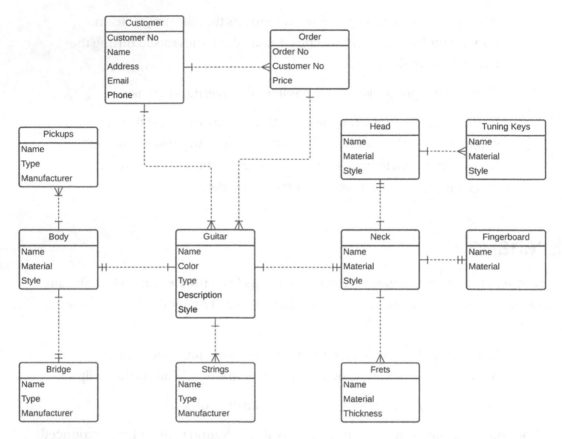

Figure 3-4. *Phase B: data architecture & management - conceptual data model*

Hanna has used a typical entity relationship diagram (ERD) to represent her conceptual model. This works perfectly for the Bright Sound Guitars' governance team, as they are familiar with this notation.

It is clear to the governance team that Hanna's application is going to store information regarding the construction of guitars, and then provide a relationship between a customer ordering a guitar and owning one.

Of course, Bright Sound Guitars would love their customers to enjoy the bright sound of many of their guitars, so the model supports a customer's ordering and owning multiple guitars.

Second, Hanna presents her logical data model. The governance team understand what she is trying to achieve with her design, so are ready to understand the next level of detail. Hanna's logical data model looks like the one shown in Figure 3-5.

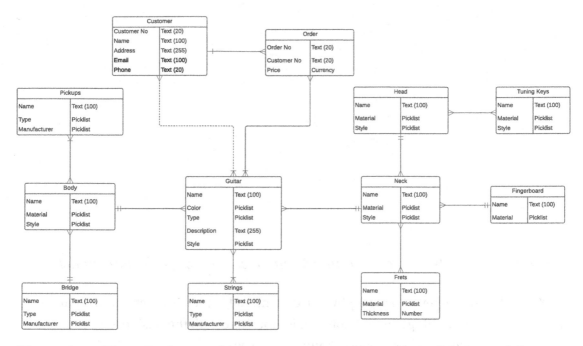

Figure 3-5. *Phase B: data architecture & management - logical data model*

Hanna has put more detail into this model, clearly showing the types of data or fields each entity is going to store. Hanna has also highlighted mandatory and optional relationships using the ERD notation, as well as refined the cardinality between entities.

The Bright Sound Guitars' governance team is now starting to build up a good picture of the application's data model that Hanna is putting together. At this point they are starting to have some concerns but want to see how this data model will be represented on the Salesforce platform. After all, there can be a big difference between models because they are aimed at different stakeholders. Hanna would have had to initially build her models with help from the business, and this means she needs them to feel confident that she has understood their requirements.

Hanna presents her last data model, which is the physical representation, as shown in Figure 3-6.

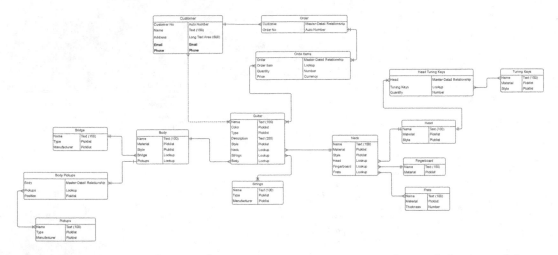

Figure 3-6. *Phase B: data architecture & management - physical data model*

Hanna has put together a great physical data model, which is much more detailed that the others, something she probably would not share with the business, but something her Salesforce developers would love to see.

Hanna's model clearly shows the master–detail and lookup relationships. This will make the governance process a lot easier for the governance team and reduce the amount of time Hanna needs to spend explaining her solution.

Having spent a short time reviewing the data models and asking Hanna questions, the governance team provides the following feedback:

1. When questioned on the use of Customer, Order, and Order Items objects, Hanna clearly states that these would be custom objects implemented on the Salesforce platform. The governance team is concerned that Hanna will recreate functionality that is already available on the platform. The governance team explains that Bright Sounds Guitars has a number of projects in the pipeline, Hanna's being the first, and wants to take advantage of as many standard features as possible. This allows Bright Sound Guitars to take advantage of features and functionality that Salesforce delivers in the releases three times each year. Hanna accepts this feedback and will review her models to take advantage of existing standard objects.

2. The governance team asks more questions around the Guitar object. One member of the governance team asks Hanna whether the Asset standard object might be a good fit. Hanna isn't sure of the exact nature of the Asset object, but accepts that this could be a good candidate, especially given the relationships with Products and PriceBooks. She feels that perhaps there are more standard objects within the platform that she could take advantage of, which would accelerate her development time, while potentially offering more functionality to her business stakeholders. The asset-tracking feature sounds like a great feature her business stakeholders could use, especially for product support issues and warranty expiration.

3. Lastly, the governance team raises a number of concerns regarding the number of objects being used to construct a guitar. Although from a business perspective these all make sense, the team wonders if picklists could be a better option. Additionally, Hanna chose to use picklists where the governance team feels an object would work better. One example of this would be the manufacturer, which was used as a picklist in several objects. The governance team feels that the use of the Account object to represent the manufacturers could be a better use of the platform's capability, especially as Bright Sound Guitars would like to track their own service requests with their suppliers for any warranty work on supplied items.

Overall, the governance team is happy with the work Hanna has produced, and given that this is her first iteration through the governance process, everyone feels like a great outcome was reached. The governance team provides a "remediate" rating against the criteria they assessed the project against. Hanna will now return to her team with the feedback and make the necessary changes. She will then present back to the governance team with her updated data models.

Summary

Phase B is focused on the data design of a project's application. This is a foundation of any application, but depending on the longevity and scale of your application it is not always relevant to take such a detailed look.

The scenario provided gave a simplistic look at how the governance process might work in your organization. Governance should be seen as a collaborative exercise to make sure that you are taking the best approach, given what you know for your organization and the business requirements.

Bear in mind that design is subjective; there is not always a right and a wrong. However, you should attempt to steer your design based on principles you define, such as reusing as much of the standard functionality as possible. This is highlighted in the scenario, where the governance team has a principle to use as many standard objects as possible. Given the size of Bright Sound Guitars and the fact that IT systems are not their specialty, they chose to keep the amount of bespoke work to a minimum and focus their efforts on delivering business benefits quickly.

Depending on the complexity of your application, you may find that all of the steps laid out in this phase will need to be completed. However, make sure you take a look with the project team to make sure you are not spending time on reviewing irrelevant areas.

The main takeaway from this phase is that a little time spent up front checking a few key principles can avoid a lot of heartache later on in the usage of your application.

CHAPTER 4

Identity & Access Management: Phase C

This phase of the Salesforce Platform Governance Method focuses on the identity and access management solution that the project team you are governing intends to put in place for its application.

Overview

Phase C should be governed by team members who understand the security controls available within the Salesforce platform as well as your company's internal security policies.

As the governing team, you should ensure that the Salesforce platform, first and foremost, is kept secure and that the correct level of access is applied to every end user of the application under governance.

Understanding how access to the Salesforce platform integrates with the wider company access policies will be critical; you cannot assume your project teams understand all the implications of their decisions. As shown in Figure 4-1, this phase is broken down into two sub-phases to ease the governance process.

© Lee Harding and Lee Bayliss 2022
L. Harding and L. Bayliss, *Salesforce Platform Governance Method*,
https://doi.org/10.1007/978-1-4842-7404-0_4

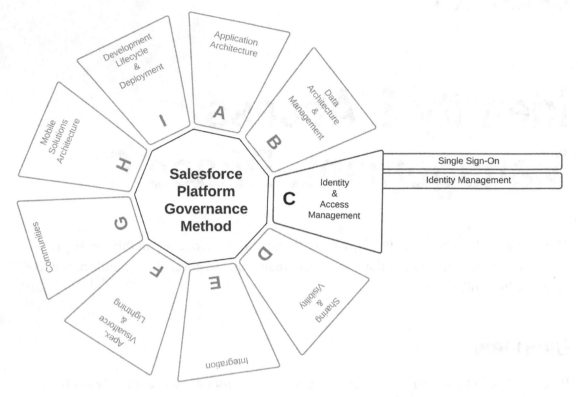

Figure 4-1. *The Salesforce Platform Governance Method: Phase C*

As with previous phases, let's start by defining what we mean by identity and access management, as it can have a few definitions, and having a clear definition will help us understand the role of governance within this phase. In the context of the Salesforce Platform Governance Method, we will again use the Gartner definition:

> *"Identity and access management (IAM) is the discipline that enables the right individuals to access the right resources at the right times for the right reasons.*
>
> *IAM addresses the mission-critical need to ensure appropriate access to resources across increasingly heterogeneous technology environments, and to meet increasingly rigorous compliance requirements. IAM is a crucial undertaking for any enterprise. It is increasingly business-aligned, and it requires business skills, not just technical expertise.*

Enterprises that develop mature IAM capabilities can reduce their identity management costs and, more importantly, become significantly more agile in supporting new business initiatives."

—Gartner[1]

To achieve a successful identity and access management implementation, you will need to understand the way in which your projects intend their users to access the application being governed. As Gartner clearly states, this is focused on providing users access to the right resources at the right times for the right business reasons. Your governance and project teams should also have a basic understanding of the differences between authorization and authentication, as shown in Table 4-1.

Table 4-1. *Authentication vs. Authorization*

Authentication	Authorization
Verifies who the user is	Determines what resources a user can access
Uses passwords or other information provided by the user	Implemented through settings that are project and/or application specific and maintained at that level
First step in provided access to an application	Takes place after authentication
Visible and changeable by the user (for example, change password)	Invisible to the user; they can access what someone has deemed acceptable for them to access

As Salesforce provides a platform that is designed with the customer in mind, access to your application may not be restricted to just employees. You can allow access to your customers as well as your employees for the right business reasons; for example, a customer portal where they can raise support cases.

The Salesforce platform provides a lot of flexibility when it comes to identity and access management, but it cannot control giving access to the wrong resources at the wrong time for the wrong reasons. That responsibility sits firmly with the project team and the governing team.

---

[1] https://www.gartner.com/en/information-technology/glossary/identity-and-access-management-iam

A prerequisite to governing the IAM aspects of a project's Salesforce application is having an initial view of what is acceptable to your organization. This usually takes the form of technical standards and policies that lay out guidance for determining what solution provides the identity solution and what solutions can provide services to users via that identity solution.

If you are an organization that has no identity provider solution, then Salesforce could deliver that for you, in which case you may look to your project team or your company's security team to define those technical standards and policies, as it is the initial project requiring them.

Single Sign-On

As shown in Figure 4-2, single sign-on is the first sub-phase on which your governance team should focus.

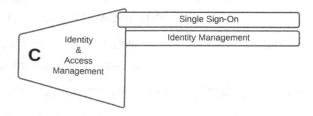

Figure 4-2. *Phase C: identity & access management - single sign-on*

Single sign-on (SSO) is a solution that provides authentication of your users and allows them to access multiple systems from one login and one set of credentials. While providing this level of convenience to the users is great from a usability perspective, it comes with some considerations that must be examined early on within the development lifecycle. There are two well-defined participants in any SSO solution, which Salesforce describes very well:

> *"When you set up SSO, you configure one system to trust another to authen-ticate users, eliminating the need for users to log in to each system separately. The system that authenticates users is called an identity provider. The sys-tem that trusts the identity provider for authentication is called the service provider."*

> —Salesforce

The role of the governance team is to determine whether the project has adhered to the technical standards and policies for single sign-on defined within your organization. Alternatively, the project may be setting the technical standards and policies for future projects if they are the first of that type within your organization. The governance team should clearly understand what part the Salesforce platform will play in the overall SSO landscape—that of service provider or identity provider (and potentially both in some cases)—and then consider the project's role within this.

If the project's application being governed adheres to existing technical standards and policies, the governance team should be aware that the application may require changes to those standards and policies.

For example, a "connected app" may be required that can only support a specific authentication solution. That solution may not be part of the technical standards already defined. This may raise questions regarding the suitability of the "connected app," but it could be the case that the "connected app" is a legacy application that has not been updated or replaced in line with the current technical standards and policies of your organization. This will more than likely be out of the project's scope of influence or even desired scope of activity, but nevertheless the team must provide a connected experience for users.

Govern whether the correct SSO components have been used in the overall application (OAuth, connected app).

Governing the use of the correct SSO configuration is very much driven from the perspective of whether Salesforce is the service provider or identity provider.

As the service provider, it will be assumed by your project that an identity provider is already in place within your organization that may offer a supported single sign-on option that uses SAML (Security Assertion Markup Language), OpenID, or the creation of a custom authentication solution.

Using SAML, authenticated users flow from the identity provider into Salesforce. Identity providers such as Microsoft's Active Directory use SAML. Users continue to use the Salesforce login page, but behind the scenes the Salesforce platform sends the users to the identity provider using a SAML request, which is then responded to by the identity provider with a SAML response containing the SAML assertion that authenticates the user.

Using OpenID, a user would select the appropriate identity provider, such as Facebook, from the options provided to the user from the Salesforce login page. This would redirect the user to the identity provider's login page. The user would then enter their login credentials into that page, and once authenticated the user would be taken back to the Salesforce platform. Salesforce supports several predefined authentication providers, such as Apple and Google.

The final option is to use Apex to create a custom authentication provider. From a governance perspective, this option would need to be carefully considered as it falls into a few governance phases, such as technical design review and approval, as well as code quality checks.

As the identity provider, Salesforce can authenticate on behalf of third-party service providers by implementing SAML or OpenID. Third-party applications need to be configured as connected apps.

If Salesforce is used as a SAML identity provider for your connected app, the project's users will log in to the third-party application using their Salesforce credentials. If Salesforce is used as an OpenID identity provider for your connected app, the Salesforce login page will be presented to the users of that third-party app for authentication.

Salesforce offers several options when considering single sign-on. As the governing team you are really focused on the following:

- If Salesforce is selected as the identity provider, have you the resources to manage and support the predicted user base and connected apps within your Salesforce resource pool at an operational level?

- If Salesforce is selected as a service provider, have you the resources to manage and support the predicated user base within your operational identity management team and considered any Just-in-Time (JIT) requirements?

- Have you automated as much as possible to allow your user base to "self-serve" for basic identity management issues, such as forgotten passwords?

- Have all parties been involved and agreed upon the solution regarding authentication across multiple applications?

Your governance team should make sure that the project has considered the following:

- The project should provide evidence that service provider–initiated SSO is working.

- The project should provide evidence of successful SSO implantation on desktop before attempted on mobile.

- The project should clearly communicate your MyDomain URL to users and provide clear instructions.

- The project should consider any impacts of IP restrictions.

- The project should have considered the look and feel of the login page when using SAML.

- The project should consider the data that is passed in the OpenID token, as this could contain sensitive information that pertains to the user. You do not want this information to be accessible, so content (key–value pairs) and connection security will be a critical factor.

Govern SSO configuration and components (SAML configuration, MyDomain, Scope Parameter Values, OpenID).

Once the project's single sign-on requirements are understood and governed, the governance team can review in more detail how the project configures each SSO component.

If Salesforce is the service provider, the project will need to work with the identity provider to gain access to the SAML information and assertion parameters. This information will include an authentication certificate and the SAML assertion parameters.

Tip   Some identity providers offer the SAML setting via an XML file or URL pointing to the file.

The project may also need to implement its own Just-in-Time provisioning, which will automatically create a corresponding user within the Salesforce platform for the authenticated user. This is required because Salesforce will need to reference a record in the User object with which to associate permissions, sharing, and ownership, among several other things. As the governance team, you will need to understand the parameters being sent within the SAML assertion from which the users will be created.

Just-in-Time provisioning can be used to perform the same function for your project's customer and partner bases if the project is to support a customer and/or partner portal of some kind. Your governance team will need to focus on the gaps in what the user-creation process delivers versus what is really required to provision a user within the Salesforce platform. Additional permission sets and other user-level configuration may need to be carefully considered.

If Salesforce is the identity provider, the project will need to configure the connected apps for each of the third-party applications or service providers where Salesforce is used for authentication.

Before Salesforce is configured as the identity provider, MyDomain should be configured. MyDomain uses Salesforce domain suffixes such as `company.salesforce.com` for Salesforce orgs' URLs. This domain affects all applications within the Salesforce org; as such, the governance team should review this implementation with the view that all projects within the organization are affected. While the impact of the change may have no effect whatsoever on some projects, it is something that is org-wide.

Changes to MyDomain will interrupt your Salesforce users briefly, so the governance team should review the schedule for this change with the project team to make sure that this change is done at a convenient time for all applications and users on the Salesforce platform.

The governance team may offer guidance as part of the security policy of your organization regarding the use of certificates. As the identity provider, Salesforce will need a certificate, either self-signed or provided by your certificate authority. Typically, the use of self-signed certificates is reserved for sandboxes, while your certificate authority is used for your production org.

Finally, as the governing team, you will need to review the scope parameter values to determine if the correct scope is being used. This could be important in terms of the data you are looking to gain access to from your identity provider.

Govern any App Launcher changes.

App Launcher provides a convenient landing page that offers your users the applications they have access to. Users will only see the applications that they are authorized to see based on their profile and permission sets.

Changes to the App Launcher should be reviewed by your governance team so that users are not surprised by any changes made. Communications may be required to prepare your users for upcoming changes. This should include connected apps that they will gain access to and any they will lose access to.

Govern mobile SSO requests.

Your governance team should be aware that some changes may be required to support single sign-on from the mobile application. These changes may be required on either or both the identity provider and the Salesforce org. Some of the areas the governance team will need to review are as follows:

- The Salesforce mobile application will only work with service provider–initiated setups.

- Salesforce recommends that single sign-on servers support TLS 1.2.

- SAML configuration needs to be added within the Authentication Configuration section of MyDomain.

As with all Salesforce org-wide configurations introduced by a single project, the governance team will need to explore the provisions being made over the lifespan of the application being deployed and then any ongoing change impacts for future application deployments. Additionally, once Salesforce has been integrated into an identity provider, any changes to that identity provider will need to consider the Salesforce platform(s) that it serves.

Govern OAuth integrating to an external platform.

Your governance team will need to have a thorough understanding of the OAuth capabilities of the Salesforce platform. OAuth can be used for several inbound and outbound integrations with external platforms.

Integrations can take the form of programmatic or declarative configurations, as detailed in Table 4-2.

Table 4-2. *Integration Authentication*

	Direction	Configuration	Code
HTTP Callouts	Outbound	Named credential	Apex
Authentication via OpenID Connect	Outbound	Connected app, authentication provider	Registration handler for authentication provider
Mobile App, Web App, Smart Devices, Middleware	Inbound	Connected app	None

Salesforce supports the following flows for OAuth authentication:

- Web Server Flow for Web App Integration

- User-Agent Flow for Desktop or Mobile App Integration

- Refresh Token Flow for Renewed Sessions

- JWT Bearer Flow for Server-to-Server Integration

- OpenID Connect Dynamic Client Registration for External API Gateways

- Device Flow for IoT Integration

- Asset Token Flow

- Username–Password Flow for Special Scenarios

- SAML Bearer Assertion Flow for Previously Authorized Apps

- SAML Assertion Flow for Accessing Web Services API

Your governance team will need to identify any potential vulnerabilities as well as adhere to your organization's security policies and technical standards. For example, your organization may not permit username–password integrations.

Govern SAML integrating to an external platform.

SAML can be used to provide your users with automatic authentication into your Canvas apps. SAML is an XML-based standard for user authentication on the Web.

The governance team will need to take a deep look into the implementation of any Canvas and Mobile SDK usage.

Govern any multi-factor authentication requirements.

Multi-factor authentication (MFA) is a solution to increase protection for user accounts. When enabled, MFA requires a user to provide two or more pieces of evidence that they are who they say they are. In most cases, two pieces of evidence or factors are used.

Traditionally, two-factor authentications were based on a factor the user knows and a factor the user owns. The factor the user knows was typically a password, and the factor the user owns was typically a token device that would provide a series of numbers that the user would type in when prompted. These numbers would change every sixty seconds.

Salesforce, as of February 2022, will enforce the use of multi-factor authentication, deeming it a necessary tool in creating a platform of trust.

From a governance perspective, the use of multi-factor authentication should focus on the operational aspects of managing MFA for your users. Your governing team should look to understand the following:

- What solution will be rolled out to users to support multi-factor authentication? There are many options, such as the Salesforce Authenticator app or the Google Authenticator app. Some are free to use (such as the Salesforce and Google solutions), while others may have financial implications.

- If a user forgets or loses their device that has the authenticator app installed, how will the user gain access? What operational solutions will be in place to facilitate this? Are your Salesforce administrators prepared for this additional workload?

Identity Management

As shown in Figure 4-3, identity management is the second sub-phase on which your governance team should focus.

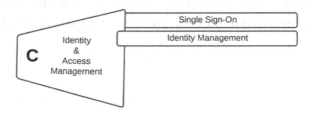

Figure 4-3. *Phase C: identity & access management – identity management*

Regardless of the authentication solution that is employed for your project and the Salesforce org in general, the Salesforce platform requires a user account to be created within the Salesforce platform.

The Salesforce platform overcomes the requirement to create a user account for every user that logs in with single sign-on (SSO) with a solution called Just-in-Time (JIT) provisioning.

JIT provisioning works with your identity provider to pass user information to Salesforce so that when a new user logs in via SSO, the JIT provisioning method automatically creates their account.

Without the use of JIT provisioning, your Salesforce administrators would need to create each user manually.

Govern any changes to user provisioning, syncing, and de-provisioning.

Your governance team will need to look at the project's requirements for changing the way users are provisioned on the Salesforce platform. This will include the de-provisioning of a user.

As users come and go from an organization, and given that Salesforce is an internet-based SaaS (Software as a Service) platform, it is important that you have not only a streamlined user provisioning solution, but also a streamlined de-provisioning solution.

When a user leaves your organization, it is imperative that their access to your systems is revoked. This is even more important for platforms such as Salesforce that are accessible from anywhere in the world (albeit other configurations could restrict this; for example, with the use of SSO). Your governance team will need to review the processes that your project is going to employ to support this, as well as any third-party products. Additionally, active users on the Salesforce platform where no actual user is present pose the risk of data's being inadvertently allocated to that user.

Your governance team may also need to review how a user's permissions are set. Some complex user provisioning solutions can be taken into account; for example, when using Active Directory, the groups the user belongs to can drive the permissions the user is provided on the Salesforce platform. Any such solutions should be governed, with your governance team playing a part in building your organization's maturity in this area.

Method

This is the formal method for Phase C of the Salesforce Platform Governance Method. The objective of Phase C is to ensure that the data aspects of the application have adhered to the technical standards and policies defined for the Salesforce platform. The areas that will be assessed during this phase are as follows:

- Single Sign-On

- Identity Management

Approach

This phase is focused on the identity and access management aspects of the application. These will form part of the technical standards and policies, but it is possible for an application to seek changes to these. For example, a connected app (external to Salesforce) may be required that can only support a specific authentication solution that is not part of the technical standards. This may raise questions regarding the suitability of the connected app, but it could be a case where the legacy application has not been replaced or updated in line with the current technical standards and policies.

Where a core org (or number of them) has been used the standards for SSO should be well defined, but it is possible for an application to specify a dedicated org where requirements dictate the need; for example, where sensitive data resides. In this case, this phase will focus on the adherence to standards for the new org.

More likely, the application being governed will be looking to use external platforms and to modify any App Launcher configurations, especially where an organization has implemented the App Launcher as the standard home page for a user and has multiple orgs in which the applications can reside. The App Launcher configuration may be a centralized task; however, this will be governed in exactly the same way as any other application/configuration change.

It is envisaged that the majority of this phase can be automated with the correct tooling, as specific configurations can be checked against the standards using static source code analysis. However, there may be a need for a subjective review, especially regarding connected apps where the configuration can be checked automatically but the requirement cannot.

Inputs

For the governance process to be a success, the project must have a number of artifacts available to the governance team for review. Suggested artifacts for Phase C of the Salesforce Platform Governance Method are as follows:

- Application configuration and source (or the repository, in the instance of using a source control system) where appropriate

- Custom settings used or created

Steps

The steps to govern the identity and access management phase will help the project team understand how users will authenticate with the Salesforce platform on which their application resides as well as the lifecycle that needs to be considered. The governance team should look to gain confidence that the identity and access management proposal works across the entire organization.

Single Sign-On

1. Govern whether the correct SSO components have been used in the overall application (OAuth, Connected App, etc.).

2. Govern SSO configuration and components (SAML configuration, MyDomain, Scope Parameter Values, OpenID).

3. Govern any App Launcher changes.

4. Govern mobile SSO requests.

5. Govern OAuth's integrating to an external platform.

6. Govern SAML's integrating to an external platform.

Identity Management

1. Govern any changes to user provisioning, syncing, and de-provisioning.

Outputs

Once all the steps have been assessed, the outputs of Phase C are as follows:

- Not Applicable – Project team has no intention of utilizing platform feature.

- Remediate – The governance team requests that the project remediates its design to accommodate the issues raised during the governance review.

- Pass – The input provided has passed this governance phase.

- Review – The input cannot be objectively measured and therefore a subjective view has been made, which will lead to a discussion with the development team to reach consensus. Although undesirable, this could be a consequence of unclear standards and policies.

Scenario

For our scenario, we are going to focus on the following two steps from the Single Sign-On aspect of the identity and access management Phase C method:

- Govern whether the correct SSO components have been used in the overall application (OAuth, Connected App, etc.).

- Govern any App Launcher changes.

Returning to our fictitious company, Bright Sound Guitars Ltd., you may recall Hanna, the project's architect. Hanna wants to introduce single sign-on for the users of the application she and her team are building. Hanna wants her users to only sign in once, and then have access to several services that she intends to leverage that are already in place at Bright Sound.

The most notable of these services is access to the stock system used at Bright Sound. Hanna introduced the stock system during her application architecture review, where she needed to create an interface between Salesforce and the stock system. However, since then her thinking has matured in the use of the stock system and she feels that for some users, it will be useful to log in to both the Salesforce platform and the stock system with the same credentials.

Hanna has put together a high-level diagram depicting the set-up she wants to implement, as shown in Figure 4-4.

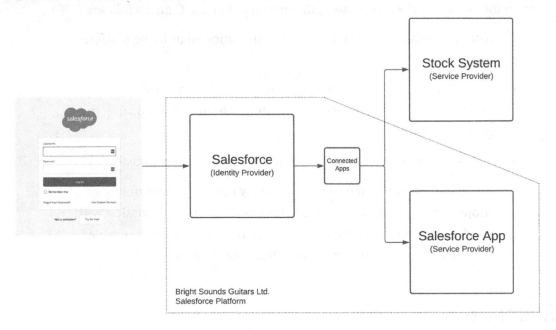

Figure 4-4. *Bright Sound Guitars single sign-on architecture*

Hanna explains that Salesforce will become the identity provider at Bright Sound Guitars, as they currently do not have one. Every system that a user requires access to needs a separate set of credentials for that user. Hanna explains that this is leading to a lot of effort for the system administrators who are helping users with login issues.

Hanna highlights that her project will configure the Salesforce platform as the identity provider. Then, she will configure a connected app for the stock system so that users will simply log in once to Salesforce and will be trusted by the connected app.

Hanna then goes on to explain that she will add the stock system into the App Launcher configuration of the Salesforce platform and make that the home page for each of her users. This way, each user will see the application they have access to whether they are part of the Salesforce platform or not.

Hanna explains that the stock system used at Bright Sound Guitars accepts identity using SAML, so this should be straightforward to configure.

The governance team likes the idea. Anything that makes the life of the users easier is a win as far as they are concerned. However, the governance team makes the following observations:

- They mention that Hanna's team will need to review IP enforcement, which they know is in place for the Salesforce platform. Hanna didn't realize that IP enforcement was in place, so must look at how this might affect the connected app.

- The governance team also mentions that they like the idea of using the App Launcher, as it's a convenient way of providing users with access to the systems they can use. However, the governance team raises a concern that not everyone at Bright Sound Guitars uses the Salesforce platform, and therefore not everyone would benefit from this feature, leaving several users accessing systems as they do today. Hanna responds with the idea that perhaps she could find a way to provide all users at Bright Sound access to Salesforce.

Summary

Phase C looks at identity and access management, with a view of simplifying life for your users by integrating the Salesforce platform into your organization's identity management solution or becoming that solution. Typically, identity and access management are driven by security policy, where your organization may have views on what is acceptable in terms of systems trusted by other systems. In the main, however, single sign-on is widely accepted in today's enterprises.

CHAPTER 5

Sharing & Visibility: Phase D

This phase of the Salesforce Platform Governance Method focuses on the sharing and visibility capabilities of the Salesforce platform.

Overview

Phase D of the Salesforce Platform Governance Method focuses on sharing and visibility, a term that Salesforce uses to refer to providing user access to the right data. The sharing and visibility capabilities of the platform do not require that your organization takes a specific approach to data accessibility; that is down to your own data security policies. However, it is always best to follow the principle of least privilege if you are in any doubt.

The principle of least privilege means that a user is given the minimum levels of access, or permissions, needed to perform their job function. This extends to systems or tools as well as users, where those systems or tools are granted the requisite access needed and nothing more. As shown in Figure 5-1, this phase is broken down into several sub-phases to aid your governance team in managing this aspect of the solution.

© Lee Harding and Lee Bayliss 2022
L. Harding and L. Bayliss, *Salesforce Platform Governance Method*,
https://doi.org/10.1007/978-1-4842-7404-0_5

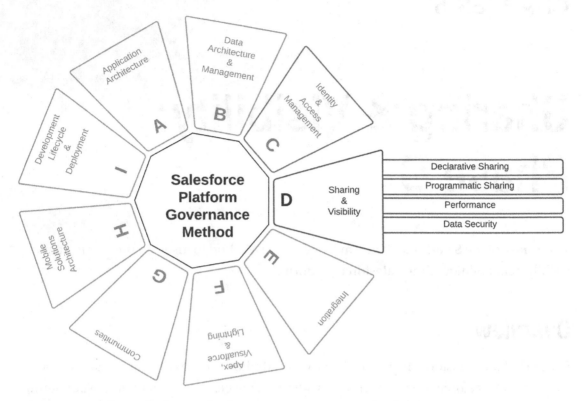

Figure 5-1. *The Salesforce Platform Governance Method: Phase D*

As with previous phases, let's start by defining what we mean by sharing and visibility, as it can have a few definitions, and having a clear definition helps us understand the role of governance within this phase. In the context of the Salesforce Platform Governance Method, we will this time use the Salesforce definition:

> *"The Salesforce sharing model is an essential element in your organization's ability to provide secure application data access. Therefore, it's crucial to architect your sharing model correctly to meet your current and future data access requirements."*

> —Salesforce[1]

Salesforce, like most applications, controls data access by starting with the user. However, Salesforce, unlike other applications, supports different types of user by way of license types.

---

[1] https://resources.docs.salesforce.com/latest/latest/en-us/sfdc/pdf/sharing_architecture.pdf

This governance phase will primarily focus on Salesforce user types that utilize the full sharing model. Other user types, such as Chatter Free or Chatter External licenses, do not follow the standard sharing model as they do not have access to core Salesforce records (standard or custom objects) or content functionality. More important, these user types do not support roles, which is a fundamental part of the sharing solution.

Additionally, high-volume users, such as those with access to a community, also do not support the sharing model because the license types associated with these types of users—Customer Community, High Volume Customer Portal, and Authenticated Website—do not support roles. However, these license types have their own sharing model, which Salesforce administrators can leverage by creating sharing sets and share groups.

Salesforce offers several solutions to control the data that users can see, as shown in Figure 5-2.

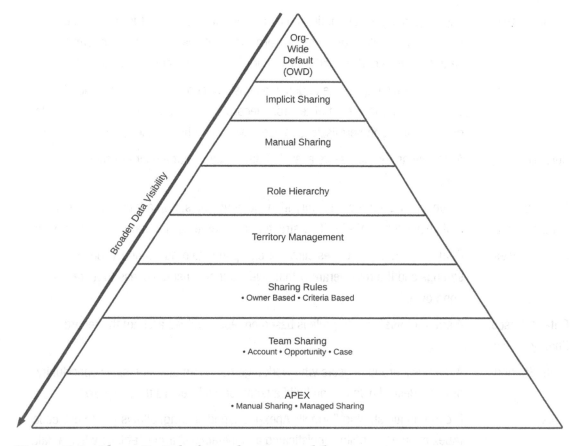

Figure 5-2. *Phase D: Salesforce sharing model*

Salesforce broadens the visibility of data with each service, starting at the lowest level of the organization-wide default for the object (standard or custom). Of course, if your org-wide default is set to full access for everyone, then there isn't much point in opening the data visibility more.

Hopefully, this is where the policy of least privilege has come into play, such that your default visibility for objects, whether standard or custom, is as restrictive as possible, only opening visibility further for specific users' job functions.

The layers of data sharing and visibility are described in Table 5-1.

Table 5-1. *Layers of Data Sharing and Visibility*

Component	Description
Org-Wide Default (OWD)	Organization-wide sharing settings specify the default level of access users have to each other's records.
Implicit Sharing	Implicit sharing is automatic. You can neither turn it off nor turn it on—it is native to the application. In other words, implicit sharing isn't a configurable setting; however, it's important for your governance team to understand.
Manual Sharing	Sometimes it's impossible to define a consistent group of users who need access to a particular set of records. Record owners can use manual sharing to give read and edit permissions to users who don't have access any other way.
Role Hierarchy	A role hierarchy represents a level of data access that a user or group of users needs.
Territory Management	When using Enterprise Territory Management, you set up a territory hierarchy that shows a model's territory structure and serves as its main interaction points.
Sharing Rules	Owner-based sharing rules allow for exceptions to organization-wide default settings and the role hierarchy that give additional users access to records they don't own.
Criteria-Based Sharing Rules	A criteria-based sharing rule is based on record values and not the record owners.
Team Sharing	A team is a group of users who work together on an account, sales opportunity, or case. Record owners can build a team for each record that they own.
Apex	Programmatic sharing (formally Apex-managed sharing) allows you to use code (Apex or other) to build sophisticated and dynamic sharing settings when a data access requirement cannot be met by any other means.

To clarify these sharing components further, your governance team has (currently) twenty-one different features within the Salesforce platform that can affect data sharing and visibility, as follows:

- Organization-wide default (OWD)

- Profile-level object settings

- Permission set–level object settings and permission set groups

- Record ownership

- Role hierarchy

- Teams (accounts, case, and opportunity)

- Queues

- Sharing rules

- Groups

- Manager groups

- Enterprise territory management

- Sharing sets

- Sharing groups

- Super user access

- Manual sharing

- Implicit sharing

- Master–detail relationship

- Account relationship data sharing

- External account hierarchy

- Programmatic sharing (Apex)

- Visualforce with Apex

This list provides a more focused approach to reviewing data sharing and visibility for your governance team. However, from the perspective of governance, the team can categorize data sharing and visibility in the following four main areas:

- Declarative Sharing – This is an area of data sharing and visibility that can be configured within the Salesforce platform without the need to write any code. This does, in fact, cover the bulk of the data sharing and visibility options.

- Programmatic Sharing – This is an area of data sharing and visibility that requires programming skills, as there is coding involved. This requires a more specialized set of skills and as such will require the governance team to have those skills also.

- Performance – This involves the impacts on the performance of the Salesforce platform through sharing data and changes to sharing data.

- Data Security – This considers the impacts to your organization's data security of any sharing and visibility requirements.

It is the governance team's goal to make sure data security is maintained. Leaning on the principle of least privilege, your governance team should feel confident that the project has taken the proper steps to ensure the right amount of data is visible to users to allow them to perform their job function and no more.

Additionally, your governance team must take a longer-term view on data governance, looking at their "crystal ball" to determine whether there could be any long-term implications of the project's sharing and visibility configuration, especially regarding enterprise objects (objects used by multiple projects, into which category Salesforce's standard objects fall). Changes to data sharing once a significant amount of data exists in the affected objects will have performance implications.

Declarative Sharing

As shown in Figure 5-3, declarative sharing is the first sub-phase for your governance team to tackle.

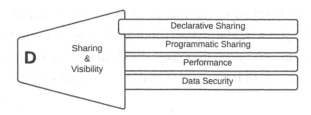

Figure 5-3. *Phase D: sharing & visibility - declarative sharing*

Most of Salesforce's data sharing and visibility capabilities fall into the Declarative Sharing category. Your governance team is looking to understand the broader impact of any data sharing and whether there is a possibility of inadvertently giving access to data to unauthorized users.

Govern the core declarative platform features that are used to meet record-level, object, and field-sharing requirements

Organization-Wide Defaults (OWDs)

OWDs define the default behavior that each object will have regarding data visibility and sharing within the Salesforce platform. OWDs are the only core feature of the Salesforce platform that allows for restrictive access; all other features open up access. An object set to `private` will restrict access to the data records of that object to the owners of those records. If you created the record, you have full access to that record. If an object is set to `read-only`, then other users will be able to see the record but not be able do anything else.

Your governance team should look to the project team to set the OWDs for any objects that have been introduced; they should be set to the most restrictive configuration, granting extra permissions with the other features discussed in this phase.

Profile-level object settings

The governance team should review the project's profile settings for any objects being introduced to the platform. The profile should be used to restrict objects' data access rather than open it up. Taking this approach, data access granularity will be easier to control.

The main driver for this approach is that profiles are a broader level of access to Salesforce. Typically you would not have thousands of profiles on the Salesforce platform, but rather a small number that gives the right access to the broadest of features you want every user to have. Access to data should then be broadened via permission sets.

Permission set–level object settings

It is easy for a project team to select the most open levels of access to keep things simple. It reduces the number of test cases required to make sure everything functions correctly for every user. However, this should be challenged by your governance team.

The project should deliver permission sets for each user persona that the project expects will use the application being governed. Although data access can be configured at the profile level, it is desirable to control data visibility through a permission set, with the profile set to be as restrictive as possible. This will allow users to change profiles (as they move around your organization), while potentially maintaining the same access to the application's data via the permission set.

Your governance team should raise concerns where a minimum number of permission sets have been proposed by your project and those permission sets offer all-or-nothing access. This will indicate that your project has not really taken the time to design data visibility against your user personas.

Record ownership

As a record owner, the user has full access to the records they have created for each object. This allows the user to `read` / `write` / `transfer` / `delete` / `share` a record they own.

Your governance team cannot do much about this configuration, but they should also question any project that is taking this approach as their data visibility and sharing solution, as this is mostly impractical and will lead to many manual-sharing scenarios.

Manual sharing

Manual sharing provides users access to certain types of record via the owner of that record manually sharing it with someone else.

Your governance team must highlight to the project team that if this is normal behavior for the users of their application, they should note that any previous manual sharing of the record by the owner performing the transfer will be lost. Additionally, your governance team should make it clear that the new user automatically has access to all records associated with the parent.

Govern the use of team functionality to meet business requirements

Role hierarchies

Role hierarchies grant extra permissions for those people who are managers of somebody else, which allows them to see the same data as the people they manage. This means that a manager will receive the same permissions for the record data that the person they manage has.

Your governance team should review whether inheriting permissions using role hierarchies has the desired outcome. This feature can be disabled for custom objects by unchecking the `Grant Access Using Hierarchies` checkbox on the OWD configuration.

Tip   Role hierarchies can have undesirable outcomes on data visibility. Take the scenario of an employee raising a case against their line manager.

Teams (accounts, case, and opportunity)

Teams allow users of the Salesforce platform to collaborate on a particular account, case, or opportunity record.

Teams can only broaden access to object records, not reduce access, and work in conjunction with sharing rules, organization-wide defaults (OWD), and other sharing methods. Team sharing is sometimes used to overcome the criteria-based sharing-rule limit (50 on the account object) or other sharing limits.

Your governance team should review the use of team sharing to uncover whether there is a hidden reason for its being proposed by the project team. If a valid use case is being proposed, then team sharing is a great way for users to collaborate temporarily. Default teams can also be configured such that users are added to a team where they regularly work with the same people.

Tip   An example of a great default team could be a Change Impact team, where a group of users can regularly collaborate around change requests handled via the case object.

Queues

Queues are a solution to more easily manage a shared workload, which is especially helpful if you have users out sick or on vacation, since if their workload is within a queue other members of that queue can pick up the work. Your governance team should pay close attention to the queue structure and hierarchy as this can cause confusion regarding data access and visibility.

Queues can be joined by specific users, roles, and public groups depending on your requirements. Queues fall under data visibility, where the object records are places in a queue for users of that queue to take ownership of the record, or the record is transferred to another queue. Role hierarchy is considered with queues, so a user that is higher in the role hierarchy than a user with access to a queue can take ownership of a record within that queue.

Your governance team is looking to be reassured that the wrong person cannot take ownership of records within a queue, or read the data within that record. Additionally, users added to a queue will be able to access all records assigned to the queue. Your governance team should look to understand how users are added to queue and what controls will be in place to control that process.

Manager groups

Manager groups can be used in manual sharing, sharing rules, and Apex-managed sharing. Manager groups can be used to share records with a management chain rather than with all managers in the same role, as with role hierarchy.

Your governance team is really looking for "accidental" exposure to data. As with most of the Salesforce platform's capabilities, they need managing and controlling. Often, over time, some of these configurations get forgotten or abandoned, until someone sees a record they should not have.

Your governance team will need to be assured that there will be proper controls in place to maintain the manager groups. Most organizations have people come and go from roles, so the process of managing user mobility within the organization needs to extend to the Salesforce platform.

Govern list view, report folder, and dashboard folder security

List view security

The Salesforce platform allows three options with regards to list view sharing:

- Only I can see this list view.

- All users can see this list view (including guest, partner, and customer portal users).

- Share list view with groups of users.

The first two options are clear: either no one can see the list view or everyone can. Your governance team should challenge the need for everyone to see the list view with your project team. This may be a legitimate business requirement but may also be a simple solution to a more complex problem.

The third option is possibly where your governance team may need to probe a little deeper. In some cases, sharing list views with a group of users makes sense, but bear in mind the following:

- If "Grant Access Using Hierarchies" is being used, managers of group members receive access to the list view.

- Managing multiple public groups with a small number of users is a burden for your Salesforce administrators.

Report folder and dashboard folder security

The Salesforce platform has a comprehensive sharing model, which extends to reports and dashboards. Reports and dashboards are stored in folders. When a folder is private to the owner, only the owner and Salesforce administrators can see the content of that folder.

Your governance team is trying to make sure that the project has considered any sharing implications with report folders and dashboard folders. Salesforce introduced enhanced folder sharing for reports and dashboards a while back, which has introduced new permissions and the way users access existing reports and dashboards.

Legacy folder sharing

Legacy folder sharing is basic, in that on creating a folder your user specifies its name but also whether it is public `read-only` or `read-write`. Additionally, the folder visibility is set, giving users one of the following:

- Accessible by all users

- Hidden from all users

- Accessible only to specific public groups, roles, and role subordinates

In this case, your project team is in a similar situation to the list view security considerations from a governance perspective.

Enhanced folder Sharing

Creating a folder with enhanced folder sharing is simpler, as you do not specify any visibility or sharing configuration, just the name of the folder. After folder creation, the user can select one of three access levels for selected users, groups, or roles, or even a combination of the following:

- View

- Edit

- Manage

Each of the access levels mentioned controls what a user can and cannot do to the content of the folder. See the resource base for more detail on this topic.

From a governance perspective, your governance team is looking to see evidence that the least-privilege principle has been applied. Warning signs are clear when a project is presenting a limited number of personas that will access the application or configuration (such as one, with full access).

Additionally, your governance team should be aware that a project may be requesting that enhanced folder sharing become enabled as part of their project. This has implications for existing configuration with legacy folders that might warrant additional clarification, such as the following:

- Clarify communications to the users where access to their reports and dashboards may change, for example:

    - If two users have View All Data, but one user has Manage Dashboards, and they collaborate on a dashboard in a public folder, the user with View All Data will move to View Dashboards in Public Folders, losing the right to edit the dashboard.

    - If a user has Manage Dashboards in legacy folder sharing, in enhanced folder sharing they will only be able to edit their dashboards in that folder; all others will be View Access.

Govern implicit sharing within the platform

Implicit sharing

The Salesforce platform has several sharing behaviors that are built into the platform that are not configurable by the project team or Salesforce administrators. Implicit sharing is one of those behaviors and has a few variations to consider, as follows:

- Account and child records

    - Parent implicit sharing – If the user has access to a parent account record, the user will have access to the associated child records based on the account owner's role.

    - Child implicit sharing – If the user has access to an account's child record, the user will have Read-Only access to that account.

- Site and portal user sharing behavior

    - Contact and account record access – The portal or site user will gain Read-Only access to their account's parent account and to all of that account's contacts.

- Service Cloud portal users – Service Cloud portal users do not
  have roles so are unable to access their data via role hierarchy.
  The user can be added to a share group to gain access to the data
  owned by the Service Cloud portal user.

- Case access – Any user that is the contact on a case has `Read` and
  `Write` access on the case.

It is easy to see that data could be inadvertently exposed with implicit sharing on
the Salesforce platform. Your governance team will need to understand or challenge
some of the scenarios that can drive implicit sharing, especially around site and portal
users. The governance team should not be particularly challenging around the business
requirements themselves, just simply whether the project has thoroughly considered the
configuration needed to deliver those business requirements.

Additionally, the implementation of sites and portals will need long-term
management. In most cases, once the sharing configuration is initially set up it
continues to work with very little interaction in the longer term; however, this can create
complacency and might be something that your governance team needs to understand.
People tend to come and go from organizations, and your governance team will need
to be assured that the knowledge around the sharing solution is clearly documented for
future team members to pick up.

Master–detail relationship

Your project team will more than likely introduce an object or two with a master–detail
relationship. On many occasions, this relationship is overlooked in terms of how it
impacts the data sharing model; however, it does. Your governance team should help the
project team with determining whether data is being inappropriately shared because of
any master–detail relationships the project has implemented.

Basically, the master–detail relationship can be viewed as a parent and child
relationship, with a parent object having a fixed relationship with the child object. This
means that the child cannot exist without a parent object, and so the owner field of the detail
(or child) object is not available as it is automatically set to that of the parent. Additionally,
this means that the detail (or child) object cannot have sharing rules, manual sharing, or
queues associated with it. Although the relationship between a detail (or child) object and
the master (or parent) is fixed, it is possible to re-parent a detail custom object to a different
parent record if the option is configured in the master–detail relationship definition.

Your governance team should be aware that the detail (or child) object inherits the sharing and security settings of the master (or parent) object. Additionally, it is not possible to set permissions on the detail object independently of the master.

You project team should understand that the detail (or child) object records will appear on the master (or parent) object's page layout, therefore allowing those records to be viewed. Your governance team should really be trying to determine whether this behavior is the desired outcome. Although this relationship type between two objects is quite convenient, it is harder to change later if your project team decides that details records should not always be visible to end users.

Account relationship data sharing

Account relationship data sharing rules provide granular control for account information sharing. These rules allow the sharing of objects related to the account, such as cases, opportunities, and contacts, to be shared with other accounts. This sharing model is independent of both the owner of the account and the access level granted.

Your governance team, if presented with this type of sharing rule by the project team, should try to understand the drivers behind using this type of sharing. Effectively, the project will be requesting that data associated with one account be shared with a different account. During the configuration of these rules, the project team can define the type of relationship the accounts have between them to provide more details as to why this type of sharing is required.

Your governance team will need to review the access level being used in the data sharing as well as the criteria that will drive the record sharing for the object type specified. Additionally, once a sharing rule has been created it cannot be modified; only its name can be changed. This means that if mistakes are made or changes are required, the rule will need to be deleted and recreated.

Govern the appropriate sharing design for the various community user types

Community users fall into two types, which are controlled by the Salesforce license allocated to that user. The two types are as follows:

- With roles
- Without roles

Users with roles will have a partner community license or a customer community plus license. Users with roles are impacted by any sharing that relies upon roles. Users without a role cannot be provided access to data that is driven by sharing that requires a role.

Sharing sets

Sharing sets grant site users access to any record that is associated with an account or contact that matches the user's account or contact. Access mapping allows you to grant access to records in a sharing set. Access mappings support indirect lookups from the user. As an example, this allows you to grant site users access to all cases related to the account that is identified on the users' contact record.

As the governing team, you must examine what records you are exposing to potential external users (i.e., site users). Sharing sets are applicable across all sites of which the user is a member. Users who have been granted access to any records via sharing sets are not influenced by the role hierarchy. There are several standard objects that can be part of a sharing set, but only custom objects with a lookup to account or contact can be part of a sharing set.

As with other sharing configurations, your governance team should pay close attention to the long-term maintenance and control of sharing sets.

Sharing groups

Sharing groups allow records owned by site users to be shared with internal and external users. This sharing solution is applicable to high-volume users, which are users with no role associated.

Your governance team will need to consider the consequences of future deactivation of any sharing groups, and how the project team intends to control and maintain these. Deactivating a sharing group removes users' access to records.

Super user access

Super user access applies to anyone with partner community or customer community plus licenses and grants access to data owned by other partner users who have the same role or a role below them.

Super user access applies to cases, leads, custom objects, and opportunities only. However, external users will only gain access to these objects if they are exposed by their profile or sharing, and the tabs are added to the site.

As the governance team, you will need to review the project's approach to exposing data via super user access. Your project's role hierarchy is critical in this process. Long-term management and maintenance of this data access method will be required. The governance team needs to make sure the project team has the proper controls in place so that data is not inadvertently accessed or visible.

External account hierarchy

External account hierarchy is a feature introduced in 2020 that allows records to be shared between Community Cloud (now referred to as Experience Cloud) users in one account and Community Cloud users in a different account. This can be useful for managing subsidiaries of businesses modeled within your Salesforce org.

Your governance team should consider the wider application usage and how the project team sees its application being used. The following are questions that your governance team should present to the project team:

- How many levels in the account hierarchy does the project expect to have? External account hierarchy supports up to five hierarchical levels.

- How many records within the account hierarchy does the project expect to have? The external account hierarchy feature introduces a new object that should contain no more than 100,000 records per Salesforce org.

- Can the account be part of more than one account hierarchy? Customer or partner accounts can only be used in one active external account hierarchy.

- Does the project foresee any account merging requirements in the lifespan of the application? Accounts used in an external account hierarchy cannot be merged with another account.

- Does the project expect to use account role optimization (ARO), as this is incompatible with extremal account hierarchy?

Govern the application of territory management

Territory management is best used for modeling a matrix reporting structure, where a user can report to multiple managers.

Your governance team should review the use of territory management to make sure that it has not been used as a replacement for role hierarchy. Often, territories are created to mirror role hierarchies. Additionally, your governance team should look out for any data-cleaning activities that are being used with territory assignment rules. And data clean-up should be performed by the built-in duplicate management features of the Salesforce platform, merging duplicate records or the use of Lightning Data.

Lastly, your governance team should make sure that the project has avoided any unnecessary sharing recalculations as these may have performance implications.

Programmatic Sharing

As shown in Figure 5-4, programmatic sharing is the next sub-phase on which your governance team should focus.

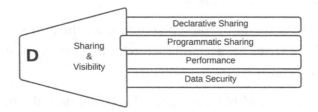

Figure 5-4. *Phase D: sharing & visibility - programmatic sharing*

Govern the core programmatic platform security features that have been used to meet sharing requirements

The Salesforce platform provides various programmatic platform security features. Your governance team should look for evidence that these have been considered by the project team for any Apex development that has taken place. These security features fall into the following categories:

- Enforcing sharing rules

- Enforcing object and field permissions

- Enforcing SOQL data filtering

- Class security

- Apex-managed sharing

Enforcing sharing rules

Apex normally runs in a system context, which basically means that the current user's permissions are not considered during the execution of the Apex code (except for code that is executed with `executeAnonymous`). However, sharing rules are not always enforced. Apex classes declared with the `without sharing` keyword will not enforce sharing rules.

If this keyword is used by your project team in its Apex development, your governance team should make sure that data is not inadvertently being exposed where it would normally be hidden from users by permissions, field-level security, or organization-wide defaults.

Your governance team should also check that a class declared as `with sharing` is not calling a different class using `without sharing`.

Enforcing object and field permissions

Apex does not enforce object and field permissions as standard. If object and field permissions are critical aspects of your project's security model, your governance team should challenge the project to overcome this default behavior.

Your project team can enforce object and field permissions by using the sObject's describe result method. Your project should consider using `Schema.DescribeSobjectResult` and `Schema.DescribeFieldResult` to understand whether the current user has `read`, `create`, or `update` access to an sObject or an sObject's fields. Your governance team should look for evidence that this extra code has been implemented correctly.

Enforcing SOQL data filtering

Another area of Apex that can create data access and visibility leakage is SOQL. The use of SOQL within Apex code is common practice. However, your governance team should look to the project team to make sure that any object- and field-level permissions are adhered to.

91

Your governance team should also look to the project team to enforce security for SOQL statements using the `stripInaccessible` method. This method will remove any fields that do not meet the permissions of the current user.

Additionally, SOQL queries can be made security aware by using the `WITH SECURITY_ENFORCED` clause.

As there are restrictions around the usage of both of these features, it is more than likely that your governance team will see both in action across Apex that must provide user-level data access that correctly adheres to the user's permissions.

Class security

A project can control which users can execute methods on Apex classes (does not include triggers) using profiles and permissions. This could be an additional level of security control that can restrict access to sensitive methods, such as a method that calculates commission payments. Although this is in the control of the project team because it will be driven by business requirements, your governance team can discuss this feature as an additional way of securing sensitive functions developed in Apex.

Apex-managed sharing

Apex sharing (more often referred to as programmatic sharing) allows the use of code to build sophisticated sharing models that might not be possible using declarative solutions.

As part of your governance, your team should make sure that the project team is providing the relevant Apex classes for recalculating sharing. These Apex classes will be executed every time a custom object's organization-wide default access level is changed.

As programmatic sharing falls within Phase F of the Salesforce Platform Governance Method, your governance team should flag the project's application as requiring further governance, as all Apex programming should be governed consistently.

The Apex sharing recalculation class must implement the `Database.Batchable` interface. Your governance team now knows that Phase F must pay attention to the best practices for developing batch Apex. Additionally, your governance team should also expect Phase I to be used to govern the project's development life cycle, specifically around source control, development standards, testing, and deployment of Apex code.

As Phase F will no doubt highlight, your project team should also deliver all the relevant Apex tests and make sure that the APEX class used for sharing recalculation is associated with the custom object via the custom object's management settings.

One of the challenges facing your governance team will be determining whether programmatic sharing has been used appropriately. As mentioned in Phase A of the Salesforce Platform Governance Method, some resources prefer to develop solutions using code rather than explore pre-existing platform capabilities. It is the role of the governance team to make sure this does not happen.

Your governance team should always challenge your projects if programmatic sharing has been used when a declarative solution could have been. This is because the programmatic solution inevitably adds more complexity to your project's application, increases the maintenance overheads, and drives a different model into your platform resourcing requirements for operational support.

There are, however, a few good reasons to use programmatic sharing, as follows:

- The obvious is that no other declarative sharing solution is available to meet the data sharing needs of the project.

- Poor performance has been experienced using declarative sharing solutions, which can occur when your project expects very large data volumes; you may also experience this for applications that have been in use for a while.

- You require team functionality for your project's custom objects.

- Your project expects data access to be dictated by an external source, such as an external system to which you are integrating.

Govern the security risks in programmatic customizations relative to data visibility, focus on difference in capabilities between programmatic sharing for standard vs. custom objects

The Salesforce platform has several security defenses built into the Lightning platform; however, just like any other platform, careless programming can bypass these defenses, thus exposing applications to security risks.

As mentioned previously, it is easy for Apex code to see the complete data available on the Salesforce platform rather than just the data that should be visible to the current user. This is not something the project team really has to concern itself with when using declarative sharing features. Your governance team will need to grasp the holistic view of the sharing solutions being proposed by your project team so as to provide a full assessment of the security implications of the project's choices.

Your project team should also pay attention to the differences in sharing standard versus sharing custom object records using programmatic sharing. Standard objects, such as Account, Contact, and so on, do not support the Apex Sharing Reason. For this reason, standard objects use the RowCause of "Manual" by default. Shares with this condition are removed when record ownership changes. Therefore, users may find they lose access to data from standard objects where programmatic sharing was used and the record ownership has changed. This is not the case for custom objects.

Performance

As shown in Figure 5-5, performance is the next sub-phase for your governance team to examine.

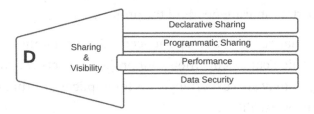

Figure 5-5. *Phase D: sharing & visibility - performance*

Govern whether the solution is scalable to and maintainable at enterprise levels

One of the primary concerns for your governance team will be the performance of the Salesforce platform. Often, the Salesforce platform becomes a business-critical platform that is used by thousands of people every day within your organization. If that is not the case today, it may well be the case in the future.

Changes to sharing data can have a significant impact on the performance of the Salesforce platform.

Caution   We have all experienced that situation where a change is made to a sharing rule that then triggers a recalculation that impacts the platform for days. Plan changes carefully and make sure the scale of the change is well understood, and consider the number of records and the number of users that are impacted by the change.

Your governance team should take time to understand the changes your project intends to deploy into your Salesforce platform. For a new application, one that has never been deployed before, you will not have pre-existing data. Sharing rules, which are hopefully part of the deployment package that the project is constructing, will have limited impact. However, if you have had a Salesforce implementation for some time, you may find that your project is leveraging enterprise objects (standard or custom). Alternatively, your project may be deploying a change to an existing application that has been in use for several years and has vast amounts of data.

Your governance team should look to understand the following:

- Whether any large quantities of data are to be loaded after any sharing rules have already been created

- Limit updates to account relationship data sharing rules that are being used by multiple account relationships. Recalculating account relationship data sharing rules for many records can take some time. If updates to active account relationship data sharing rules are necessary, space them out to avoid performance issues. Also, shared data may not be immediately available after you make the updates.

- Avoid bulk contact reparenting operations.

- For optimal data processing, position users who own many records at the top of an external role hierarchy.

- Salesforce has a recommended limit of 50 million records for custom objects.

- If possible, load your data before you set up account relationship data sharing rules. Loading data after you create account relationships and account relationship data sharing rules activates the sharing rules. If it is necessary to load data after account relationship data sharing rules have been created, load no more than 1 million records per day.

- Salesforce automatically recalculates sharing for all records on an object when its organization-wide sharing default access level changes. The recalculation adds managed sharing when appropriate.

- Every time a custom object's organization-wide sharing default access level is updated, any Apex recalculation classes defined for associated custom objects are also executed.

- Where bulk changes are to be made, such as role hierarchy changes, has the project considered deferring automatic sharing recalculation?

However, even for "green-field" deployments of applications, your governance team should take a long-term view of data sharing, considering any data volume estimates presented by the project team during Phase B of the Salesforce Platform Governance Method.

Data Security

As shown in Figure 5-6, data security is the next sub-phase of the Salesforce Platform Governance Method that should be focused on.

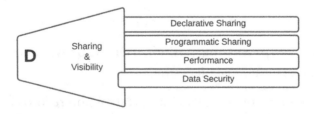

Figure 5-6. *Phase D: sharing & visibility - data security*

Govern any specific secured data implementation on the Salesforce platform

Your governance team will need to understand whether the project has any specific data protection requirements. These are generally business dependent, but normally fall into the category of data requiring additional protection for some reason. The reason could be regulatory or just specific to your business.

If your project has specific requirements to secure data for any reason, your governance team will need to understand how that data protection will be implemented so that they can determine whether that requirement is in fact fully met.

The project should provide personas for the usage of the application they are building or the configuration they are delivering. These personas should provide the levels of data security required. An example of business-type data that may require additional levels of protection could be credit card numbers. The project may provide several personas that can view a lot of data, but only certain personas are trusted to see the customer's credit card number. Additionally, Salesforce administrators, typically the custodians of the Salesforce platform, may not be allowed to see this particular information.

Govern the use of "classic" encryption fields in the Salesforce platform and the limitations that need to be taken into consideration

The Salesforce platform's classic field encryption provides a convenient solution to protecting data within fields that your project wants to keep private. As previously mentioned, the use of a credit card number field might fall into this category. Only specific users will normally have access to a customer's credit card number. It is not something that every user should be able to see.

Users with the `View Encrypted Data` permission will be able to see the data within the field. However, there are a few areas that your governance team should explore if a project is using encrypted fields, as follows:

- If a user with the `View Encrypted Data` permission grants login access to another user, that user will see encrypted fields in plain text.

- Encrypted fields are limited to 175 characters.

- Encrypted fields are editable regardless of whether the user has the View Encrypted Data permission. The project must use validation rules, field-level security, or page layouts to prevent this.

- Encrypted data fields can still be used in validation rules and Apex regardless of whether the user has the View Encrypted Data permission.

- Existing custom fields cannot be converted into encrypted fields, nor can encrypted fields be converted into another data type.

- The project should only use encrypted custom fields when the business requires an extra level of security due to processing overheads and search-related limitations.

Method

This is the formal method for Phase D of the Salesforce Platform Governance Method. The objectives of Phase D are to ensure that the data sharing and visibility aspects of the application have been thoroughly considered. The areas that will be assessed during this phase are as follows:

- Declarative Sharing

- Programmatic Sharing

- Performance

- Data Security

Approach

This phase is focused on governing the data sharing and visibility aspects of an application or configuration. In some part, these will be driven by security policies already in place within your organization. If that is not the case, these security policies may be a deliverable of the project itself, effectively setting the standards for future application development.

As this phase may contain Apex source code, your governance team will inform the project team that they are subject to subsequent governance phases if Apex source code is part of the project's application or configuration.

Your governance team should not seek to reject any sharing the project deems necessary to deliver the business requirements, but rather should explore with the project team that the correct platform feature has been used and that consideration has been made regarding the impacts of data sharing on the wider data security of the platform.

Where enterprise objects have been impacted in the sharing and visibility solution, the governance team should be confident that a wider impact analysis has taken place on the projects impacted by the changes being proposed. Remember that enterprise objects are standard or custom objects in use by more than one project or application within your organization.

Inputs

For the governance process to be a success, the project must have a few artifacts available to the governance team for review. Suggested artifacts for the governance team to review for Phase D of the Salesforce Platform Governance Method are as follows:

- Application configuration and source (or the repository in the instance of using a source control system) where appropriate

- User personas, detailing permissions and data sharing and visibility requirements

- Security policy (if defined by the project)

- Clear definitions around sensitive data

Steps

The steps to govern the sharing and visibility phase will help the project team understand how users will gain access to the data held within the Salesforce platform. The governance team should ensure that the project team has used a least-privilege principle for data access and be assured that data security is maintained.

Declarative Sharing

1. Govern the core declarative platform features that are used to meet record-level, object, and field sharing requirements.

2. Govern the use of team functionality to meet business requirements.

3. Govern list view, report folder, and dashboard folder security.

4. Govern implicit sharing within the platform.

5. Govern the appropriate sharing design for the various community user types.

6. Govern the application of territory management.

Programmatic Sharing

1. Govern the core programmatic platform security features that have been used to meet sharing requirements.

2. Govern the security risks in programmatic customizations relative to data visibility, focus on difference in capabilities between programmatic sharing for standard vs. custom objects.

Performance

1. Govern that the solution is scalable to and maintainable at enterprise levels.

Data Security

1. Govern any specific secured data implementation on the Salesforce platform.

2. Govern the use of "classic" encryption fields in the Salesforce platform and the limitations that need to be taken into consideration.

Outputs

Once all the steps have been assessed, the outputs to Phase D are as follows:

- Not Applicable – This phase in the Salesforce Platform Governance Method is not applicable to the project.

- Remediate – The governance team requests that the project team remediates its design to accommodate the issues raised during the governance review.

- Pass – The governance team has found no issues or concerns with the project's proposal and therefore the project has passed this governance phase.

- Review – The governance team has found the inputs cannot be objectively measured and therefore a subjective view has been made, which will lead to a discussion with the project team to reach consensus. Although undesirable, this could be a consequence of unclear standards/policies.

Scenario

For our scenario we are going to focus on one step from the Declarative Sharing group of the sharing and visibility Phase D method. This step is as follows:

- Govern the core declarative platform features that are used to meet record-level, object, and field sharing requirements

Returning to our fictitious company, Bright Sound Guitars Ltd., you may recall Hanna, the project's architect. Hanna wants to provide an overview of the sharing model she wants to put in place. Hanna wants her users to have access to as much data as possible, as she feels that the more data the users can see, the easier their jobs will be.

Hanna proposes a simple sharing configuration for her project's application. She recommends the following two user personas:

- Standard User – Someone who has access to all data and can see and do everything

- Administration User – Someone who is like the Standard User but is known as the administrator.

Hanna highlights that this is really the starting position, and she doesn't really have a good handle on exactly the types of users her project's application will have. She wants to allow the application to "bed in" for a few months before really tackling data visibility and sharing.

The governance team reflects on what Hanna is proposing and sympathizes with her situation. They do realize how difficult it is to get the data visibility and sharing model right in the first instance. However, the governance team counters Hanna's proposal with a few suggestions, as follows:

- Given that Bright Sound Guitars is operating a least-privilege principle to data access, the governance team knows that the business area that Hanna's application is going to be deployed to has a very good role hierarchy in place. The team suggests that Hanna review her personas along the lines of the following:

  - Contact Agent – Users have access to the data records they own. Users can manually share data records with other users where required, but this must be supported with an approval process from their line manager.

  - Team Lead – Users have access to their own records and by using the role hierarchy can access the data of the contact agent that reports to them.

  - Department Lead – Using the role hierarchy, the department lead can see the entire department's data.

  - The governance team would like to see sharing automated, and express that manual sharing can lead to a lot of overhead in terms of knowing who can see what. They feel that with a little more investigation, Hanna will see a pattern that could drive a sharing rule.

Hanna likes what she is hearing and takes the advice away to work with the business to understand more around the personas they have in their department and what data those personas can and cannot see. She feels like she understands more about the use of roles and how that could help expose data to broader user groups without the complexity of manually sharing data. The sharing rule is a great idea, and she already has an idea as to why one contact agent may involve another.

Summary

There is no doubt that the Salesforce platform offers a magnitude of sharing capabilities. Some might say it is too flexible. It is easy to see that with all the different features available to share data and broaden data visibility a Salesforce platform could become quite complex to manage.

The key principle to remember is the principle of least privilege. Taking that principle, you must work through the options to deliver the data visibility and sharing model that your project requires. Pay close attention to limitations that each feature has, as some may not be an issue from the offset, but may become an issue further in the lifespan of the project.

Consider all the consequences that are a result of sharing. Keep a holistic mindset, especially around the use of sites and communities (now referred to as Experience Cloud).

CHAPTER 6

Integration: Phase E

This phase of the Salesforce Platform Governance Method focuses on the integration capabilities of the Salesforce platform and the external systems with which your projects intend to integrate.

Overview

Integration is a key capability of the Salesforce platform. It is designed to bring as much customer-related information together in one place as possible. The more you know about your customers, the better you can serve them.

Part of that customer-centric strategy is to provide numerous ways for Salesforce to integrate with any external systems that an enterprise may already have in use. The Salesforce platform is one of the most open platforms available today in terms of integration. With that level of openness comes some work for your organization to govern. Not that you are looking to restrict what your projects do in terms of integrating with external systems, but you will need to understand at a holistic level the flow of data and the connected systems you have.

As shown in Figure 6-1, Phase E has a few sub-phases to help your governance team focus its activities.

© Lee Harding and Lee Bayliss 2022
L. Harding and L. Bayliss, *Salesforce Platform Governance Method*,
https://doi.org/10.1007/978-1-4842-7404-0_6

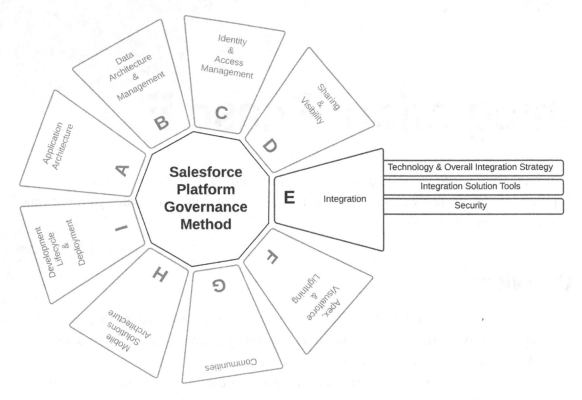

Figure 6-1. *The Salesforce Platform Governance Method: Phase E*

As with previous phases, let's start by defining what we mean by integration as it can have a few definitions, and having a clear definition helps us understand the role of governance within this phase. In the context of the Salesforce Platform Governance Method, we will this time use the Gartner definition:

> *"Integration services are detailed design and implementation services that link application functionality (custom software or package software) and/or data with each other or with the established or planned IT infrastructure. Specific activities might include project planning, project management, detailed design or implementation of application programming interfaces, Web services, or middleware systems."*

> —Gartner[1]

---

[1] https://www.gartner.com/en/information-technology/glossary/integration

Salesforce has provided a great starting point for integrating external systems in the form of integration patterns. These patterns address key archetype integration scenarios and can help accelerate your approach to integrating an external system. The patterns are broad enough that you could categorize your integration requirements into one of the patterns shown in Table 6-1.

Table 6-1. *Salesforce Integration Patterns*

Pattern	Usage
Remote Process Invocation – Request and Reply	This pattern is probably the ideal integration technique to use with an external system. Salesforce invokes a process on your external system and waits for that process to complete; the response can then be used to determine success or failure and act accordingly.
Remote Process Invocation – Fire and Forget	This pattern is useful for integrating with external systems that need to be informed or act as part of a business process, but completion and response are not required. Salesforce can continue to perform the business process regardless of the external systems' success or failure.
Batch Data Synchronization	This pattern is useful for sending and receiving large quantities of data that you want to reside in two or more different systems. Each system has its own copy of the data. The data is synchronized on a regular interval, typically daily.
Remote Call-In	This pattern allows an external system to call a Salesforce process to create and maintain data or perform a process of some sort. You could consider this the opposite of remote process invocation, as the instigation of the interface is triggered by the external system rather than the Salesforce platform.
UI Update Based on Data Changes	This is a useful integration pattern from an end user's perspective, where the user interface is automatically refreshed based on data changes.
Data Virtualization	This pattern allows Salesforce to expose data that is stored externally as if that data were held within the Salesforce platform. It's useful when large amounts of data sit outside the Salesforce platform and you do not want to duplicate that data within the Salesforce platform using the batch data synchronization pattern.

The Salesforce integration patterns are a starting point and a neat way to categorize your integration requirements with the Salesforce platform. However, because you can use Apex to integrate with external systems, your projects can create all manner of solutions to meet the nuances of your organization and the systems within it.

The flexibility of the Salesforce platform when it comes to integration makes governance more important than ever. Your governance team will be looking to understand the flow of data from one system to the other, which system owns the data, and, when changes occur to that data, how those changes flow back into the correct systems.

As the patterns suggest, integrations can take many forms; some integrations will be triggered by data changes, while others will be slower data movement–type integrations. Additionally, you could use a few patterns in concert.

Note   It is common that some legacy systems provide a basic integration capability. On several occasions you will find that the batch data synchronization and remote process invocation patterns are used together. For example, when dealing with stock information, the stock is loaded into the Salesforce platform via the batch data synchronization pattern and then stock "status" is updated on the external system using either of the remote process invocation patterns.

What is important is recognizing when integration sprawl is happening—multiple systems all trying to talk to each other with more and more complex coordination requirements and eventually a lack of data integrity. This situation will be harder and more costly to unpick than taking the time to define an integration strategy and standards up front.

Your governance team should be instrumental in defining your organization's integration strategy and standards and managing the deviations from those standards. There will more than likely be scenarios that challenge the standards in place within your organization because it is unlikely that every system you use will have the capabilities required to meet your standards.

Finally, if your governance team covers more than just the Salesforce platform, they are probably familiar with a much broader range of integration patterns (such as the 65 integration patterns detailed in Gregor Hohpe and Bobby Wool's book, *Enterprise Integration Patterns*). If this is the case, your governance team will probably need to provide some degree of translation between your enterprise integration patterns and the Salesforce integration patterns, mainly because your Salesforce capability will have learned the Salesforce approach to integration, driven by the Salesforce training and certifications.

Technologies & Overall Integration Strategy

As shown in Figure 6-2, technology and overall integration strategy is the first sub-phase on which your governance team should focus.

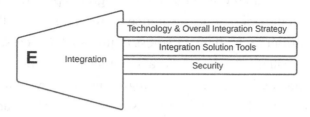

Figure 6-2. *Phase E: integration - technology & overall integration strategy*

Govern the enterprise integration landscape and overall integration strategy, with associated risks, trade-offs, and business and technical considerations

Your governance team will need to govern the overall integration landscape within your organization by using a clearly defined integration strategy. Your strategy will provide the acceptable patterns that your organization can accommodate, and each pattern will come with trade-offs and risks. These trade-offs and risks must be clearly articulated to the business by the project team.

Every time an integration is made between two or more separate systems, you are accepting an intrinsic link between those two or more systems. What happens to one system may influence the other systems integrated with it. Your governance team needs to understand this situation, because simple operational processes such as updates to systems for security patches or simply new releases may have an impact on other integrated systems.

Your governance team should not dictate to the project team that an integration cannot occur, as the project should be driven by business requirements. As such, denying an integration could create a business impact that may be unacceptable to your organization. Instead, your governance team must maintain order and standardization over the following areas:

- Data Custody – Which system is a custodian of the data? This system is the primary owner of the data and therefore the primary source of "truth" for that data. This is important for the business to know (if they do not know already) because not all integrations offer "instant" interactions, and therefore knowing which system has the most up-to-date view of the data is an important piece of information.

- Business Risks – Can the systems being integrated provide the business with the operational resilience required to deliver the business requirements? If the business requires 24/7 access, your project team will need to know if that is achievable by the systems delivering the business processes. Integrating with a system that is offline over the weekend, when the business requires 24/7 access, will not be acceptable to the business.

- Technical Standards – Has the project delivered the integration solution in line with your organization's technical standards? For example, has the project used the organization's integration solution already in place, such as Salesforce's MuleSoft or Dell's Boomi products, because your integration standards require no peer-to-peer integrations?

- Integration Patterns Used – Has the project used the appropriate integration pattern(s)? This is sometimes driven by the systems being integrated, but can also be driven by project deadlines where several integration solutions are available, and the project selects the pattern that's easiest to implement, sometimes presented as a "minimal viable product" approach but tends to remain for the lifetime of the application.

- Security Compliance – Security plays a part in practically every aspect of systems design. The Salesforce platform is no exception. Integration between two or more systems requires security consideration: how the systems authenticate, how that authentication is tracked, how data is transmitted, how changes to data are tracked. Your governance team will need to spend some time working with the project to understand how these questions are being tackled.

Your governance team will need to address the preceding items, helping the project team to understand the risks associated with the integration patterns selected. Your project team should provide your governance team with a clear scope or set of requirements that is driving the integration to begin with. This will help your governance team understand what your project team is trying to achieve and assess the project based on those criteria.

Tip   One area that is typically overlooked is the quality of the data. Often, the project and business have overlooked that data quality may not be as good as expected. This drives all sorts of integration challenges, especially when one system is controlling the data an end user enters versus receiving data from a system that does not provide such controls.

One example that happens very regularly is using restricted picklists in the Salesforce platform. These are great for controlling the options available for the end user to select. Color is a good example of a picklist. However, your external system may not use a picklist for this information, allowing the end user to enter a color as "free" text. Your integration will be challenged by this simple problem of mapping a free text field with a controlled field in the Salesforce platform.

Another example is a field that is mandatory on the Salesforce platform versus a field that is not mandatory on the external system. Again, this simple problem creates complexity within your integration solution. Your project will have to work with the business to provide a solution for this.

Broadly, the risks associated with the integration patterns suggested by Salesforce are shown in Table 6-2.

Table 6-2. *Integration Pattern Risks*

Pattern	Risks
Remote Process Invocation – Request and Reply	• Your external system must respond within the Salesforce platform's timeout limit; otherwise, the process will fail. • External calls are subject to Apex synchronous transaction governor limits. Care should be taken that your process stays within those limits. • The small timeout values may drive the volume of data that can be transmitted, while variation in data volume may create failures in the process. • State management needs to be addressed, where errors on the external system result in transactional integrity on the Salesforce platform. • Transaction complexity could become an issue over time. This pattern is particularly useful for simple transactions and not complicated processes. • Pay attention to the Salesforce platform's governor limits, which are easily breached if the integration is not clearly defined. • Keep in mind the external systems' integration capabilities and how they might change over time. For example, a system may support SOAP today, but have a roadmap to move to a RESTful API in the future, retiring the SOAP interface.
Remote Process Invocation – Fire and Forget	• State management needs to be addressed, where errors on the external system result in transactional integrity on the Salesforce platform, made more complex in the "fire and forget" pattern because your two systems are not performing a synchronous process, which means that failures on the external system need to inform the Salesforce platform with information to tie the transactions together (such as an external ID). • Pay attention to the Salesforce platform's governor limits, which are easily breached if the integration is not clearly defined. • Keep in mind the external systems' integration capabilities and how they might change over time. For example, a system may support SOAP today, but have a roadmap to move to a RESTful API in the future, retiring the SOAP interface.

(continued)

Table 6-2. (*continued*)

Pattern	Risks
Batch Data Synchronization	• Your batch processes must complete within the batch window. • You need to understand the business requirements for system availability. Your batch processes should not execute while you have active users. • Pay attention to the Salesforce platform's governor limits, which are easily breached (such as DML limits) if your project has not considered data volumes and processing times. Batch sizes can help keep your batch processes within the limits but will extend the time for your complete batch to complete.
Remote Call-In	• Your external system must complete within the Salesforce platform's session timeout limit; otherwise, the process will fail. Keep in mind any SOQL queries also have individual timeout limits. • The small timeout values may drive the volume of data that can be transmitted, while variation in data volume may create failures in the process. • State management needs to be addressed, where errors on the external system result in transactional integrity on the Salesforce platform. Use external ID to maintain a consistent key between systems.
UI Update Based on Data Changes	• Custom user interfaces are required in Salesforce to implement this pattern, adding technical risk to the project and increased testing requirements.
Data Virtualization	• Your external system must respond within the Salesforce platform's timeout limit; otherwise, the process will fail. • The small timeout values may drive the volume of data that can be transmitted, while variation in data volume may create failures in the process. • State management needs to be addressed, where errors on the external system result in transactional integrity on the Salesforce platform. Use external ID to maintain a consistent key between systems. • Pay attention to the Salesforce platform's governor limits, which are easily breached if the integration is not clearly defined.

Your governance team should pay attention to any trade-offs between the integration patterns and how that marries with the business requirements delivered by the project. There is always a trade-off in every integration pattern, and it is likely that whichever pattern is selected will be not perfect.

Usually, trade-offs come in the following forms:

- Data Consistency – Data is rarely updated in real-time in today's integration solutions; it is typically too expensive to achieve this. Real-time has morphed into the phrase *near-time*, where data is updated as quickly as it can be given the processes involved and the communication routes required. This does lead to some degree of data skew between the different systems. The slower the data updates occur, the greater the chance of data skew.

- Data Volumes – The quicker you want to have data reflected across different systems, the lower the data volumes should be. Where important status indicators are required between systems, such as stock status, the approach should be to keep the data volume as small as possible. For example, if you are changing the status of a stock item, the data could contain just the stock identifier and the status, rather than any other data that is not really required to maintain stock status.

- Data Frequency – The frequency at which data changes can be an issue with regards to the data volumes and consistency. You will not want to create a "chatty" integration solution for data records that change regularly as this will consume your Salesforce platform limits and may not be accommodated by your external system.

Given these trade-offs, your project will have had to undergo some design consideration, which may have driven several integrations to be developed to accommodate all the business requirements. The trade-offs to consider are shown in Table 6-3.

Table 6-3. *Integration Data Requirement Trade-offs*

Requirement	Trade-off
Data Consistency – HIGH	Data Volume – LOW Data Frequency – HIGH
Data Volume – HIGH	Data Consistency – LOW Data Frequency – LOW
Data Frequency – HIGH	Data Consistency – HIGH Data Volume – LOW

Your governance team should look at the overall integration landscape, really focusing on the following principles:

- Reduce data duplication – Ideally, you should not be duplicating data in multiple systems. This is not always an achievable principle, but one that should always be front of mind. Only duplicate data if it is critical, and then only duplicate data that changes infrequently.

- Reduce communication frequency – You do not want to flood your network or your systems with lots of communications. Communications should be kept to a minimum, as highly "chatty" integrations could have a detrimental impact on the systems being integrated since they may not be capable of accommodating the additional workload put upon them.

- Reduce peer-to-peer integrations – You want to avoid propagating peer-to-peer integrations. Where you only have a small number of systems within your enterprise, it is unlikely you could justify the expense of an integration solution, but where you have several systems, all needing to share data and integrate processes, you should really consider using an enterprise integration solution.

Govern the data backup/archiving/data warehousing integration strategies

Governing data backup, archiving, and data warehouse integration strategies focuses on the storing of data outside the Salesforce platform and how that is going to happen.

Your project team may not have considered this requirement because most such teams think that your data backup requirements are taken care of by Salesforce. To some degree that is true. Obviously Salesforce is running the Salesforce platform in a manner that delivers the service its customers expect; however, this is different from data backup, archiving, and warehousing at the project or business level.

Your organization may have a data backup, archiving, or warehousing strategy already in place, but this will differ massively from how Salesforce provides for backups of its own services.

From a governance perspective, you can broadly define your backup, archiving, and data warehousing strategies as shown in Table 6-4.

Table 6-4. *Backup, Archiving, and Data Warehousing Strategies*

Strategy	Definition
Data Backup	The solution to store data outside the Salesforce platform for the purposes of recovering data lost inadvertently. This could be due to human error, maliciousness, or defects in coding, configuration, or integration. For example, you create an integration that updated account information that inadvertently updated the wrong fields.
Data Archiving	The solution to store data outside the Salesforce platform for a period (usually several years) to meet compliance requirements. Typically, the data being archived is removed from the system that the data came from, but this is not always the case.
	Archiving data can be a great way to retain current information in the Salesforce platform rather than historical data that is no longer relevant to the business but must be retained.
Data Warehousing	The solution to copy data from the Salesforce platform into another data management platform for the purposes of reporting or business intelligence requirements

Given the simplified definitions in Table 6-4, your governance team will be looking to identify how the project will integrate with solutions to deliver those requirements out of the box, as the Salesforce platform does not provide built-in integrations for these.

Of course, Salesforce has provided some simple tools that could be used for the most basic of implementations, and that might be perfect for your organization. Currently, Salesforce provides native backup solutions with the following:

- Data Export – A basic solution built into the Salesforce platform that allows the project to export data either "now" or as scheduled. However, the term *now* does not mean the Salesforce platform will export the data there and then; your project will need to wait for the job to be queued and executed. The project selects the objects in scope for export, and the Salesforce platform will export the contents of those objects. Your project will have 48 hours to retrieve the exported data files, after which time Salesforce will delete them.

- Data Loader – An external application for the desktop PC. The application provides various features for data unloading and loading. The added attraction of this application is that you can use filters, which means you can be more selective over the data retrieved. The data is saved directly onto your desktop PC in a character-separated-values file format.

It is obvious to see that the solutions offered by Salesforce for data backup require some level of manual intervention and probably lack the capabilities that most businesses require for a robust data backup solution. However, they are good enough for a growing enterprise to start with.

As the solutions offered by Salesforce are quite basic, the levels of integration are basic too. However, your project may be looking to introduce a more robust solution for data backup, archiving, and data warehouse.

If your project needs a more sophisticated solution, there are two options to pursue, as follows:

- Use the Salesforce APIs.

- Use a third-party solution specifically designed for the Salesforce platform.

Your project team may have the capability to develop its own solution using the Salesforce APIs, and your governance team will need to govern this solution as they would any other application developed on the Salesforce platform.

Using a third-party solution offers a pre-built answer to your backup and archiving needs. Generally, data warehousing can occur from the data that is backed up, as you have already extracted the data; tacking this into a data warehouse solution has no impact on the Salesforce platform.

Govern whether the appropriate integration strategy and standard integration patterns have been used

Where possible, your governance team must ensure that your projects have kept to the standards. For the Salesforce platform, the standard integration patterns help with that. Each pattern provides several different approaches that the platform supports.

Your governance team should make itself familiar with these patterns or utilize expertise from elsewhere, such as offer projects or even Salesforce advisory services, to effectively govern the project's use of the relevant integration patterns.

There will be situations where a project has had to integrate with an system external to the Salesforce platform that does not provide the facilities to cleanly use a standard Salesforce feature to integrate. In the main, though, even those outlying situations can be categorized into one of the standard Salesforce integration patterns. However, your governance team will need to have a dispensation process that allows projects to create a bespoke integration via Apex or alternative that works for the business requirement. The dispensation should be offered for a period, after which a review should happen to determine if the solution selected is still the only approach available.

Throughout the lifecycle of an application, it is more than likely that your organization will see its IT landscape change, so the dispensation approach allows everyone to revisit non-standard or out-of-policy solutions regularly and determine whether anything has changed within your IT landscape that could offer alternatives.

Most integrations will follow a similar strategy. There are always outliers, but the following is a good set of principles to think about:

- Verify what data needs to exist within the Salesforce platform.

- Understand which external system that data will come from.

- Decide on the frequency at which the data will arrive within the Salesforce platform from the external system.

- Configure the data model within the Salesforce platform to receive the external system's data.

- Control access to fields that are specific to managing the integration, and use external IDs if possible.

Govern the integration components involved in a flow and consider transaction management and error and exception handling

Flows offer a declarative solution to develop complex processes. In some way, flows are very close to the principles of developing a program in Apex, as they offer many of the constructs you would expect to develop using Apex.

To that end, Flow has become a commonly used solution to create complex business logic on the Salesforce platform. Salesforce has also provided a means to integrate with external systems from a flow by using the following integration options:

- Platform Events

- External Objects

- Custom Lightning Components

- Enhanced External Services

- Apex

The principles of integration are the same as previously discussed; however, there are some subtle considerations for your governance team in terms of whether the integration is executed from the server side or client side, as well as whether the integration is synchronous or asynchronous, as shown in Table 6-5.

***Table 6-5.** Integration Considerations from Flow*

Option	Server Side	Client Side	Synchronous	Asynchronous
Platform Events	Yes	No	No	Yes
External Objects	Yes	No	Yes	No
Custom Lightning Components	No	Yes	Yes	Yes
Enhanced External Services	Yes	No	Yes	No
Apex	Yes	No	Yes	Yes

There are two main areas here to consider for your governance team that may be something that has been overlooked by the project team.

Firstly, server side versus client side. This may be obvious to some, but basically you are deciding whether the integration executes from your desktop/laptop PC via the browser for client side, or from the server side (i.e., within Salesforce's data centers). The only technical solution that offers client-side integration is the Lightning components (whether traditional [Aura] Lightning components or more modern [JavaScript] Lightning Web components). The important matter here from a governance perspective is that the performance and reliability aspects shift.

For client-side solutions, your organization is very much responsible for making sure that the browser deployed to your desktop/laptop PC runs consistently for all users across all usage scenarios. For example, if you have users who can access your Salesforce instance via VPN from a café using their three-year-old laptop, then that experience may differ from a user sitting in your main office on your internal network using the latest laptop offered by your organization. This basically means that your external system needs to be more tolerant of transaction timelines as they will be affected by the network and compute performance of whatever device the client-side integration is executing upon.

For server-side solutions, your organization relies upon Salesforce to execute the integration in a timely manner. You are less concerned with network bandwidth (as that too is Salesforce's problem). Your laptop/desktop PC performance is not so important because it does not execute the integration. However, server side is consuming limits on the Salesforce platform, so you have a trade-off to consider.

Secondly, synchronous versus asynchronous. This basically decides whether the execution of your integration "blocks" the execution of your flow (i.e., the flow must wait for the integration to complete) or the integration is "non-blocking," allowing your flow to continue to execute while the integration executes independently. These are important factors to consider from a governance perspective, as you may have to implement additional transactional controls to correct any asynchronous processes that fail.

Integration Solution Tools

As shown in Figure 6-3, integration solution tools is the next sub-phase for your governance team to look into.

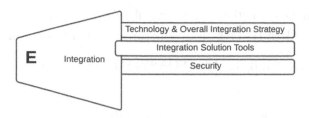

Figure 6-3. *Phase E: integration - integration solution tools*

Govern the use of the appropriate platform-specific integration technology for integration with external systems

Once your project team has learned the types of integration that are needed to meet the business requirements, it will have several choices to make regarding the technology available to them.

The Salesforce platform, as you would expect, offers a few technologies that can be used to deliver the integration patterns described earlier. Although some might say there are no wrong approaches, there are some that will deliver the desired outcome better than others.

The following describes the integration technologies available to your projects and whether the technology is optimal for the integration pattern. Although Salesforce provides a more conservative view on what is acceptable, your governance team should take a harder view, simply because any compromise drives workload later on in the application's lifespan, and it is worth tracking any integration that was not optimal.

Remote Process Invocation – Request and Reply

The Salesforce platform offers a few platform-specific technologies to support the Remote Process Invocation – Request and Reply integration pattern, as follows:

- Enhanced external services (optimal)

- Lightning component initiating an Apex SOAP or REST callout synchronously (optimal)

- Visualforce page initiating an Apex HTTP callout synchronously (optimal)

- Trigger that is invoked by Salesforce platform data changes initiating an Apex SOAP or HTTP callout synchronously (suboptimal)

- Batch Apex initiating an Apex SOAP or HTTP callout synchronously (suboptimal)

Your governance team is looking to make sure the project has considered the limits associated with each technology listed as well as considered potential failure conditions, such as timeouts and errors. Additionally, transactional integrity should be considered by the project team in the event of those failure conditions.

The actual technical approach will be controlled by the capability of the external system, but your governance team must determine whether the best approach has been taken given those external system limitations. A few technical solutions proposed are suboptimal, and therefore should be used with caution as there is usually a high number of trade-offs and restrictions.

Remote Process Invocation – Fire and Forget

The Salesforce platform offers a few platform-specific technologies to support the Remote Process Invocation – Fire and Forget integration pattern, as follows:

- Process-driven platform events (optimal)

- Customization-driven platform events (suboptimal)

- Workflow-driven outbound messaging (suboptimal)

- Outbound messaging and call-backs (suboptimal)

- Lightning component initiating an Apex SOAP or HTTP callout asynchronously (suboptimal)

- Trigger that is invoked by Salesforce platform data changes initiating an Apex SOAP or HTTP callout asynchronously (suboptimal)

- Batch Apex initiating an Apex SOAP or HTTP callout asynchronously (suboptimal)

There are a few options for the Remote Process Invocation – Fire and Forget integration pattern, and your governance team may need to be considerate of the capabilities of the external system in terms of trying to coordinate transactions via error or failure scenarios. It may be that the best the project can achieve is a batch integration using Apex, with very little idea as to whether the data made it to the external system's data stores or not.

However, your governance team is always going to be looking to the project team to achieve the best outcome given the constraints of all systems.

Batch Data Synchronization

The Salesforce platform offers a few platform-specific technologies to support the Batch Data Synchronization integration pattern, as follows:

- Change data capture (optimal)

- Data replication using bulk API (optimal)

- Data replication using non-bulk API (suboptimal)

- Remote call-in (suboptimal)

- Remote process invocation (suboptimal)

Any integration for large amounts of data that does not use one of Salesforce's solutions built specifically for that purpose is going to be suboptimal. Your governance team will need to understand the drivers behind any suboptimal integration patterns chosen by your project.

There are a few reasons that your governance team should encourage alternatives, mainly for consumption of platform limits and the number of records being changed. Your project's use cases will vary, of course, so there may be good reason to perform a record-level data replication integration. However, your governance team should raise the potential problems this could cause and have the project team discuss the mitigations they have.

Remote Call-in

The Salesforce platform offers a few platform-specific technologies to support the Remote Call-in integration pattern, as follows:

- SOAP API (optimal)

- REST API (optimal)

- Apex web services (suboptimal)

- Apex REST services (suboptimal)

- Bulk API (optimal for bulk operations)

Your project may have the requirement to provide a method for your external systems to make a call into the Salesforce platform to retrieve data. There are many reasons for this to occur, but mainly a call-in denotes the Salesforce platform as the primary owner of the data being requested.

Out of the box, the Salesforce platform exposes its objects, standards, or customers via a REST interface. This is the most simplistic solution to supporting call-in integrations. However, if more complex processing is required before the data being requested is ready—for example, the data needs to be reformatted into a particular structure—then Apex REST services could be the right option. However, your governance team will need to subject the project to further governance phases to support the Apex coding introduction.

UI Update Based on Data Changes

The Salesforce platform offers the following platform-specific technology to support the UI Update Based on Data Changes integration pattern:

- Streaming API (optimal)

There will be a few programmatic elements to this integration solution; therefore, your governance team will need to review this not only from an integration perspective, but also from a code quality perspective.

Data Virtualization

The Salesforce platform offers a few platform-specific technologies to support the Data Virtualization integration pattern, as follows:

- Salesforce Connect (optimal)

- Apex web services (suboptimal)

- Apex REST services (suboptimal)

Your governance team must make sure the project team understands the implications of data virtualization. On the surface this can be a very straightforward solution to implement, especially if Salesforce Connect is suitable. However, the project team should be confident that they have understood any longer-term implications around the data's being virtualized and where that data resides currently. Will this data be available for the lifespan of the application the project is building? Will the data format remain consistent for the lifespan of the application that the project is building? Additionally, where Salesforce Connect is being used, it may be prudent to understand Salesforce's longer-term support for the connector you are planning to use.

Govern the usage of the Lightning platform integration APIs and features and determine whether they have been appropriately used

Salesforce offers many APIs, and as previously mentioned some are more suited than others to specific integration patterns.

Your governance team will need to address any areas where your project team has overstepped the intended capability of any given Salesforce platform API; for example, using a Lightning component to integrate with an external system to extract large volumes of data.

Caution   The example given may sound silly to some, but this does happen. Not everyone who creates applications or configurations for the Salesforce platform has the right level of knowledge to tackle the task at hand. Even large system integrators do not always have the most experienced resources working on your projects. It is always worth checking.

Security

As shown in Figure 6-4, security is the next sub-phase for your governance team to focus on within the integration phase.

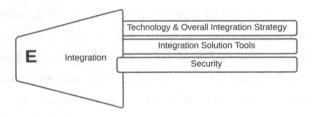

Figure 6-4. *Phase E: integration - security*

Govern how security requirements are met at each of the integration layers

Security is a paramount consideration in any application development or configuration on the Salesforce platform. Your data is an important part of your organization, and as such you will want to make sure it is safe and secure. Previous phases of the Salesforce Platform Governance Method tackled the broader security and data access governance, but your governance team will need to apply some of the thinking from those previous phases into this phase.

The main difference that your governance team will need to consider when applying security to an integration is making sure that security is considered and applied at all levels of your project's integration.

The typical layers of an integration that require security considerations are as follows:

- Authentication – Your governance team will need to make sure that your integration has implemented the proper authentication solution. In most cases this will require credentials of some sort to be passed from the external system to the Salesforce platform to allow further communications to occur.

- Data Access – Your governance team will need to provide the right level of access to the external system that is integrating with the Salesforce platform. This should not be a broad full-access grant, but something that is tailored for the specific use case of the integration.

- Data Transmission – Your governance team will need to make sure that any data transmissions from the external system to the Salesforce platform are done using the proper encryption. Remember that the Salesforce platform is an SaaS product accessible from anywhere in the world.

- Traceability – Your governance team will need to make sure that any changes made to data by the external system integrating to the Salesforce platform are logged or traceable in some way so that it is clear what has changed and when.

As with any security requirements, the credentials used to allow communications from one system to another should be controlled and maintained just like any other access to your systems. Therefore, your governance team will want to learn from the project team how the credentials used to authenticate the external system with the Salesforce platform are maintained in line with your organization's security policies; for example, password change requirements.

Your governance team will need to consider the integration and the capabilities of the external system or platform. If your project is extracting data from the Salesforce platform to store elsewhere for further processes, that data should be secured.

Caution   It can be very easy to overlook data security once the data leaves the Salesforce platform. One example that is constantly arising is the extraction of data for the purposes of business intelligence. That data being extracted from the Salesforce platform and moved into a database of some kind has a very open access policy.

Method

This is the formal method for Phase E of the Salesforce Platform Governance Method. The objectives of Phase E are to ensure that the integration aspects of the application have been thoroughly considered. The areas that will be assessed during this phase are as follows:

- Technologies and Overall Integration Strategy

- Integration Solution Tools

- Security

Approach

This phase is focused on governing the integration aspects of an application or configuration. You may have integration strategy and standards already defined within your organization, which should be applied to your Salesforce platform implementation as well. Alternatively, the design patterns provided by Salesforce cover the main use cases you are likely to come across if you do not have these already defined.

Your project team could present you with Apex source code as part of its integration solution, so your governance team will need to inform the project team that it is subject to subsequent governance phases because of this.

Ultimately, integration can be a complex and difficult part of any project. On the surface the integration may sound straightforward, but very often an integration becomes complex very quickly or compromises must be made to accommodate the capabilities of both sides of the integration. It is likely that some incompatibility will arise that will drive these compromises.

Your governance team should pay close attention to security throughout its assessment of the project's application or configuration. Security is often only considered from one perspective during the integration. Your governance team should take a holistic view of how security will be applied, perhaps looking at the lifecycle of the data that the integration is focused on to provide a level of assurance that security has been applied consistently across the entire integration requirement.

Your governance team will need to be sympathetic toward any deviation from the standard policy or best practice within your organization if that deviation is driven by lack of capability in the systems involved. The business should drive the requirement, but also carry the risk associated with any suboptimal approaches taken. Your governance team should highlight this to the business sponsors of the project under governance to make sure that although the project team has done everything it can to provide the best possible integration, any suboptimal areas are accepted as business risk.

Inputs

For the governance process to be a success, the project team must have a few artifacts available to the governance team for review. Suggested artifacts to review for Phase E of the Salesforce Platform Governance Method are as follows:

- Application configuration and source (or the repository in the instance of using a source control system) where appropriate

- Integration architecture, detailing the systems involved and the flow of data

- Security policy (if defined by the project)

- Clear definitions around sensitive data

Steps

The steps to govern the integration will help the project team understand how its application and ultimately the Salesforce platform will participate in any integrations with external systems. Your governance team is looking not only to protect the assets of your company, especially the data, but also to protect the holistic view of data integrity across all systems deployed within your organization.

Technologies and Overall Integration Strategy

1. Govern the enterprise integration landscape and overall integration strategy, with associated risks, trade-offs, and business and technical considerations

2. Govern the data backup / archiving / data warehousing integration strategies

3. Govern whether the appropriate integration strategy and standard integration patterns have been used

4. Govern the integration components involved in a flow and consider transaction management and error and exception handling

Integration Solution Tools

1. Govern the usage of the appropriate platform-specific integration technology for integration with external systems

2. Govern the usage of the Lightning platform integration APIs and features and determine whether they have been appropriately used

Security

1. Govern how security requirements are met at each of the integration layers

Outputs

Once all the steps have been assessed, the outputs to Phase E are as follows:

- Not Applicable – This phase in the Salesforce Platform Governance Method is not applicable to the project.

- Remediate – The governance team requests that the project team remediates its design to accommodate the issues raised during the governance review.

- Pass – The governance team has found no issues or concerns with the project's proposal and therefore the project has passed this governance phase.

- Review – The governance team has found the inputs cannot be objectively measured and therefore a subjective view has been made, which will lead to a discussion with the project team to reach consensus. Although undesirable, this could be a consequence of unclear standards/policies.

Scenario

For our scenario we are going to focus on the following two steps from the Technologies and Overall Integration Strategy of the integration Phase E method:

- Govern the enterprise integration landscape and overall integration strategy, with associated risks, trade-offs, and business and technical considerations

- Govern whether the appropriate integration strategy and standard integration patterns have been used

Back with our fictitious company Bright Sound Guitars Ltd., Hanna Snyder, the project architect, suggested during the application architecture (Phase A) governance session that her project would be implementing an integration between the Salesforce platform and the stock control system in use at Bright Sound Guitars. This is shown in Figure 6-5.

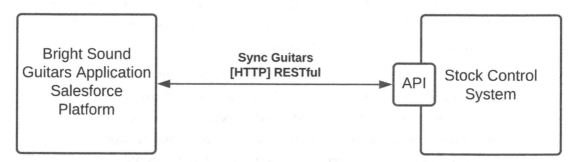

Figure 6-5. *Bright Sound Guitars integration architecture*

Hanna has worked with her developers, Ranveer Shah and Caitlyn Horton, to tackle the suggestions raised during that previous governance session. Hanna is now ready to present to the governance team a more detailed view of her integration between the Salesforce platform and the Stock Control System.

On further analysis by her team of developers, it was discovered that the stock control system has two APIs: one that provides the current stock, and another that allows the stock status to be updated for a single stock item. Hanna has updated her diagram with the additional detail, as shown in Figure 6-6.

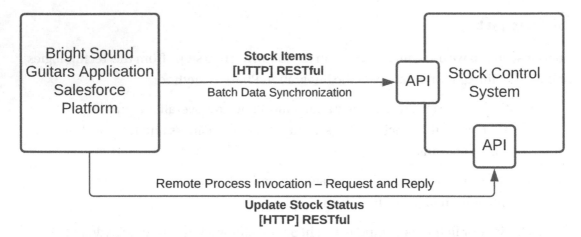

Figure 6-6. *Bright Sound Guitars detailed integration architecture*

Hanna introduces Caitlyn to the governance team so that Caitlyn can talk the team through her solution.

Caitlyn first talks in more detail about the stock items that will be retrieved from the stock control system into the Salesforce platform. Caitlyn has chosen the Batch Data Synchronization pattern for the following reasons:

- The stock control system only supports one API to retrieve stock. Caitlyn needs the stock to be within the Salesforce platform so that the business can perform an end-to-end sales process. She will update the Product2 object with the stock from the stock control system, enhancing that object to contain a field that holds the external ID used by the stock control system. That way, any changes to the stock can be reflected accurately with the Salesforce platform.

- As Caitlyn will need to update the price book for any new products added, and the fact that she needs to do some basic manipulation and verification of the data being received from the stock control system, she will implement this integration using Apex.

- The API for the current stock from the stock control system provides several stock items per page. Caitlyn will need to call the API for each page of stock, incrementing the page she needs until she reaches the final page of stock. She then knows she has all the stock available. However, Caitlyn does not know how many pages of stock are available until she makes the first API call for the first page.

The returned payload provides an attribute that provides the total number of pages. Therefore, Caitlyn suggests having an Apex function that always attempts a retrieval of the first page from the stock control system's API so that she knows up front how many times she will call the API. She needs to know this to optimize her batch processes and recursion to retrieve all stock.

- Finally, Caitlyn suggests that she can trigger an update to the stock control system via a trigger on the Salesforce platform so that the business can deactivate products when they know they are no longer for sale rather than use the external system to perform the same function.

Caitlyn talks the governance team through how she sees the integration working, as shown in Figure 6-7.

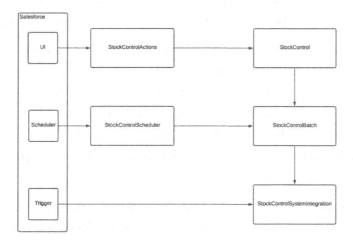

Figure 6-7. *Bright Sound Guitars integration design*

Caitlyn suggests that there will be three parts to this integration, as follows:

- A batch process that is scheduled and retrieves all the stock from the stock control system each night, updating the Salesforce platform

- An action that she wants to add into the Salesforce platform's user interface so that a manual stock transfer can occur

- A trigger that will update a specific item within the stock control system when its status is changed on the Salesforce platform

Caitlyn will develop a few Apex classes to support the features she wants, plus use a few other Salesforce platform technologies to support the button she wants to add to the user interface and custom fields she needs. Caitlyn wants to contain all the Apex callouts within one class so that maintenance is easier in the longer term.

The governance team likes the solution and praises Caitlyn for the level of detail she has brought to them. This has made the governance team's task much easier as they can clearly see that Caitlyn has considered the Salesforce integration patterns and thought through the solution. However, the governance team highlights the following:

- The batch process could be difficult to control in terms of knowing how many times it will need to call out to the stock control system. As this is a limitation of the stock control system, they understand that Caitlyn has done the best she can. However, they highlight that Caitlyn will need to make sure that she considers the DML statements and call-out sequence, as well as "bulkify" as much as possible so that multiple statements are being recursively used.

- The open-endedness of the stock synchronization will make it difficult to determine the batch window needed to complete a stock transfer, so the governance team recommends that Hanna and Caitlyn look at the current stock records within the stock control system to model this. Also, filtering out any unwanted records from the stock control system that are not relevant to the Salesforce platform would be beneficial.

- The governance team can see that all communications with the stock control system are initiated from the Salesforce platform. They like the fact that the control sits within the Salesforce platform to determine the appropriate time to perform a stock synchronization. However, they mention to Hanna that she may need to review the availability of the stock control system to make sure her project is not attempting a stock synchronization during a time when the stock control system is not available.

- Finally, the governance team mentions that the business should be made aware that the stock will only be updated on a nightly basis and therefore they are trading off data volume against data consistency. It could be that when Bright Sound Guitars performs its monthly stock updates, these might not be immediately available within the Salesforce platform, although the governance team acknowledges that Caitlyn is going to develop a manual option for stock synchronization.

Overall, the governance team is happy with what they have been presented by the project team and thank Hanna and Caitlyn for a job well done. They feel comfortable that once the comments have been addressed the project team will be able to progress in its development.

Summary

Phase E tackles the governance of a project's integration solutions, from architecture design through to implementation. Having completed this governance phase, you have checked that the project has adhered to the standard integration patterns, considered security, and accepted the trade-offs associated with each integration pattern. Additionally, you have learned the limitations of any external systems and how these limitations have to be overcome to meet the business requirements.

You have highlighted to your project team any areas of concern within the integration solution and are confident that the team will remediate your concerns.

CHAPTER 7

Apex, Visualforce & Lightning: Phase F

This phase of the Salesforce Platform Governance Method focuses on the programmatic side of the Salesforce platform, which includes the Apex, Visualforce, and Lightning development capabilities.

Overview

The Salesforce platform offers a large amount of configurability and automation without the need to resort to a traditional programming language. However, some projects will inevitably have requirements that can be best met by using the Salesforce platform's programmatic features.

Your organization may have policies in place to help guide projects as to the appropriate time or reason to choose a programmatic solution over the declarative options available. Given that Flow is rapidly growing into a viable alternative to developing Apex code, those policies may be updated regularly. As shown in Figure 7-1, this phase is broken down into sub-phases to help your governance team provide focused feedback to your projects.

© Lee Harding and Lee Bayliss 2022
L. Harding and L. Bayliss, *Salesforce Platform Governance Method*,
https://doi.org/10.1007/978-1-4842-7404-0_7

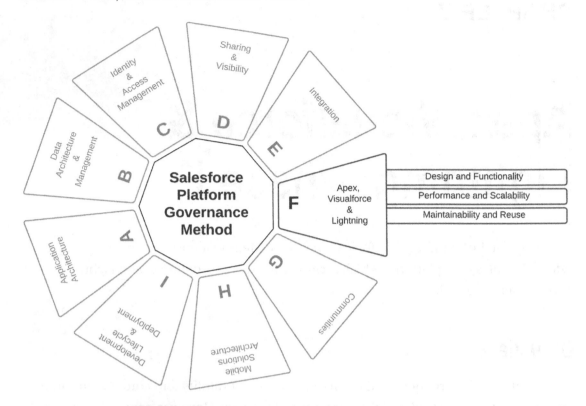

Figure 7-1. *The Salesforce Platform Governance Method: Phase F*

As with previous phases, let's start by defining what we mean by Apex, Visualforce, and Lightning so that we are clear as to what we are governing. In the context of the Salesforce Platform Governance Method, we will use the Salesforce definitions, as they are Salesforce technologies. First, Apex:

> *"Apex is a strongly typed, object-oriented programming language that allows developers to execute flow and transaction control statements on the Lightning platform server in conjunction with calls to the Lightning Platform API. Using syntax that looks like Java and acts like database stored procedures, Apex enables developers to add business logic to most system events, including button clicks, related record updates, and Visualforce pages. Apex code can be initiated by Web service requests and from triggers on objects."*

> —Salesforce[1]

---

[1] https://developer.salesforce.com/docs/atlas.en-us.apexcode.meta/apexcode/apex_intro_what_is_apex.htm

Next, we'll define Visualforce as the following:

"Visualforce is a framework that allows developers to build sophisticated, custom user interfaces that can be hosted natively on the Lightning platform. The Visualforce framework includes a tag-based markup language, similar to HTML, and a set of server-side 'standard controllers' that make basic database operations, such as queries and saves, very simple to perform."

—Salesforce

Finally, we will define the Lightning term as the following:

"The Lightning Component framework is a UI framework for developing single page applications for mobile and desktop devices.

As of Spring '19 (API version 45.0), you can build Lightning components using two programming models: the Lightning Web Components model, and the original Aura Components model. Lightning web components are custom HTML elements built using HTML and modern JavaScript. Lightning web components and Aura components can coexist and interoperate on a page."

—Salesforce

If your project team has delivered a component or solution using the programmatic capabilities of the Salesforce platform, it will be using all or a combination of the following:

- Apex

- Lightning component (Web or Aura)

- Visualforce

Your governance team will need to understand some of the nuances of these technologies, especially when looking at the future usage of the Salesforce platform and recognizing that reusable components may be elevated to enterprise level from a project level.

As with all source code–driven development, your project team should seek to manage the software assets properly, and your governance team will look to understand how this is achieved. A more mature organization may have an existing source code repository and version control system in place. For those embarking on their first Salesforce application development, this is something that you may be looking to implement for the first time.

The following provides a brief description of the Salesforce platform technologies, but by no means serves as a replacement for the thorough understanding of these technologies that will be required to properly govern this part of the Salesforce Platform Governance Method. As such, your governance team should look to call upon experts within your organization who can help review the solutions developed by your project teams in their specific areas.

Visualforce

Visualforce uses a markup language that is very similar to HTML for designing pages, and then Apex code for supporting database operations and business processes. Typically, there are four parts to a Visualforce solution, as follows:

- Visualforce Page – A markup language like HTML is used to design the content and layout of the page or user interface.

- Custom Controller – Apex code will process all the server-side operations implemented within the Visualforce page.

- JavaScript – Optionally used to perform any client-side processing and user interface manipulations.

- Apex Extension – Further processing can be optionally achieved in Apex extensions, which are not supported within a standard controller.

Apex

Apex is a programming language that is very similar to Java. It is a strongly typed, object-oriented language that allows developers to execute complex processes to leverage the Salesforce platform's abundant APIs. Apex can be initiated from triggers on objects, where data changes or database actions can trigger Apex code to be executed, or from a Web service.

Apex is executed server side and can open up complete flexibility in terms of what can be achieved on the Salesforce platform. It is used in the platform in two areas:

- Apex Triggers – Apex triggers can be configured to perform processing on data before or after changes to records,; for example, inserting a new record could initiate an Apex trigger.

- Apex Classes – Classes are a template to create Apex objects. Classes contain methods, variables, other classes, and so forth. Using Apex, complex business processes can be accomplished that can not only operate upon internal Salesforce platform data, but also make call-outs to external systems.

Developing a program in Apex is no different to developing in any language, with coding standards and naming conventions in place so that any developer feels at home debugging or enhancing code developed by previous programmers. However, one area where Apex does differ from most other programming languages is that unit testing is enforced. The Salesforce platform will not allow Apex code to be deployed to your production org without your project's Apex test classes exercising at least 75% of the Apex code you are deploying. This is considered good practice in most other programming languages, but is enforced on the Salesforce platform due to the platform's multi-tenancy nature.

The need to develop unit test classes in Apex is sometimes overlooked by inexperienced developers, as this is not enforced when actually developing on your sandboxes.

This need for Apex test classes adds additional overhead to the governance process because it is additional code that must be reviewed against the development standards, and of course it will need to be managed and maintained in exactly the same way as the rest of your project's Apex code.

Lightning Components

When Salesforce introduced the Lightning user interface (UI) for its core platform (often referred to as Salesforce, SalesCloud, ServiceCloud, or CRM), it also delivered a new technology to allow developers to build bespoke components for that UI for use in their own applications alongside those delivered by Salesforce.

Lightning components can be developed using two different technologies. The original used what Salesforce called the Aura framework and was introduced by Salesforce around 2013. This open source framework essentially provided the features and functions that underpinned Salesforce's new Lightning UI. This version of Aura was archived in 2019, although it is still supported by Salesforce. It could be considered a legacy solution even though this is not the position taken by Salesforce.

Aura was replaced by Lightning Web Components (LWC) around 2019, which uses the current standards in Web technology. You could consider Aura as a proprietary JavaScript framework while LWC uses standard JavaScript capabilities. As such, developing solutions using LWC is a more familiar experience to Web developers than using Aura was. Additionally, some might say that LWC performs much better than Aura-based components.

As of the writing of this book, both Lightning component solutions are available to your projects, and they can interoperate. However, while you can embed an LWC within an Aura Lightning component, you cannot do the opposite because of the bespoke nature of the Aura framework.

Design and Functionality

As shown in Figure 7-2, design and functionality is the first of the sub-phases in the Apex, Visualforce, and Lightning governance phase.

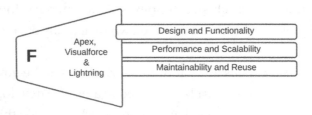

Figure 7-2. *Phase F: Apex, Visualforce & Lightning - design and functionality*

Govern the continuum of UI options actually used against those available on the platform (buttons, mashups, Canvas, Visualforce pages, and Lightning components)

The Salesforce platform offers more configurability than most people can probably remember, and the number of ways in which to initiate bespoke functionality is no exception.

As mentioned previously, Lightning components offer nearly unlimited possibilities, with Lightning Web Components being made even more extensible with the introduction of standard JavaScript libraries such as chart.js, among countless others. However, your governance team will need to understand why a bespoke component was built when a standard component may have delivered the same business outcome. This is important because your bespoke solution will require ongoing maintenance and support, potentially needing to be revisited in the future as the Salesforce platform progresses in its relentless release cadence. In comparison, an inbuilt feature once configured will more than likely require less support and maintenance in the longer term.

This is especially true when integrating with external systems. It is sometimes easy to think only of the data level of integration, making call-outs as necessary when data is required and building a bespoke user interface to interact with that data. An alternative may be to deliver the external system as a Canvas app embedded within the Salesforce UI and then have Salesforce interact with that external application's user interface. Of course, this is not always possible, or perhaps more often than not a complete set of functions cannot be delivered to the end user due to limitations in the external system's user interface.

If the necessary knowledge cannot be found within your governance team, the team will need to call upon the appropriate resources to learn what is possible on the Salesforce platform versus what has been proposed by the project team. Ultimately, your governance team is trying to protect your organization from unwanted cost in the longer term as a result of having components developed that basically replicate existing standard functionality.

Caution   Our experience has shown us time and again that this basic governance step is not taken. Many organizations that we have worked with over the years have duplicated built-in functionality, either because of unfamiliarity with the Salesforce platform or because the organization has a team of developers that "always do it that way." However, all of these organizations get frustrated when every new release of the Salesforce platform forces them to revisit their bespoke code. If you are in an organization that is still using the "Classic" user interface because migrating to Lightning is not possible, it is likely you are dealing with this situation.

Govern the sharing and visibility model in code solution

The Salesforce platform will run Apex in the system context, which basically means that it does not consider the user's permissions when executing the code. This makes sense in most cases because the code your project team has developed may need to operate across the entire data set and not just the data visible to the user.

Your governance team will need to pay close attention to the sharing and visibility model that is utilized within your code. The importance of data visibility was highlighted in Phase D of the Salesforce Platform Governance Method and as such should be your governance team's initial attempt at governing this area. However, during this phase your governance team is looking for evidence that what was uncovered during the Phase D assessment has in fact been implemented.

Govern the code against security best practices to ensure all Visualforce and Apex code is developed per OWASP standards

As with all platforms that provide a programmatic solution to tailoring end-user functionality, there is always the possibility of inadvertently exposing your organization to security risks. The Open Web Application Security Project (OWASP) provides a set of standards that should be adhered to when developing an application that is exposed to the Web. As the Salesforce platform is an SaaS platform, it is accessible from the Web (in fact, this is the only way it is accessible), and as such any code that is developed by your project is also exposed. Of course, the Salesforce platform offers guard rails when you are using declarative and basic configuration, but once you move into developing on the platform using Apex or other technologies you are opening yourself up to vulnerabilities unless the proper standards are applied.

OWASP provides a top ten Web application vulnerability list, which is just as applicable to the Salesforce platform as any other platform used to develop applications. At the time of writing this book, the top ten vulnerabilities according to OWASP[2] are as follows:

- Injection

- Broken authentication

- Sensitive data exposure

- XML external entities

- Broken access control

- Security misconfiguration

- Cross-site scripting

- Insecure deserialization

- Using components with known vulnerabilities

- Insufficient logging and monitoring

Given this list, it is easy to see how your project could run into some issues that need to be addressed.

Caution   Security misconfiguration is a common problem. There are a number of causes of this. Inexperienced Salesforce administrators might think providing everyone full access is easy and a "quick fix" to some problem. More often than not, the analysis around personas isd completely overlooked or a last-minute "guess." Understanding the correct access (remembering the least-privilege principles) is paramount to the ongoing security of your data and hence your business.

---

[2] https://owasp.org/www-project-top-ten/

Your governance team should be aware of the OWASP standards or their own organization's standards to be assured that the project has considered and implemented the proper controls for their bespoke code.

Tip   Webhooks have become a popular solution that sends a "nudge" from an external system that an action has taken place that may be of interest to your application. This is mostly implemented using a public site within the Salesforce platform that calls an Apex class automatically with no authentication. Make sure you have secured that Apex class.

Govern the object-oriented design principles and design patterns that were adhered to when developing the solution (Singleton, etc.)

Apex is an object-oriented language and as such adheres to object-oriented design principles. Lightning components use JavaScript, which is an object-based language; however, some of the principles around object-oriented design still apply.

Note   Object-oriented development was introduced circa 1966, many decades before the Salesforce platform was even thought about, so it is not something that is new. However, it is surprising how many developers use an object-oriented programming language without fully understanding the principles of object-oriented programming.

Your governance team should have a thorough understanding of object-oriented design or access to resources that can perform this governance step on their behalf.

The main thrust of this step is for your governance team to determine whether the appropriate design principles have been applied to the project's development. Have classes been appropriately used and designed, with appropriate methods encapsulated using `public` or `private`? Have attributes also been suitably encapsulated?

A good indication that your project's development team does not fully understand the principles of object-oriented design is the misuse of or complete disregard for the following:

- Inheritance – child classes inherit data and behaviors from a parent class

- Encapsulation – containing information in an object, exposing only selected information

- Abstraction – only exposing high-level public methods for accessing an object

- Polymorphism – many methods can do the same task

The misuse of these principles can be quite easy to identify. If your project is duplicating functionality within several classes, inheritance has probably been overlooked, or possibly abstraction should have been considered. Declaring every attribute and method of a class `public` can indicate the encapsulation was not fully understood. If many methods have been created that have different names but fundamentally perform similar functions, just using different attributes, then polymorphism is possibly misunderstood.

There are other aspects of the Apex language that could also lead to bad object-oriented design, such as the use of `static` or the inadvertent creation of a singleton.

Your governance team is really looking at the maintainability of the programs developed by your project's development team. Object-oriented design principles are fundamentally designed to simplify the reusability of functionality, while protecting the inadvertent modification of that reusable code. This should provide your project teams with accelerated delivery, while minimizing repeated testing.

Tip   It is very common to see a single Apex class with many functions that are performing unrelated processes. While this is more common than is desirable, it does not break the Salesforce platform. Adhering to object-oriented principles is something that is helpful to your organization and that ultimately will deliver a more maintainable code base with lower occurrences of repeated code, which on a platform with a limited number of resources available to your projects (including the lines of Apex code) is always a good thing.

Govern the appropriate use of the Model-View-Controller pattern

The Model-View-Controller pattern is commonly used for developing user interfaces that divide a program into three interconnected components. This is done to separate internal representations of data from the ways the data can be presented to and accepted from the end user.

The model represents the data and its storage, while the controller represents the processing applied to that data, such as a business process. The view is the representation of the data to the end user.

The Model-View-Controller design pattern can help you gain reusability from your investment in developing code. Your projects can deliver multiple user interfaces onto a single controller without having to re-engineer that controller.

Visualforce enforces the Model-View-Controller pattern in that it has a mark-up language very similar to HTML that controls the user representation, which is the view. A controller represents the processing of the data inputted by an end user before it is updated in an object, which represents the model.

Using Lightning components, whether Aura or LWC, the programmer could bypass this pattern, as they could in theory make a direct call from the client to a back-end server-side API, as an example.

Your governance team should be familiar with the MVC design pattern and look for instances where this pattern should have been used. Obvious examples breaching this design pattern are Lightning components that perform business logic, handle the display to the end user, and then push the data model directly to a basic Apex server-side class that really doesn't do anything.

Govern any Apex controllers against the technical standards (extensions to standard controllers and custom controllers)

All Salesforce platform objects come with a pre-built standard controller, even custom objects. These standard controllers provide the basic functionality that is required by the Salesforce user interface to interact with the object that the standard controller is associated with. For example, if you hit the Save button on an account using the standard Salesforce user interface, the behavior will be the same as if you had your own button within your Visualforce page that triggers a save. You associate the appropriate controller within the Visualforce markup.

As you would expect, the Salesforce platform allows your project teams to create their own custom controller or extend a standard controller.

The main difference between a custom controller and an extension to a standard controller is that your project team will need to develop all the functions it requires within a custom controller, whereas by extending a standard controller, the project inherits the standard functions and then can apply additional functions.

Tip   Remember that as with all Apex code, controllers will run in the system context and will not take user permissions into account unless explicitly stated.

Your governance team must be capable of reviewing the use of extended and custom controllers to determine whether they have been used appropriately. Additionally, your governance team should be assured that data visibility and access have been appropriately considered, given the system context within which Apex code normally executes.

Additionally, your organization may have guidelines and standards to adhere to. If your project teams are building many custom controllers, your governance team will need to consider appropriate standards for naming the functions within those controllers. From a maintenance perspective it would not be wise to have each project use different standards.

Govern the usage of custom settings and synchronous vs. asynchronous patterns, and all the available execution contexts (e.g., batch, trigger, callout, etc.)

Your project may have used custom settings to store configuration information or perhaps credentials for authentication with external systems. Your governance team should review the need for custom settings and the purpose behind the decision; for example, if credentials are being stored, why was this preferred over the use of a named credential?

In the main, custom settings provide some flexibility in terms of how the custom setting data relates to the current user or otherwise. Additionally, when creating sandboxes, the custom settings data is not replicated. Custom settings are effectively a custom object in terms of the Salesforce metadata and should follow your organization's naming conventions and standards.

As with most modern platforms, the Salesforce platform allows code to be executed synchronously and asynchronously. The main difference is that when code is executed asynchronously the code that triggered the asynchronous code will continue to execute regardless of what the triggered code is doing.

Your governance team will need to assure themselves that the project team fully understands the implications of this, especially in the context of making call-outs to external systems. Additionally, the synchronous code should be reviewed to understand whether this is constructed in the correct manner. If the user is kept waiting due to synchronous code, this is possibly not going to be a great user experience. Additionally, the Salesforce platform will not allow Apex code to run continuously, but rather will timeout long-running processes. Your governance team will need to know whether the project team has taken these issues into account, especially when making external calls, where response time is not always guaranteed.

The Salesforce platform can run Apex in a number of contexts. Each context introduces limitations and requires some awareness of what is possible for the developer when constructing code. For example, you cannot perform Data Manipulation Language (DML) statements before making a call-out to an external system, which might be frustrating to some, especially when multiple call-outs are made and it is desirable to write the data into Salesforce objects.

Additionally, while the Apex code is running in a batch context, your developers are restricted in the number of DML statements they can perform. Therefore, performing DML within loops for Apex that are intended for batch execution is not acceptable. Your governance team should be looking for assurance that the project team has taken the correct steps to "bulkify" their Apex code if it is destined for execution in a batch context.

Apex triggers are a powerful solution to performing additional processing before or after data is inserted, updated within, or deleted from the Salesforce platform. In many cases, the same actions can be performed using Flow or Process Builder. Your governance team should be assured that your project team is using triggers appropriately, and not diluting the implementation across multiple platform capabilities.

Tip   It is very easy to use multiple Salesforce platform solutions to deliver similar functionality. Triggers could be considered one of these areas. It is wiser to standardize your usage of Flow, Process Builder, and triggers (or any other platform automation) so that all your project teams and ultimately the developers know what the appropriate use is. This will avoid their having to look in several places to make changes, or needing to debug trigger-related functionality.

If Apex triggers are a preferred solution to performing actions based on a specific set of circumstances, your governance team should recommend using a trigger framework. This is especially the case if multiple project teams are looking to add trigger code to a number of standard or enterprise objects. This will avoid projects' clashing with one another in code, as well as make sure that each project's trigger code is discrete.

Govern the usage of batch Apex and the flex queue

As previously mentioned, your governance team should focus its attention on any batch Apex delivered by the project team. Your governance team should pay close attention to the following:

- Any batch job that is invoked from a trigger. Your project team must be able to assure your governance team that the trigger will not add more batch jobs than the allowable limit.

- The actual execution timeframe requirement. Salesforce only places the batch job in the queue.

- Any stateful requirements. Instance member variables are reset to their initial states at the beginning of each transaction unless specified.

- The use of `@future`. Methods declared with the `@future` decorator are not allowed to be called from batch Apex.

- Email notifications for running batch Apex jobs, especially if the batch Apex is part of a managed package.

- Filter the `AsyncApexJob` object records. With every 10,000 `AsyncApexJob` records, Apex creates an `AsyncApexJob` record of type `BatchApexWorker` for internal use; your project should filter these out of any queries.

- Testing has considered governor limits and ensured that the batch has completed before continuing testing.

- Sharing recalculation. The execute method should delete and then recreate all Apex-managed sharing for optimal sharing accuracy.

- Any Salesforce service maintenance downtime. Running batch jobs are rolled back and restarted during maintenance.

- The number of batches your project will create. Having more than 2,000 unprocessed requests from a single Salesforce org causes additional requests from the same Salesforce org to be delayed.

- Minimize call-out times and tune queries as much as possible. Your project should make sure the batch jobs execute as quickly as possible. Longer executing batch jobs will delay other queued batch jobs.

Developing batch processes take careful planning and consideration regarding the number of batch jobs created and the size of each of those batch jobs. It is very easy to hit issues in production if the amount of data being processed has not been considered carefully.

Govern the Apex / Visualforce solution against the governor limits

As with all aspects of the Salesforce platform, governor limits apply to Apex and Visualforce, perhaps even more so. The governor limits for Apex and Visualforce have a larger impact on the execution of your code than does a consumption of resources within a 24-hour-type limit, as seen in other limitations of the platform.

Your governance team should have a good understanding of the main governor limits that commonly affect Apex and Visualforce, and with Apex, the contexts in which the Apex is being used.

Salesforce categorizes Apex governor limits as follows:

- Per-Transaction Apex Limits

- Per-Transaction Certified Managed Package Limits

- Lightning Platform Apex Limits

- Static Apex Limits

- Size-Specific Apex Limits

- Miscellaneous Apex Limits

Visualforce limits are slightly simpler than the Apex limits, and are mainly focused on the number of records the Visualforce page is dealing with or the amount of data.

Your governance team is basically looking to be assured that the project team has made a concerted effort to understand the use of the Visualforce and Apex code that they have developed and that it will accommodate those use cases. Additionally, your governance team will want to understand the edge cases that the project team has considered so that it is clear as to when problems may be seen in the production environment. This at least will give the operations teams something to monitor, and they can raise the appropriate concern if production workloads are edging toward causing problems with the project's implementation.

Govern the order of execution of transactions within the platform (specifically against pre-existing triggers)

The Salesforce platform can have numerous automation processes running when something happens to an object. This could be due to data changes or the insertion of a new object record. As you would expect, Salesforce has implemented an order of execution to the processes that can be triggered by changes occurring on the platform.

The order of execution is important as it determines what Salesforce processes will be triggered and in what order. When a record is saved with an insert, update, or upsert statement, Salesforce performs the following events in order:

1. Load the record.

2. Run system validation to check the record for page layout–specific rules, field definition, and maximum field length.

3. Execute flows that make a "before-save" update.

4. Execute all before triggers.

5. Run most custom validation rules.

6. Execute duplicate rules.

7. Save the record to the database without committing the data.

8. Execute all after triggers.

9. Execute assignment rules.

10. Execute auto-response rules.

11. Execute workflow rules.

    a. If there are workflow field updates, then update the record again.

    b. If the workflow field updates introduced new duplicate field values, execute duplicate rules again.

    c. If the record was updated with workflow field updates, fire before and after update triggers one more time (and only one more time) in addition to standard validation.

12. Execute processes and flow.

13. Execute escalation rules

14. Execute entitlement rules.

15. Execute record-triggered flows that are configured to run after the record is saved.

16. If the record contains a roll-up summary field or is part of a cross-object workflow, perform calculations and update the roll-up summary field in the parent record. Parent record goes through save procedure.

17. If the parent record is updated, and a grandparent record contains a roll-up summary field or is part of a cross-object workflow, perform calculations and update the roll-up summary field in the grandparent record. Grandparent record goes through save procedure.

18. Execute Criteria-Based Sharing evaluation.

19. Commit all DML operations to the database.

20. Execute all after-commit logic, such as sending email.

The after commit logic can consist of a number of processes that require the order of execution to be completed before they can be executed. These processes are as follows:

1. Send all emails.

2. Execute asynchronous Apex (@future methods).

3. Execute asynchronous Sharing Rule processing (for >25,000 records).

4. Outbound messages are placed in the queue.

5. Calculate index, such as search index.

6. Render file previews.

7. Publication of platform events (if configured).

The order of execution can create a lot of confusion if it is not clearly understood, and can generate many hours of debugging if the results your project team expects are not what is being experienced.

Your governance team cannot change any of these things, but what is clear is that the order of execution should be considered. Your governance team will be looking for assurance that the project team understands the implications of this order and how it affects their solution. Specifically, your governance team should be asking the project team the following:

1. Has the project team fully understood any changes that might have occurred with each release of the Salesforce platform?

2. Has the project team understood the details behind the order of execution?

3. Has the project team adhered to a "rule of thumb," such as one trigger, one process per object?

4. Do the project team and operations team understand how to use the debug log to troubleshoot if required? Pay close attention to "***CLOSE TO LIMIT***" debug log entries.

5. The project team should avoid situations that could cause a loop in the order of execution; if unavoidable they should be clear of the implications.

6. Your project team should consider the use of `trigger.old` with care.

Lastly, your governance team should be assured that your project team has performed the relevant testing, taking into account edge cases and with sufficient data volumes.

Govern the quality of test coverage (required for production deployment, call-out testing is a special case)

Test coverage is critical to the successful deployment of your project's Apex code. As mentioned previously, the Salesforce platform enforces test coverage on Apex code. Your project's Apex code must reach a test coverage of 75% before it is allowed to be deployed into the production org.

Tip   It is good practice to take a test-driven development approach. You cannot avoid creating test classes and meeting the 75% test coverage requirement. Your project team should consider the test classes just as important as the business logic they are implementing within the Apex code. Do not leave this until the last minute. Integrate your test class development with your development plan and treat it as equal to any other code you develop. Also, remember you are not trying to reach 75%—it is not a score to obtain. You are fundamentally trying to test your code.

Your governance team should review the test coverage results from your project's test deployment. Where code has not been covered by the test classes, your governance team should review to understand whether this is acceptable or not. Where call-outs are made, the project team should put in additional effort to simulate the endpoints in the call-out.

Ultimately, your governance team is looking to understand whether the project has taken the development of Apex test classes seriously, or simply manufactured tests to meet the 75% code coverage requirement.

Govern the approach to error/exception handling

Most programming code includes a significant amount of error and exception handling. It is widely accepted that up to 90% of a program's code will be error and exception handling code rather than business logic. The Apex programming language is no different.

Your governance team will need to be assured that the project team has implemented sufficient error and exception handling within its code so that the end user does not experience errors and therefore report them to the operations team.

As an example, try/catch blocks should be placed around any SOQL. It is easy during development to assume that a consistent result will be seen, given the limited data most development environments have. However, once the code is deployed into the production org, it is often the case that issues arise because the developer made certain assumptions and therefore did not properly check for error conditions.

Tip   Using the LIMIT 1 on SOQL to bring back a single object and then perform processing on that object is a great shortcut, but remember that your project is relying on a single object's always being returned, which might not always be the case.

Your governance team should be wary of any hard coding within the Apex code; for example, making assumptions around the name of a `RecordType` when creating a new object record of a certain type.

Equally, your test classes (as discussed earlier) should be testing that error and exception handling has been implemented correctly.

Performance and Scalability

As shown in Figure 7-3, performance and scalability is the next sub-phase on which your governance team should focus.

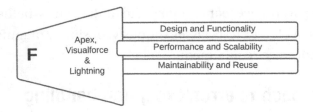

Figure 7-3. *Phase F: Apex, Visualforce & Lightning - performance and scalability*

Govern that performance and scalability best practices have been considered within Visualforce pages and Apex code (performance profiling, use of static resources)

The Salesforce platform comes with a few tools that are at your project team's disposal to help them understand the performance and scalability of the Visualforce pages and Apex that they have delivered. The basic tools are shown in Table 7-1.

Table 7-1. *Performance & Scalability Tools*

Tool	Description
The Developer Console	The original "go to" tool for all developers that didn't want to use the Eclipse IDE. The developer console is still heavily used today, but Visual Studio Code and its extensions are rapidly catching up. However, as the developer console is part of the Salesforce platform, it is easy to access and requires no configuration or setup. The developer console provides a number of panels dedicated to analyzing performance. Based on detailed execution logs, which you can open by using the Log Inspector associated with the Logs tab, you can view the graphical timeline of the overall request, the aggregated performance of an operation, and statistics on governor limits, as well as drill down to the executed units.
Debug Logs	A debug log records database operations, system processes, and errors that occur when you execute a transaction. The system generates a debug log for a user every time that user executes a transaction that is included in the filter criteria. The level of detail each log contains can be adjusted. Although the debug log files appear as plain text, it is difficult to interpret their raw log lines. If your projects are using Visual Studio Code as the main development tool, a number of extensions exist that can analyze Salesforce debug logs.

(continued)

Table 7-1. (*continued*)

Tool	Description
Workbench	Workbench is a Web-based suite of tools available from the developer community. Designed for administrators and developers, this tool allows you to describe, query, manipulate, and migrate both data and metadata in the Salesforce platform directly in your Web browser. Workbench also provides many advanced features for testing and troubleshooting the Salesforce platform's APIs.
Architecture Development Center	The Architecture Developer Center is a library of best practices for architecting sound implementations on the Salesforce platform. On this page, your projects can find links to many white papers, webinars, and blog posts related to performance optimization. These resources can help your projects determine what to look for when performance profiling their application, as well as see how to apply best practices to overcome performance-related challenges.

Your governance team is looking to be assured that the project team has taken the time to consider and test the performance of its application. Your project team may be using the standard tools mentioned previously, or your organization may have invested in alternatives. Whatever solution your project teams have available to them, performance testing—similar to the unit testing of Apex code—should be a key deliverable in your projects.

Your governance team should look to the project team to provide evidence that such testing has occurred and to deliver a report that details the outcomes of your project team's testing efforts. Your performance test report should contain the details shown in Table 7-2.

Table 7-2. *Performance Test Report Contents*

Area	Description
Governor limits analysis	The project team should be providing analysis of its execution logs to highlight the LIMIT_USAGE keyword, demonstrating that there are no areas that are close to reaching any governor limits.
Sharing settings	The project team should demonstrate that they have iterated their performance testing to consider users of differing roles coupled with a reasonable data volume to identify that sharing calculation overheads are not an issue. Testing as a system administrator with full access to all data effectively bypasses any sharing recalculation as the user already has full access.
Database caching	The project should provide its performance test results, ideally with a baseline benchmark with no cache in effect. The project should run a test several times, demonstrating the effect of caching and the initial overhead that the user will experience.
Indexes	Your project is not able to force the Salesforce platform to use an index; however, the project can demonstrate that there is a performance improvement by swapping out index fields in a query with custom fields that are not indexed. This creates a baseline performance for comparison and evaluation of the index's effect of the query.
Load testing	Load testing, where multiple concurrent users are simulated on the Salesforce platform, is a key part of performance testing. As your project team has no real control over the performance of the Salesforce platform beyond its own customizations, the team is really looking to understand any impact on governor limits, such as long-running Apex (more than five seconds). Your project will need to raise a support case with Salesforce before performing load tests.

As with most governance roles for any other platform, your governance team is trying to establish that the project team has undertaken its due diligence in terms of understanding the impact its application has on the Salesforce platform given the potential usage it is going to see.

It may be that your project team has created an application for a specific set of users at a specific scale, or at least is comfortable that the application will work as expected up to a particular usage. This is a good approach in setting boundaries for application usage. Taking this approach could trigger future testing if, for example, your company acquires another and you are suddenly increasing your user base.

Govern the Apex and Visualforce performance to include LDV scenarios (Pagination, JavaScript remoting)

Your governance team may come across a project that uses large data volumes (LDVs); however, the definition of a large data volume is not exact. Your project team may be looking to create tens of millions of records with a relatively simple custom object, or hundreds of thousands of records with a very complex object.

Your governance team is looking to understand the steps your project team has taken to accommodate its large data volumes. In most cases, when dealing with LDVs, it is normal for processes to take longer to execute; after all, there are many more records that could be affected by any changes that your project's users make or other processes that the project creates.

The Salesforce platform provides some features that your project team can take advantage of when dealing with large data volumes. JavaScript remoting provides your developers with the ability to create asynchronous calls to your Visualforce controllers so as to lazy-load data, or load data as it becomes relevant to the end user. Pagination allows your project to request pages of information rather than everything, providing your end users with the ability to move through pages of data at their own pace, rather than long lists of data that take a while to load.

Your governance team will be looking for assurance from the project team that where large data volumes are expected, the project has taken steps to provide a means for the end user to interact with that data in a sensible manner.

Govern the use of external web technologies and complementary UI technologies

With Visualforce and Lightning components your project teams can leverage libraries that are available from multiple developers. Lightning components have made it easier than ever to add libraries to the Salesforce platform's user interface to create a user experience that end users now expect from a modern Web-based application.

Your governance team will need to pay close attention to the external libraries and technologies that your project team has utilized and from where these external libraries and components have come. The AppExchange is a great source for Lightning components that can be "plugged" into your project's Lightning pages. Additionally, if your project team is building its own Lightning components, then third-party JavaScript libraries may be of use to provide specific features and functionality.

Although your governance team is not going to try to restrict what the project team is attempting to deliver, it will need to be assured that the proper commercial and support requirements have been reviewed across the entire project's solution. Where a third-party JavaScript library is in use, the project team should be able to provide assurance that the library complies with your company's commercial and security requirements. It is likely that your supplier or purchasing department may need to be involved to put the correct procedures in place to pay any subscription costs for using the third-party components and libraries.

Your security team may need to review the data policy of the third party to be assured that there is no possibility of data leakage and that the third party is a reputable organization.

Additionally, your governance team will be looking to understand any support requirements for business needs across all the components that are being used in the development of the solution.

Maintainability and Reuse

As shown in Figure 7-4, maintainability and reuse is the next sub-phase on which your governance team should focus.

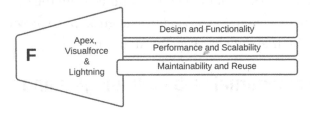

Figure 7-4. *Phase F: Apex, Visualforce & Lightning - maintainability and reuse*

Govern multi-language support and determine the appropriate solution has been used to support globalization

Your governance team will need to understand the language capabilities of the Salesforce platform.

Depending on your company's language requirements, your project team has three options in terms of language support on the Salesforce platform, as shown in Table 7-3.

Table 7-3. *Multi-language Support*

Area	Description
Fully supported languages	Languages in this category are fully supported by the Salesforce platform. All Salesforce features and user interface text appear in the chosen language.
End-user languages	Provide a solution for an end user to select a language other than the default. Salesforce provides translated labels for all standard objects and pages, except admin pages, Setup, and Help. Unsupported labels appear in English.
Platform-only languages	In situations where the Salesforce platform does not provide a default translation, platform-only languages can be used to localize apps and custom functionality that your project builds on the Salesforce platform. Your project team can translate items such as custom labels, custom objects, and field names. Your project team can also rename most standard objects, labels, and fields. Informational text and non-field label text aren't translatable.

To provide further flexibility, the Salesforce platform provides a tool called the translation workbench. When enabled, this tool allows your project team to specify languages for translation, assign translators, and manage those translations through the workbench or bulk translation.

As language support can have a great effect on the end-user community, your governance team will need to be assured that the project team has understood the language requirements from the business, then compared those requirements to the capabilities of the Salesforce platform given the three options mentioned previously. If additional work is required to provide translations, then additional testing will be required. Your business will also need to understand what is possible and any limitations for specific languages.

Govern the options and techniques used to make programmatic components maintainable and reusable on the platform (custom settings, skeleton templates, custom metadata types)

Creating maintainable and reusable components is the desire of nearly all development projects. It is unlikely that any programmer sets out to deliver code that is impossible to maintain. However, not all programmers intend for their programs to be reusable.

163

Creating reusable components typically requires more thought and effort than building a component meant to be used solely at the project level. However, your governance team may be the only group within your company that has a holistic view of all the projects and what is being built. Recognizing reusability could save your company significant money, while delivering functionality to the business more quickly.

However, implementing reusability within your company may not be as straightforward as many would hope. Once a component becomes reusable, it usually means that more than one project makes use of the component. This simple action typically makes way for the inevitable question: "Who will maintain the component on an ongoing basis?"

Initially, your company may be able to support reusable components at the project level, depending on the workload of the project-allocated developers and the impact of issues and enhancements from other projects using the component.

If your company has identified a number of reusable components, it may be time to consider a centralized development team that has the sole task of maintaining and enhancing, and potentially delivering, new components in the future to all other projects. This configuration does, however, come at additional cost.

It is good practice for your governance team to keep in mind that what your project team is developing may one day be reused somewhere else. This helps elevate the quality and avoids those "good enough" scenarios. That is not to say that your governance team should go to extremes to make sure everything developed within your company could be reused, but it should at least make some effort to keep that possibility alive.

Code standards should be in place and adhered to. This is especially true for Apex, where you are aiming for all code to at least follow the same standards in naming convention and code layout. This will provide for a more easily maintainable code base, in that all developers will be able to read the code that other developers have written without getting frustrated that every class they look at is different. Your coding standards should extend to comments and any header-type documentation that should be present at the top of every class's source code. Providing useful information about the changes that have occurred to a specific Apex class via the use of the header and a brief change list could save other developers a lot of time trying to understand what has happened to the code and why.

Tip   Creating a simple header for each Apex class is a great way to introduce developers to what the class is going to support. Additionally, using a basic change list within this header that details the name of the developer, the date, and a brief description of the reason for the change can help dramatically when dealing with source control systems and merging code into other branches. The change list can give a developer an instant view of whether they are merging in the right direction. Additionally, the comments within your Apex code do not contribute to the consumption of your Apex allowance, so why not?

Salesforce has implemented a few solutions to assist developers in creating reusable components in Visualforce. Some are more flexible than others and are as shown in Table 7-4.

Table 7-4. *Reusability Solutions*

Solution	Description
Define custom components	This is an approach that is similar to encapsulating Apex code in methods that can be reused by many programs. By encapsulating a common design pattern in a custom component, it can be reused by one or more Visualforce pages.
Define templates with `<apex:composition>`	This approach allows your projects to define a base template that will allow for portions of that template to change when implemented. This approach should be used when you want to maintain an overall structure on a page, but need the content of individual pages to be different.
Referencing an existing page with `<apex:include>`	This approach allows the entire contents of a Visualforce page to be inserted into another page. This approach should be used when your project team wants to replicate the same content in multiple areas.

Your governance team should make sure that your project team has used the correct solution given what the project is trying to achieve. Make sure that any custom components are not used to define reusable Visualforce pages. Your project should use one of the two templating methods to reuse the content of an entire Visualforce page.

If your project team is looking to store configuration settings that control the behavior of the application it is building, your governance team may need to review the approach the project team has taken. If your project team is creating a packaged solution, then there are features that can be used on the Salesforce platform to accomplish managing application configuration, but they may not be completely appropriate for certain situations, as shown in Table 7-5.

Table 7-5. *Managing Application Configuration*

Solution	Description
Custom objects	This approach might be one of the easiest to implement, but custom objects should be focused on business outcomes rather than application configuration. It is unlikely that your project will be creating numerous records for configuration; therefore, this solution would not be appropriate. Additionally, for packages, your project will be unable to distribute the configuration data without additional scripts to populate the data in the customer objects.
Custom Settings (List)	This approach provides the same settings for every user, which may not be the desired functionality. Custom settings are similar to custom objects but do not require the developer to query the object; the data is accessible directly.
Custom Settings (Hierarchy)	This approach is similar to custom settings (list); however, the settings can be different from user to user. From a developer perspective this is a useful solution for holding configuration settings. These settings are not packageable, so an alternative approach to creating a default set of configuration settings will be required (such as an install script).
Custom Metadata	This approach is probably the best option. Your project can package the values, and end users can deploy them. However, there are specific Apex functions to access the metadata, such as `Metadata.DeployContainer`, which are asynchronous. Your project should develop a customer user interface for the end user to simplify the management of your application's configuration.

Ultimately, your governance team is looking to be assured that the project has used the appropriate solution to meet the business requirements, taking into account maintainability and best practices on the Salesforce platform. Additionally, it may be that your governance team needs to take into account an element of pragmatism to assist the project team in meeting project timelines. Taking a dispensation approach for any areas where a project has strayed from best practices may be a good approach, allowing the project to meet project timelines and refactor any areas where corners may have been cut to meet a deadline.

Method

This is the formal method for Phase F of the Salesforce Platform Governance Method. The objectives of Phase F are to ensure that your project teams have used the Salesforce platform's programmatic capabilities, adhering to best practices to ensure the application being developed can be maintained and operational on the Salesforce platform unhindered in the future. The areas that will be assessed during this phase are as follows:

- Design and Functionality

- Performance and Scalability

- Maintainability and Reuse

Approach

It is not unusual for Apex, Lightning components, and Visualforce pages to be numerous and lengthy. It may be possible for your governance team to manually check the source code delivered by your projects, but it is likely not very practical. Therefore, an automated static code analysis solution (such as PMD) should be considered. This will take time to configure and set up within your organization, but the advantages for your development teams will be huge. These types of governance checks can be executed early within your application development lifecycle, which means your developers will get feedback early in their development process. This will allow your project teams to correct any deviation from standards in the code before it becomes expensive and impacts the timeline.

Ideally, given the timeline, your organization could integrate the code quality governance processes within the continuous delivery and continuous integration pipelines. However, if this is not something your organization can accommodate initially, then it should be possible for your developers to manually code check using tools such as PMD.

As always, your governance team is not a blocker to progress, but rather helps the business get the most out of the Salesforce platform, which does not support any form of application containerization. Therefore, your governance team is trying to ensure that multiple projects co-exist on the Salesforce platform in harmony, while additionally helping your project team deliver a quality solution that will serve your business for the future.

Inputs

For the governance process to be a success, the project team must have a few artifacts available for the governance team to review. Suggested artifacts to review for Phase E of the Salesforce Platform Governance Method are as follows:

- Application configuration and source (or the repository in the instance of using a source control system) where appropriate

- Development standards and best practices

Steps

Properly following the steps to govern your projects' Apex, Visualforce, and Lightning components will help the project team deliver a quality solution that can confidently support your business for the foreseeable future. Additionally, you must ensure that the application being developed will operate without problems throughout Salesforce's frequent update process.

Your application will have to withstand three substantial platform releases each year. Ultimately, your business will want to have these updates applied without causing any issues with your applications.

Design and Functionality

1. Govern the continuum of UI options used against those available on the platform (buttons, mashups, Canvas, Visualforce pages, and Lightning components)

2. Govern the sharing and visibility model in the code solution

3. Govern the code against the security best practices to ensure all Visualforce and Apex code is developed per OWASP standards

4. Govern the object-oriented design principles and design patterns that were adhered to when developing the solution (Singleton, etc.)

5. Govern the appropriate use of the Model-View-Controller pattern

6. Govern any Apex controllers against the technical standards (extensions to standard controllers and custom controllers)

7. Govern the usage of custom settings and synchronous vs. asynchronous patterns, and all the available execution contexts (e.g., batch, trigger, callout, etc.)

8. Govern the usage of batch Apex and the flex queue

9. Govern the Apex / Visualforce solution against the governor limits

10. Govern the order of execution of transactions within the platform (specifically against pre-existing triggers)

11. Govern the quality of test coverage (required for production deployment; call-out testing is a special case)

12. Govern the approach to error/exception handling

Performance and Scalability

1. Govern performance and scalability best practices have been considered within Visualforce pages and Apex code (performance profiling, use of static resources)

2. Govern the Apex and Visualforce performance to include LDV scenarios (pagination, JavaScript remoting)

3. Govern the use of external Web technologies and complementary UI technologies

Maintainability and Reuse

1. Govern multi-language support and determine whether the appropriate solution has been used to support globalization

2. Govern the options and techniques used to make programmatic components maintainable and reusable on the platform (custom settings, skeleton templates, custom metadata types)

Outputs

Once all the steps have been assessed, the outputs to Phase F are as follows:

- Not Applicable – This phase in the Salesforce Platform Governance Method is not applicable to the project.

- Remediate – The governance team requests that the project team remediates its design to accommodate the issues raised during the governance review.

- Pass – The governance team has found no issues or concerns with the project team's proposal and therefore the project has passed this governance phase.

- Review – The governance team has found the inputs cannot be objectively measured and therefore a subjective view has been made, which will lead to a discussion with the project team to reach consensus. Although undesirable, this could be a consequence of unclear standards/policies.

Scenario

For our scenario we are going to focus on two steps: one from the Design and Functionality section and the other from the Maintainability and Reuse section of Phase F. These steps are as follows:

- Govern the usage of batch Apex and the flex queue

- Govern the options and techniques used to make programmatic components maintainable and reusable on the platform (custom settings, skeleton templates, custom metadata types)

Back with our fictitious company Bright Sound Guitars Ltd., Hanna Snyder, the project architect, suggested during the application architecture (Phase A) governance session that her project would be implementing an integration between the Salesforce platform and the stock control system in use at Bright Sound Guitars.

During the integration (Phase E) governance session, Hanna's developer, Caitlyn, mentioned that they intended to develop the integration between the Salesforce application and the stock control system using Apex. Caitlyn suggested that there would be three parts to this integration, as follows:

- A batch process that is scheduled and retrieves all the stock from the stock control system each night, updating the Salesforce platform

- An action that she wants to add into the Salesforce platform's user interface so that a manual stock transfer can occur

- A trigger that will update a specific item within the stock control system when its status is changed on the Salesforce platform

On reviewing the code, the governance team first highlights that the batch appears a little open ended. It is unclear as to the number of batches that could be created and how large the batches are.

The governance team recommends placing some protection around the batch code so that platform limits are not breached, proper error handling is implemented, and alerts are available to the operations team if the batch is unable to run correctly.

The governance team then moves onto the maintainability of the Apex code that Caitlyn and the team have developed. The governance team highlights a few issues that could use fixing, which they believe will help with the longer-term maintainability of the code.

First, the governance team likes the comment header that the development team has put together, as shown in Figure 7-5, but have a few recommendations.

Figure 7-5. *Code header comment*

They recommend enhancing the header comment to include a change log. This will help the development team quickly see what has changed during any merge conflicts, as shown in Figure 7-6. Additionally, they noticed that the developers may have cut and pasted the header into each file, and have inadvertently kept the same description for every file.

Figure 7-6. *Code header comment updated*

With the updated header, the project team should easily be able to identify the latest changes and avoid any conflicts during a branch merge.

Second, the governance team moves onto standards for the naming of variables, as shown in Figure 7-7.

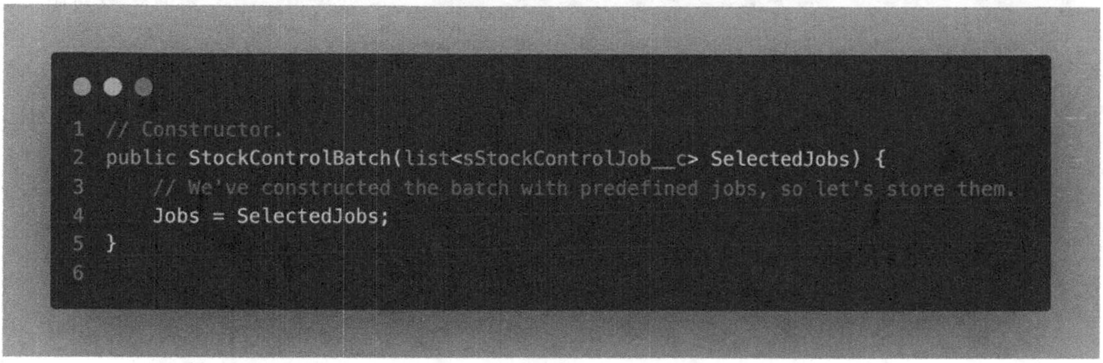

```
1  // Constructor.
2  public StockControlBatch(list<sStockControlJob__c> SelectedJobs) {
3      // We've constructed the batch with predefined jobs, so let's store them.
4      Jobs = SelectedJobs;
5  }
6
```

Figure 7-7. *Variable naming*

The governance team mentions that the preferred naming convention for variables is to use `camelCase`. Although there are a few standards for naming variables, the governance team has asked all development teams to follow this standard, as shown in Figure 7-8. It is also a core rule for the Apex PMD rule set.

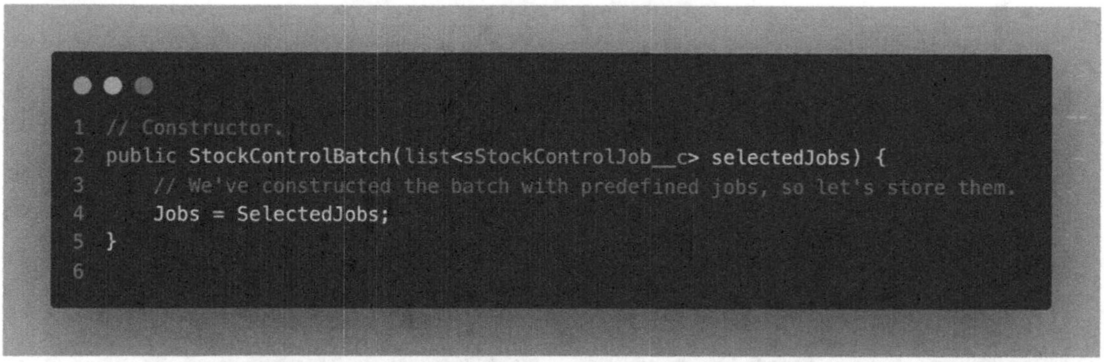

```
1  // Constructor.
2  public StockControlBatch(list<sStockControlJob__c> selectedJobs) {
3      // We've constructed the batch with predefined jobs, so let's store them.
4      Jobs = SelectedJobs;
5  }
6
```

Figure 7-8. *Variable naming updated*

Although the naming of variables appears to be a trivial requirement, it helps differentiate a variable from a class, for example. Also, making sure every developer follows the same standards helps with maintainability because all developers will feel comfortable with the code they are looking at.

The governance team notices the use of Global for the class declaration, as shown in Figure 7-9.

```
1  into the Salesforce platform.
2  */
3
4  global without sharing class StockControlBatch implements Database.Batchable<SObject>, Database.AllowsCallouts {
5      private list<StockControlJob__c> Jobs;
6
7
8      // Constructor.
9      public StockControlBatch(list<sStockControlJob__c> SelectedJobs) {
10         // We've constructed the batch with predefined jobs, so let's store them.
11         Jobs = SelectedJobs;
12     }
13
14
```

Figure 7-9. *Use of Global*

The governance team raises this with Caitlyn, wondering why this class was declared as Global. The governance team understands that the schedulable class that Caitlyn's team has put together is correct. Caitlyn spots that this Global designation is an error, perhaps carried over from another cut-and-paste mistake. The code is changed as shown in Figure 7-10.

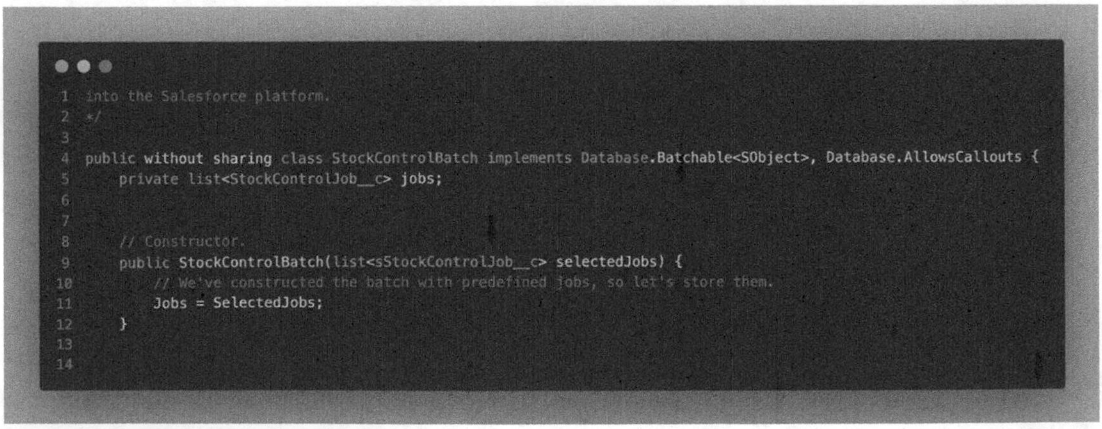

```
1  into the Salesforce platform.
2  */
3
4  public without sharing class StockControlBatch implements Database.Batchable<SObject>, Database.AllowsCallouts {
5      private list<StockControlJob__c> jobs;
6
7
8      // Constructor.
9      public StockControlBatch(list<sStockControlJob__c> selectedJobs) {
10         // We've constructed the batch with predefined jobs, so let's store them.
11         Jobs = SelectedJobs;
12     }
13
14
```

Figure 7-10. *Use of Global updated*

The use of Global affects whether a class is accessible from any other code on the Salesforce platform. Although not a critical issue, if the project does decide to move to a packaged solution it may need to be changed. The project may as well make the class declarations correct for their purposes.

The governance team takes Caitlyn and Hanna through the rest of their comments. Caitlyn is pleased with the feedback, and once all the changes have been implemented, she feels that the code has improved in quality and readability. Caitlyn knows that any issues in production are going to have to be picked up by her and her team, so she appreciates anything that can avoid this situation.

Summary

Developing on the Salesforce platform is not unlike doing so on any other development platform. However, because the Salesforce platform is a multi-tenant architecture, controls have been put in place by Salesforce to protect each tenant from one another. This adds some complexity to project development.

Phase F tackles the governance of a project's programmatic solutions, making sure standards have been followed and platform considerations have been made. Having completed this governance phase, you have checked that the project team has adhered to development standards, considered whether the platform capabilities they have used align with the original intent for these capabilities, and worked within the platform constraints that exist.

You have highlighted to your project team any areas of concern within the programmatic solutions they have created and are confident that the project will remediate your concerns.

CHAPTER 8

Communities: Phase G

This phase of the Salesforce Platform Governance Method focuses on your projects' use of communities within the Salesforce platform.

Overview

Communities are delivered using Salesforce's Experience Cloud (recently rebranded from Community Cloud) product, which is built into the Salesforce platform. Experience Cloud offers a number of community solutions depending on your target audience. These audiences are typically categorized as follows:

- Customer

- Partner

- Employee

These three community types cover the main user groups that you would expect to interact with your business in one way or another. For clarity, customer communities are those users that are buying services or products from your company and looking for support or help; these could be businesses (B2B) or consumers (B2C). Partner communities are those users that collaborate with your business to sell and support services or products. Employee communities are the people that work for you and may require access to information via a portal.

Essentially, the Salesforce platform is an SaaS (Software as a Service) solution that is delivered to the end user via a browser. You could argue that the community within the Salesforce platform is just another view delivered by that SaaS solution.

This phase is further broken down into sub-phases to aid your governance team and the task of governing your projects, as shown in Figure 8-1.

L. Harding and L. Bayliss, *Salesforce Platform Governance Method*,
https://doi.org/10.1007/978-1-4842-7404-0_8

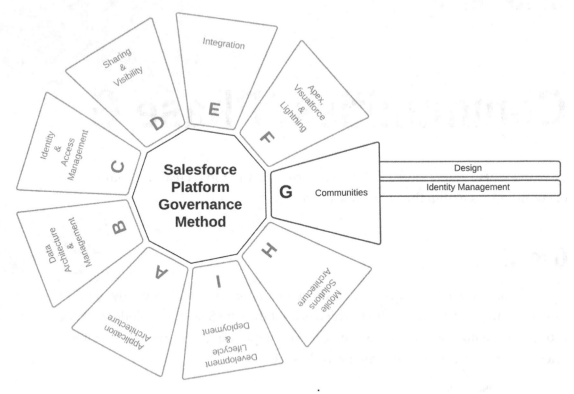

Figure 8-1. *The Salesforce Platform Governance Method: Phase G*

As with previous phases, let's start by defining what we mean by a community so that we are clear about what we are governing. In the context of the Salesforce Platform Governance Method, we will use the Gartner definition:

> *"A constantly changing group of people collaborating and sharing their ideas over an electronic network (e.g., the Internet). Communities optimize their collective power by affiliation around a common interest, by the compression of the time between member interactions (i.e., communicating in real time), and by asynchronous 'postings' that potentially reach more participants and permit more reflection time than real-time interactions."*
>
> —Gartner[1]

---

[1] https://www.gartner.com/en/information-technology/glossary/community

If your project is delivering a community solution as part of the overall application, your governance team will need to be assured that the project has put the correct measures in place to control the visibility of data. Additionally, a community that is externally focused, such as a customer or partner community, has some responsibility for delivering your brand image. A bad experience using your customer community could cause brand damage and lose your business customers. Equally, upsetting partners could create long-lasting damage for your business as well as your partners' businesses.

Internally focused communities have a responsibility to deliver a great experience for your employees, as frustrating your employees with a badly delivered and poorly thought out community could cause your employees to look elsewhere for a job.

Although your governance team is unlikely to have input into the structure or functionality of the Salesforce community, they should be aware of branding guidelines and of course take a keen interest in any quality aspects of the project's community. Your governance team will be protecting your company's public image to some extent.

Design

As shown in Figure 8-2, design is the first sub-phase for your governance team to tackle.

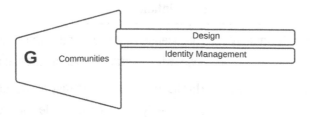

Figure 8-2. *Phase G: communities - design*

Govern the license types associated with the sites and communities

Depending on the target audience for your community, there are a number of different license types available. Your governance team should be looking for assurance that the project has selected the correct license for their particular use case, and that they have considered the quantity of licenses required.

As previously mentioned, there are three categories of Salesforce community, as follows:

- Customer Community – Allow your customers (B2B and B2C) to engage with both your company and other customers via an online portal.

- Partner Community – Provide your resellers, distributors, and brokers limited access to the Salesforce platform to pass you leads and work on sales projects with your sales team.

- Employee Community – Provide employees limited access to your data within the Salesforce platform. Use this license type to build custom applications for your employees when they do not require a full Salesforce license.

Each community category has one or more license types associated with it, and these types dictate what is available to your community users. Additionally, some license types increase limits placed on the platform, as shown in Table 8-1.

Table 8-1. *Salesforce Community License Types*

Community	License	Description
Customer	Customer Community	This license type is generally associated with a B2C use case, with a large number of external users.
	Customer Community Plus	This license type is generally associated with a B2B use case, typically for non-sales support requirements. Additionally, this license is appropriate if a customer requires access to records that are not linked to their own account or needs to view dashboards and reports or have delegated administration rights.
Partner	Partner Community	This is similar to customer community but also offers your users access to data that relates to your sales processes, typically leads, opportunities, quotes, and campaigns, among others.

(continued)

Table 8-1. (*continued*)

Community	License	Description
Employee	Lightning Platform Starter	Similar to customer community but offering your users access to some standard objects, such as accounts, contacts, cases, and activities. Objects relating to the sales process are not available. Additionally, cases are limited to internal and employee cases and not those raised by customers. This license provides access to 10 custom objects, so may be limiting depending on the complexity of your project's application. Also, the number of API calls per day per community member is 200 regardless of Salesforce platform edition.
	Lightning Platform Plus	Builds from Lightning starter but provides access to more customer objects, with the limit of customer objects being raised to 110, which allows for a much more rich and complex application or number of applications. Additionally, there are some API call limits raised with this license type with Enterprise Salesforce platform editions having 1,000 API calls per day per community member and 5,000 API calls per day per community member for Unlimited editions of the Salesforce platform.

Your governance team will need to look at the longer-term requirements of your project and question whether the correct license type has been used given the roadmap for the project's application.

If your project is delivering a new application for your employees to access via an employee community, and that application is on the verge of consuming 10 custom objects, your governance team may see this as a potential future problem.

Tip   In general, upgrading licenses is not a problem; however, it is not usually possible to downgrade licenses.

Your governance team will also want to review the license consumption holistically, as multiple projects may be delivering communities, which will not be looking at the overall license position for your company. Pooling licenses may provide a better commercial position when discussing license requirements with Salesforce.

Govern the sharing usage for partner, customer, and employee community users

There are many ways to provide data access and visibility of objects and records to your community users.

The Salesforce platform provides various layers that will determine access, beginning with the baseline access (external organization-wide defaults) controlled by profiles and permission sets. The Salesforce platform then provides many out-of-the-box capabilities to share records with external users based on their license type. Your project should document their sharing requirements and review what is possible with sharing to help them plan better and provide your governance team with the assurance they need.

Your governance team is looking for assurance that your project has taken the time to gather data sharing requirements and documented their approach for each of their communities and license types. As a general rule, your governance team will be looking to the project team to assure them that the following have been undertaken:

- The project has planned their sharing model.

- The project has defined their sharing requirements.

- The project has determined the sharing options they should use.

- The project has updated their sharing requirements with the sharing option they will implement.

The project team has planned its sharing model

There are several areas to review when your project team plans its sharing model for external users. The Salesforce platform allows your project to control access to data at many different levels, previously discussed in Phase D of the Salesforce Platform Governance Method. From an external perspective, these are shown in Table 8-2.

Table 8-2. *Community Sharing*

Area	Description
External Organization-Wide Defaults	Baseline access similar to internal org-wide default to set a different default access level for external users. When you first enable external organization-wide defaults, the default internal access and default external access are set to the original default access level. As of the Spring 2020 release, the external org-wide defaults are enabled by default in all new orgs to better secure your data. If you have an existing org and you plan to share records with external users, then you must enable the external org-wide defaults.
Role Hierarchy: Customer Community Plus and Partner Community, Channel Account, and External Apps licenses	These are role-based licenses, which means access to records rolls up the hierarchy. The role hierarchy automatically grants record access to users above the record owner in the hierarchy. You can control sharing access using hierarchies for any custom object, but not standard objects.
Sharing Rules	Use sharing rules to extend sharing access to users in public groups, roles, or territories. Sharing rules give particular users greater access by making automatic exceptions to your org-wide sharing settings.
Sharing Sets	Sharing sets let you take a lookup, such as account, contact, or user from the community user, and match it to records in your Salesforce org that also have that lookup value.
Manual Sharing	Sometimes it's impossible to define a consistent group of users who need access to a particular set of records. In those situations, record owners can use manual sharing to give read and edit permissions to users who don't have access any other way.

The project team has defined its sharing requirements

Your governance team will need to see evidence that the project team has clearly defined its sharing requirements. It is not possible to determine the best approach to sharing data with external users without first defining and documenting these requirements.

A template should be used to help the project team document its sharing requirements, which will also help the governance team in its assurance role given the team can clearly see the requirement and the reasons behind the data being shared. Figure 8-3 shows an example template.

Business Requirement	Community License Type	Sharing WHAT?	Owner	Sharing WITH?	Sharing HOW?
Document your business requirement here.	Partner Community Customer Community Customer Community Plus Guest	sObject (Cases, Files, Opportunities etc.)	Customer Internal Guest Partner etc.	Customer Internal Guest Partner etc.	
Document your business requirement here.	Partner Community Customer Community Customer Community Plus Guest	sObject (Cases, Files, Opportunities etc.)	Customer Internal Guest Partner etc.	Customer Internal Guest Partner etc.	
Document your business requirement here.	Partner Community Customer Community Customer Community Plus Guest	sObject (Cases, Files, Opportunities etc.)	Customer Internal Guest Partner etc.	Customer Internal Guest Partner etc.	

Figure 8-3. *Project sharing requirements*

The template in Figure 8-3 provides an example of a project sharing requirement document, which captures the following:

- The business requirement for external sharing

- The community license type that will be used

- The object being shared

- The owner of the record

- The user or group the object is being shared with

- The sharing option that has been selected as most appropriate to meet the business requirement

If multiple projects are creating communities, your governance team may need to centralize the overall sharing requirements so that it is easy to understand the holistic sharing solution. The template could be extended to add the project team to provide this.

A simple Salesforce platform application could be constructed to deliver this template to be completed online by the project team, which could feed directly into a company-wide view of your sharing model and provide easier reporting. Additionally, this could also highlight any pre-existing sharing configurations.

The project team has determined the sharing options it should use

Once your project has defined and documented its business and sharing requirements, the project team can review the available options based on the license type.

Your governance team should be looking to the project team to deliver a solution that is available declaratively, and only if there is no available solution should they move to a custom sharing solution. The available sharing options are shown in Table 8-3.

Table 8-3. *Sharing Options*

Sharing Option	Customer Community	Customer Community Plus	Partner Community	External Application
Sharing Sets	Yes	--	--	Yes
Share Group	Yes	--	--	--
Folders (Reports and Libraries)	--	Yes	Yes	Yes
Sharing Rules	--	Yes	Yes	Yes
Manual Sharing	--	Yes	Yes	Yes
Partner Role Hierarchy	--	Yes	Yes	Yes
External Account Hierarchies	--	Yes	Yes	Yes
External Delegated Admin	--	Yes	Yes	Yes
Super User	--	Yes	Yes	Yes
Account Relationships (Account Relationship Data Sharing Rules)	--	Yes	Yes	Yes
Account and Opportunity Teams	--	Yes	Yes	Yes
Apex Managed Sharing	--	Yes	Yes	Yes

Your project team should use the Salesforce External User Sharing Resource Matrix (https://sfdc.co/KdVbE) to help plan its external sharing model. This matrix will help your project team determine what sharing capabilities are available based on the community license type, external organization-wide sharing defaults, and more. Your project team will follow ten basic steps to determine the appropriate sharing option for each business requirement:

1. Select the community license type and update the object access. Each license type comes with baseline access or entitlements. By design, the out-of-the-box object permissions of user profiles associated with community licenses are rather restricted. Document the object.

2. Review the external organization-wide defaults—baseline access similar to "Internal Org Wide-Default"—to set a different default access level for external users. When your project team first enables external organization-wide defaults, the default internal access and default external access are set to the original default access level, which is Private.

3. Does the account role hierarchy provide the record access? Customer community plus, partner community, and external apps licenses are role based, which means access to records rolls up the hierarchy. When your project team enables the first external user on a partner account, a user role hierarchy is created for that account. This role hierarchy rolls up to the account owner. The three partner user roles in this hierarchy are partner user, partner manager, or partner executive. When your project team creates contacts on the partner account and converts them to external users, assign one of these roles to them.

4. Extend access with sharing sets. A sharing set grants community or portal users access to any record associated with an account or contact that matches the user's account or contact.

5. Use sharing groups to share records owned by high-volume community users. Sharing groups allow you to share records owned by high-volume community and portal users with internal and external users. Sharing groups apply across communities or portals and are associated with sharing sets.

6. Enable account and opportunity teams. An account team is a team of users who work together on an account. Set level of access for account, opportunity, and case objects. Set up a default opportunity team of coworkers you typically work with on opportunities, with a role for each member and special access to your opportunities. Set up a default account team and a default opportunity team.

7. Use declarative sharing rules to extend access to users in public groups, roles, or territories. Sharing rules give particular users greater access by making automatic exceptions to org-wide sharing settings.

8. Grant access with account relationships or point-to-point relationships with granular data access. Grant record access to partner or customer accounts and protect confidential data by sharing only select information. Channel account managers can use account relationships and account relationship data sharing rules to target how information is shared and who it's shared with.

9. Set up external account hierarchies, which work like Salesforce role hierarchies. Account records belonging to child accounts in an external account hierarchy share data with the parent accounts in that hierarchy. As a result, data can be shared without creating sharing rules.

10. Don't forget about built-in sharing behavior (a.k.a. implicit sharing). There are a number of sharing behaviors that are built into Salesforce applications. This kind of sharing is called implicit because it is not configured by administrators; it is defined and maintained by the system to support collaboration among members of sales teams, customer service representatives, and clients or customers.

Your governance team may want to review this matrix to be assured that the project team undertook a comprehensive review to determine the appropriate sharing option to use for each business requirement.

The project team has updated its sharing requirements with the sharing option it will implement

Once your project team has reviewed the sharing matrix and determined the most secure and efficient way to share records based on their business requirements, the team should update its sharing requirements' "Sharing HOW?" column, as shown in Table 8-4.

Table 8-4. *Project Sharing Requirements Updated*

Business Requirement	Community License Type	Sharing WHAT?	Owner	Sharing WITH?	Sharing HOW?
Document your business requirement here.	Partner Community Customer Community Customer Community Plus Guest	sObject (Cases, Files, Opportunities etc.)	Customer Internal Guest Partner etc.	Customer Internal Guest Partner etc.	
Document your business requirement here.	Partner Community Customer Community Customer Community Plus Guest	sObject (Cases, Files, Opportunities etc.)	Customer Internal Guest Partner etc.	Customer Internal Guest Partner etc.	
Document your business requirement here.	Partner Community Customer Community Customer Community Plus Guest	sObject (Cases, Files, Opportunities etc.)	Customer Internal Guest Partner etc.	Customer Internal Guest Partner etc.	

As previously mentioned, your governance team should implement a companywide sharing requirements document (or application) if you have multiple projects.

Govern the different UI / UX capabilities to style a community

Your governance team has a long-term view of all projects being delivered. They understand that the applications built for their company may be in use for years after the project team has moved on to new projects or even different companies. With this in mind, your governance team will want to understand any areas where the project team has made changes that might expose the company to future challenges as the Salesforce platform is enhanced over the years.

Salesforce makes three releases of its core platform every year. With those releases are packages with thousands of enhancements and completely new capabilities. Additionally, over time we can expect UI / UX updates, just as the original UI (now known as Classic) changed into Lightning, and also how Lightning changed from the Aura-based technology to the Lightning Web Components technology.

Given the relentless pace of change and the ever evolving user interface that people expect, and the fact that technology will no doubt be delivering new devices that will run the platform, your governance team needs to make sure that your company can consume all these future Salesforce features without challenge or disruption.

Caution   When Salesforce introduced Lightning, the migration from Classic to this new interface was a big problem for some companies. Those that heavily modified their applications and moved beyond the safe boundaries that Salesforce has in place suffered greatly. There are companies still struggling today to move away from the Classic user interface because of this. Your company does not want to be in this position in the future.

Although Salesforce categorizes its community extension as customer, employee, or partner, many companies have gone beyond that out-of-the-box experience to deliver something truly bespoke. However, your governance team should look out for any project that has put a lot of effort into changing their community way beyond the standard framework that Salesforce delivered.

For example, overriding CSS is not recommended. The best way to update any styling requirements for your components is to use the Theme panel in Experience Builder.

Use the CSS Editor in Experience Builder to add custom CSS that overrides the default template and theme panel styles. You can also use it to make minor changes to the appearance of out-of-the-box components, such as padding adjustments.

Use custom CSS sparingly. Future releases of template components might not support your CSS customizations. Additionally, Salesforce customer support cannot help resolve any issues with custom CSS.

If your project has had to make a lot of customizations for styling, you are likely to see an issue in the future when updates to the template you have used are made by Salesforce. This could leave your community stuck on a template or template version and require major investment from your company to move away from your customized template into a supported template.

Your project team should assure your governance team that any styling changes have been absolutely necessary, and document them clearly so that future teams and support personnel can troubleshoot problems if they arise.

Govern the mobile considerations for communities

To provide the best experience for your customers, your project should make every effort to ensure your community works well on a mobile device. Your governance team will look for assurance that your project has undergone usability testing of your community. It is more likely that consumer-based communities will be accessed from mobile devices. However, given the plethora of devices and network variances, your project team will have to review its community solution, taking into account the following:

- The reduction of page load times

- The usability of the page given the different screen form factors

It is unlikely that your project will be able to test for every device and screen factor, but some effort should be made to make sure the user experience is largely a good one.

Your governance team should be assured that the project team has made sure images are optimized for mobile devices (which should be enabled by default) as well as hid non-business critical components.

Identity Management

As shown in Figure 8-4, identity management is the next sub-phase that your governance team will assess.

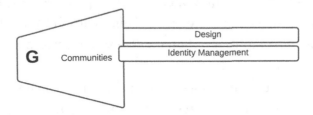

Figure 8-4. *Phase G: communities - identity management*

Govern how identity management is handled within communities: provisioning, syncing, and de-provisioning

Your project team has several options for authenticating customers and employees in your community site. Customers are users with community, customer portal, external identity, or partner portal licenses. By default, they can log in with the username and password that Salesforce assigns them for the Experience Cloud site.

Your Salesforce org's employees are users with full Salesforce licensing capabilities. These users follow the employee login flow using their Salesforce username and password.

Beyond these default settings, your project team can configure SAML, third-party authentication providers, or OAuth to authenticate and authorize all users accessing your site. Your project team can also configure self-registration or Just-in-Time (JIT) to use Login Discovery, which makes it easier for users to authenticate.

Your governance team may look for assurance around license consumption for self-registering users onto the community.

For consumer community sites, your governance team will want to review the process for provisioning and de-provisioning users. Not all identity solutions, if your project is using an external identity provider, support de-provisioning of users. Additional functionality may need to be delivered by your project team to overcome this.

Govern the use of external identity (Facebook, Google, etc.) if appropriate

Employees and customers can access a community site through a third-party authentication provider. For example, if your project configures Facebook as a third-party authentication provider, your users can log in to Facebook through a link on the community site login page. Facebook authenticates the user, allowing them access to the site.

Salesforce provides a simple way to set up several common authentication providers, such as Facebook, GitHub, Google, LinkedIn, Salesforce, and Twitter, instead of creating your own app on the third-party site.

Your company may have security policies in place that provide your project teams with guidance on acceptable external identity providers. Your governance team will want to be assured that the project team adhered to this policy.

If no such policy exists, your governance team may review the community in terms of data exposed and functionality available before deciding whether a particular external identity is acceptable. However, for most consumer use cases, it is common that social media providers are acceptable providers, and your project team will want to make authentication as straightforward as possible for their main customer base.

Method

This is the formal method for Phase G of the Salesforce Platform Governance Method. The objectives of Phase G are to ensure that your project teams have used the Salesforce platform's community capabilities properly and are not inadvertently exposing any data to the wrong people.

There is an element of taking a least-privilege view when it comes to data visibility, but that requires that your project teams have determined the business requirements for driving data sharing and visibility.

Additionally, your governance team is looking be assured that the project is delivering a maintainable community, something that will continue to operate throughout the Salesforce release cycle. Given that, the areas that will be assessed during this phase are as follows:

- Design
- Identity Management

Approach

This phase requires that your project team supplies a number of artifacts for the governance team to review. Your governance team will be looking to approve your project team's solution as quickly as possible, without necessarily knowing all the details of your community. With this in mind, governing the use of community could take the approach of an initial review where your project team presents the overall community approach and outlines the basic business requirements. With that review over, your project team could then dive into the details of the business requirements and complete the templates, delivering the artifacts to your governance team for a second review.

Inputs

For the governance process to be a success, the project team must have a few artifacts available to the governance team for review. Suggested artifacts for the governance team to review for Phase G of the Salesforce Platform Governance Method are as follows:

- Project sharing requirements
- Project completed Salesforce external user sharing resource matrix

- Project sharing requirement options

- Project bespoke styling requirements

Steps

The steps to govern your project team's community site will help the team to deliver a quality solution that can confidently support your customers for the foreseeable future without damaging your brand, or a partner community site that helps all parties be successful in their business. Your employee community site will be somewhere your employees will find what they need to help them in their jobs.

Whichever community your project is building, it will have to withstand three substantial platform releases each year. Ultimately, your business will want to have these updates applied without causing any issues with your community sites.

Design

1. Govern the license types associated with the sites and communities

2. Govern the sharing usage for partner, customer, and employee community users

3. Govern the different UI / UX capabilities to style a community

4. Govern the mobile considerations for communities

Identity Management

1. Govern how identity management is handled within communities: provisioning, syncing, and de-provisioning

2. Govern the use of external identity (Facebook, Google etc.) if appropriate

Outputs

Once all the steps have been assessed, the outputs to Phase G are as follows:

- Not Applicable – This phase in the Salesforce Platform Governance Method is not applicable to the project.

- Remediate – The governance team requests that the project team remediate its design to accommodate the issues raised during the governance review.

- Pass – The governance team has found no issues or concerns with the project's proposal and therefore the project has passed this governance phase.

- Review – The governance team has found the inputs cannot be objectively measured and therefore a subjective view has been made, which will lead to a discussion with the project team to reach consensus. Although undesirable, this could be a consequence of unclear standards/policies.

Scenario

For our scenario we are going to focus on one of the steps from the design section of the communities Phase G method. This step is as follows:

- Govern the different UI / UX capabilities to style a community

Hanna Snyder, the project architect from our company Bright Sound Guitars, has brought a proposal to the governance team regarding the use of a community site for their customers. The business wants to provide a support portal for their guitars, where customers can seek technical advice and raise cases when things not going well with the guitars they have purchased.

On the surface, the governance team cannot find any issues with Hanna's suggestion and on first review gives Hanna the all clear that she is onto a great solution and everything makes sense. Hanna goes back to her project team and starts her detailed requirements capture and design of the community portal.

On returning to the governance team a few months later, Hanna has brought with her Ranveer Shah, her Salesforce developer, and Darren Perry, her business analyst. Darren does a great job of presenting the community portal and all the functionality that they intend to deliver to the customers.

Things are going great during the governance review until Darren presents the community wireframes and UI mock-ups. Darren has really taken customization of the community to a new level.

Ranveer explains the lengths to which he has gone in order to tailor the community user interface and experience to meet Darren's requirements. Ranveer has CSS being overridden throughout, tailoring the look of the community beyond recognition from the original Salesforce template. He also used high-definition images throughout, as they felt these gave the best view of the guitars, especially those with the high-gloss finish.

The governance team raises a major concern with the amount of customization that Ranveer has done. This level of customization would leave Bright Sound Guitars exposed when Salesforce updates the template or changes any of the CSS classes they have used within the template. This could leave Bright Sound Guitars stuck in the past in terms of the template, not being able to upgrade without a major investment from the project team to remediate any issues.

Hanna steps in and agrees. She raised the issue early on that the levels of customization were too high and did not significantly improve the usability of the community portal; however, Darren did not agree.

Using a mock-up of the community, the governance team tests the site from their mobile phones. The load times are atrocious and unlikely to win any favors from their community of customers.

Darren admits that this might drive away users rather than encourage the community spirit for which he was hoping. Hanna suggests that the team go back to review the amount of customization to see how a compromise can be reached.

Summary

Creating a community for your customers is a big responsibility. In some respects, it should be no different than doing so for your employees, but the main difference is that your employees could accept issues, or some level of "clunkiness," that your customer just will not.

Phase G tackles the governance of your community requirements, focusing on maintainability and data sharing and visibility. Once a community is out in the public, it is much harder to manage failures and could create brand damage for your company.

During this phase you have highlighted to your project teams the areas of concern and provided feedback as to what needs to be done to bring the community project to an acceptable level to pass governance.

CHAPTER 9

Mobile Solutions Architecture: Phase H

This phase of the Salesforce Platform Governance Method focuses on the use of the Salesforce platform and your applications on a mobile device.

Overview

There are a few options available to your project teams when it comes to using a mobile device to access your application or Salesforce configuration. Your project can choose to use Salesforce's own mobile application, originally called Salesforce1 but now known as simply Salesforce, or take things much further and create their own mobile application, using the Salesforce mobile API to access the data and processes stored within the Salesforce platform.

Salesforce has tried to accommodate every use case in the use of mobile devices: those businesses that just want a simple solution that to some degree can mirror the main Salesforce platform's browser experience all the way to those who want to create a bespoke application that allows the business to have maximum control over the end result.

This flexibility provides some complication to your governance team. In some cases they may have to govern your project's solution just as they would any other programmatic solution, or have a light touch because the project team has chosen to access their functionality via the Salesforce mobile application.

As with previous phases of the Salesforce Platform Governance Method, this phase is broken down into sub-phases to ease governance, as shown in Figure 9-1.

© Lee Harding and Lee Bayliss 2022
L. Harding and L. Bayliss, *Salesforce Platform Governance Method*,
https://doi.org/10.1007/978-1-4842-7404-0_9

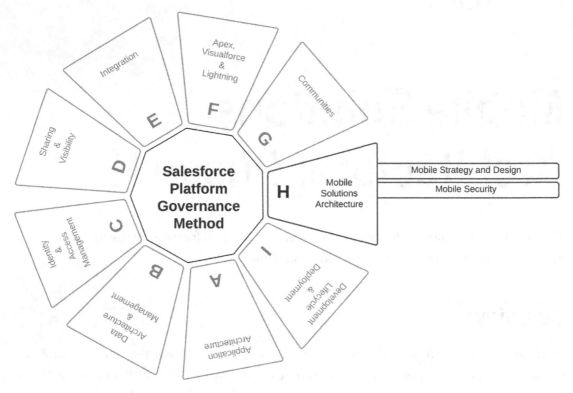

Figure 9-1. *The Salesforce Platform Governance Method: Phase H*

As with previous phases, let's start by defining what we mean by a mobile solutions architecture so that we are clear about what we are governing. As mobile solutions architecture is not really any different than any other solution architecture, we can drop the mobile part, and therefore for the context of the Salesforce Platform Governance Method, we will use the Gartner definition:

> *"A solution architecture (SA) is an architectural description of a specific solution. SAs combine guidance from different enterprise architecture view-points (business, information and technical), as well as from the enterprise solution architecture (ESA)."*

—Gartner[1]

If your project team is delivering a mobile solution as part of their overall Salesforce platform implementation, your governance team will need to understand initially the approach your project is taking. As previously mentioned, Salesforce has developed a

---

[1] https://www.gartner.com/en/information-technology/glossary/solution-architecture

number of options in the mobile solutioning space, some targeted at businesses that just want to deliver the basics to allow their end users to access key information on the move, while other solutions give developers complete control over what they do and how they do it (within the boundaries of using the appropriate Salesforce APIs).

Your governance team will want to review the process by which your project team came to the decision regarding what Salesforce technology to use. This is mainly because your governance team will be looking for the longer-term support and maintenance requirements as well as the resources needed. Developing a bespoke mobile application using, for example, Apple's Swift development system might meet the business requirements, but will require your company to have those skills available for the long term to maintain and enhance the original. It is worth investing the time up front to determine whether your business requirements could be met using a simpler approach.

Mobile Strategy and Design

As shown in Figure 9-2, mobile strategy and design is the first sub-phase to be assessed by your governance team.

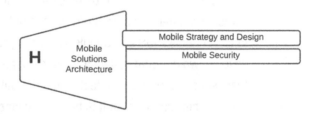

Figure 9-2. *Phase H: mobile solutions architecture - mobile strategy and design*

Govern the mobile solution for use of the appropriate mobile platform: HTML5, Native (iOS / Android), hybrid solutions, or Salesforce mobile app

As touched upon previously, your project team has a few options available to them when considering a mobile solution for their Salesforce platform application; however, these are really distilled into two types:

- Salesforce's mobile app

- Salesforce's mobile SDK

Salesforce's mobile app provides a simple solution for delivering your applications and configuration built on the Salesforce platform to your mobile users. You can consider the Salesforce mobile app as really providing your end users with a similar experience to the one they have using the platform on a desktop PC via a browser. This solution is really targeted at your employees.

Salesforce's mobile SDK provides a far richer development experience. It provides developers with the tools to develop mobile applications that your company can distribute through the Apple App Store or the Google Play Store, or others. These mobile apps can be used by employees, customers, or your partners. When using the Salesforce mobile SDK, your developers have a few choices regarding how they construct the mobile application itself, as shown in Table 9-1.

Table 9-1. *Mobile Development Solutions*

Mobile Development Solution	Description
Native	Mobile apps built specifically for a mobile device's operating system. Each operating system that your company wants to support will require your development team to create a completely different application. For example, if you wanted to target Apple's iOS and Google's Android you would have to develop two different mobile apps and support and manage them separately. There are technologies available that can simplify this situation, but it is best to assume that every platform your company wants to support will require a separate application to be developed and tested. Your developers will use tools such as Apple's XCode or Google's Android Studio.
HTML5	Mobile apps built to be as portable as possible across the available mobile platforms. These apps are developed using the popular Web technologies HTML5, JavaScript, and CSS and are delivered using the mobile Web browser. Using these popular technologies provides the greatest flexibility when targeting multiple devices and platforms.

(continued)

Table 9-1. (*continued*)

Mobile Development Solution	Description
Hybrid	Hybrid apps, as the name suggests, are mobile apps built using HTML5 and JavaScript, but these are wrapped inside a thin container that provides native access to Salesforce's platform features. You can decide to have your HTML and JavaScript code local or remote, which allows your developers to store data locally on the device or remotely on the server.
React Native	A React native mobile app uses a specialized scripting language and an older version of JavaScript (ES6 / 2015). CSS is handled via JavaScript code. React native provides access to the standard Salesforce mobile SDK features.

One of the challenges your project team will face before developing their mobile application using one of the preceding options is defining the business requirements they need to support. As some of the options presented are not native to the mobile platform you may target, your application may not have access to the mobile platform features it desires. Here is a summary of the features as Salesforce sees them, which are available depending on the development approach taken, as shown in Table 9-2.

Table 9-2. *Mobile Platform Feature Access*

	Native, React Native	HTML5	Hybrid
Graphics	Native APIs	HTML, Canvas, SVG	HTML, Canvas, SVG
Performance	Fastest	Fast	Moderately Fast
Look and feel	Native	Emulated	Emulated
Distribution	App Store	Web	App Store
Camera	Yes	Browser dependent	Yes
Notifications	Yes	No	Yes
Contacts, calendar	Yes	No	Yes

(*continued*)

Table 9-2. (*continued*)

	Native, React Native	HTML5	Hybrid
Offline storage	Secure file system	Not secure; shared SQL, key–value stores	Secure file system; shared SQL (through Cordova plug-ins)
Geolocation	Yes	Yes	Yes
Swipe	Yes	Yes	Yes
Pinch, spread	Yes	Yes	Yes
Connectivity	Online / offline	Mostly online	Online / offline
Development skills	Swift, Objective-C, Jaca, Kotlin; JavaScript (React native only)	HTML5, CSS, JavaScript	HTML5, CSS, JavaScript

Your governance team will be looking for assurance from your project team that the business requirements that need to be met are done so in the best way. This will be reviewed on a number of factors, as follows:

- Development skills within your organization and the ability to maintain the mobile app in the longer term

- Time scales required to deliver the mobile app; the HTML5 option removes the App Store requirement and therefore could be quicker to market

- Offline storage requirements, especially with regard to securely storing data

- Access to underlying mobile platform functions, such as the camera

- Application performance. Are your customers going to expect a mobile application that performs and is responsive?

- Look and feel. Customers can be put off from using a mobile app if the user interface does not adhere to their native mobile's UI.

In the main, your governance team will not be looking to dictate to the project team the best approach, though they will be looking to understand the longer-term support for the project's mobile app. Additionally, where a native solution is chosen your project will be required to participate in the normal software development governance processes, especially with regard to coding standards.

Testing may also be something of a consideration, and building a mobile app using HTML might be a slightly easier solution to test over a native solution.

Govern the authentication / authorization (including SSO), offline storage, and sync requirements

The Salesforce platform's connected app is the primary means by which to connect a mobile app to the Salesforce platform. Your governance team will be looking for assurance that the project team has not deviated from this solution to authenticate their mobile app. If they have, then further assurance will be required to understand how the project team intends to handle authentication of a mobile app to the Salesforce platform.

The mobile SDK can use the SmartStore feature to store data locally for offline use. The lifespan of data within the SmartStore is tied to the authenticated user. If access is revoked, the data held within the SmartStore is purged. Your governance team will want to review the project's use of SmartStore to determine whether the appropriate data has been stored and the lifespan requirement of any refresh tokens.

Your project may have opted to support advanced authentication, which is a configurable option and requires either MyDomain to be configured or Mobile Device Management (MDM). Advanced authentication will require additional solutions for the MDM aspects, which will be used to distribute your mobile app settings. Additionally, using advanced authentication will prompt your users with a full-screen login page, which may leave some of your users confused, and they will be given the impression that they have left your application.

Your governance team should review the overall approach to authentication to determine whether your project is within your company's security policy and whether the data that will be stored on the mobile device is secured, as well as whether that authentication will be implemented correctly. These areas of mobile app development will be the same whether your application is targeted at your employees or customers. However, you are likely to experience a greater number of users when targeting customers; therefore, your risk exposure could be greater.

Govern the use of Salesforce mobile app declarative design

Your project team may have opted to use Salesforce's mobile app to deliver the functionality they require to their end users. This is a great solution that can provide the functionality quickly without the need to do a large amount of bespoke development. Just like with the Salesforce platform, however, your project will have to accept the look and feel as is, as well as a few limitations, as follows:

- The Salesforce mobile app does not support standard or custom Salesforce apps.

- You cannot use the console or agent console.

- There is no advanced currency management.

Additionally, some fields will behave differently on the Salesforce mobile app than on the browser-based Salesforce platform, such as the following:

- The division field is unsupported.

- Combo boxes are not supported. The text field element is available, but not the picklist part.

- User-defined lookup filters are not supported.

- Creating a record from a lookup field is not supported.

- Owner lookup fields always display the name of the record's owner regardless of the user's sharing permissions (this occurs on the Salesforce platform as well as on the mobile app).

- Disabled picklists are not greyed out.

- Phone number formatting is not supported.

- Creating or editing existing list views is not supported.

- Record editing in a list view is not supported.

- Multi-record selection in a list view is not supported.

- Mass actions are not supported.

- List views are not automatically updated when data changes.

- Kanban and split view are not supported.

- Collapsing sections on a record view is not supported.

- Some related lists are not available, such as the following:

    - Content deliveries

    - External sharing

    - Related content

- List buttons are not supported in some related lists; for example:

    - Open activities

    - Activity history

    - Approval history

    - Contact roles

    - Partners

- The notes and attachments' related list is not fully supported.

- Uploading files is not supported.

It is clear to see from the previous list of limitations that there are a few considerations that need to be made. Your governance team should help the project team explore the use cases to make sure that the limitations are acceptable and do not detract from the original intent of the application itself. In the main, most of the limitations mentioned are acceptable. If you have a completely mobile workforce that only has access to a mobile device, then further consideration may be required. For many use cases, however, the Salesforce mobile app is a good compromise between accessing data and updating records when on the move versus using a laptop.

Mobile Security

As shown in Figure 9-3, mobile security is the next area of focus for your governance team.

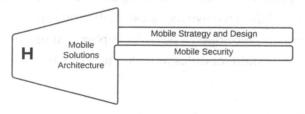

Figure 9-3. *Phase H: mobile solutions architecture - mobile security*

Govern how the project has secured the mobile application and its data, including offline data encryption

There are a few techniques to use for securing the Salesforce mobile app and the data it uses. These techniques are as follows:

- Control the access to and security of the mobile application using

  - profiles;

  - permission sets;

  - passcodes; and/or

  - login IP ranges.

- Control what the user can do once inside the mobile application using configuration, as follows:

  - FORCE_EMAIL_CLIENT_TO

  - DISABLE_ACTIVITY_TIMELINE (iOS)

  - SHOW_OPEN_IN

  - SHOW_PRINT (iOS)

  - ENABLE_SHARE

  - DISABLE_EXTERNAL_PASTE

Your governance team will need to review the features that are allowable for your users so as to assess the potential security implications. For example, allowing a user to cut the data held in a Salesforce record and paste it into an external application may be unacceptable to your company. Any changes to the mobile application configuration will not take immediate effect on a mobile device. The application must be either exited (force quit) or the user must log into a new session. This can be forced by revoking all access to the mobile application, then re-enabling access. This in effect will force every user to reauthenticate and then receive the latest configuration.

If your project team has developed a bespoke application using the Salesforce mobile SDK, there are two main modules provided by the SDK, as follows:

- SmartStore is an offline storage solution that saves encrypted Salesforce data to the mobile device.

- MobileSync provides a mechanism for synchronizing Salesforce records with local records stored in SmartStore. This module effectively takes care of retrieving and upserting data.

- Key-value stores are an alternative solution to SmartStore, designed for simpler storage requirements.

SmartStore is a useful solution to storing the data your mobile application may need for offline use. It is also tied into Salesforce authentication. If this is revoked, the storage is removed along with the secure data. However, SmartStore provides a Global SmartStore that is not tied to a user's authentication. Your governance team will be looking to the project team to provide a view of what data is being stored locally on the mobile device and in what configuration. Data stored in a Global SmartStore will require your project team to explicitly remove it.

Method

This is the formal method for Phase H of the Salesforce Platform Governance Method. The objectives of Phase H are to ensure that your project has thoroughly considered the implications of accessing Salesforce platform data from a mobile device using a mobile app.

Your project's mobile app can be developed in a few ways, depending on businesses requirements. As you are effectively opening up your Salesforce platform to a different set of users, it is imperative that security and data visibility are considered. Additionally, due to potential offline requirements, your project team may be looking to store data on a mobile device for offline access. Your governance team is looking to be assured that any lost devices do not pose a security issue for you company. Given that, the areas that will be assessed during this phase are as follows:

- Mobile Strategy and Design

- Mobile Security

Approach

This phase requires that your project team supplies a few artifacts for the governance team to review. Your governance team will be looking to approve your project's solution as quickly as possible, without necessarily knowing all the details of the mobile app being developed.

With this in mind, governing the mobile app will take the approach of an initial review, where your project team presents the overall mobile app development approach, such as whether it is a native, hybrid, or HTML app, and outlines the basic business requirements.

With that review over, your project team could then dive into the details of the business requirements and talk in more depth about their approach to authentication, data visibility, and offline data storage and security. Your project team should look to include these requirements in a sharing matrix, as discussed in Phase I.

Inputs

For the governance process to be a success, the project team must have a few artifacts available to the governance team for review. Suggested artifacts for the governance team to review for Phase H of the Salesforce Platform Governance Method are as follows:

- Project sharing requirements

- Project completed Salesforce external user sharing resource matrix

- Project sharing requirement options

- Mobile app development approach

- Offline data requirements and storage

- User authentication solution

Steps

The steps to govern your project's mobile app will help the project team deliver a quality solution that your business can be confident meets your security requirements and has considered the secure storage of offline data.

Your project will develop a mobile application that is supportable in the long term by selecting the appropriate technology in which to develop the mobile application.

Mobile Strategy and Design

1. Govern the mobile solution for use of the appropriate mobile platform: HTML5, native (iOS / Android), hybrid solutions, or Salesforce mobile app

2. Govern the authentication / authorization (including SSO), offline storage, and sync requirements

3. Govern the use of Salesforce mobile app declarative design

Mobile Security

1. Govern how the project has secured the mobile application and its data, including offline data encryption

Outputs

Once all the steps have been assessed, the outputs to Phase H are as follows:

- Not Applicable – This phase in the Salesforce Platform Governance Method is not applicable to the project.

- Remediate – The governance team requests that the project team remediates its design to accommodate the issues raised during the governance review.

- Pass – The governance team has found no issues or concerns with the project's proposal and therefore the project has passed this governance phase.

- Review – The governance team has found the inputs cannot be objectively measured and therefore a subjective view has been made, which will lead to a discussion with the project team to reach consensus. Although undesirable, this could be a consequence of unclear standards/policies.

Scenario

For our scenario we are going to focus on one of the steps from the Mobile Strategy and Design section of the Mobile Solution Architecture Phase H method. This step is:

- Govern the mobile solution for use of the appropriate mobile platform: HTML5, native (iOS / Android), hybrid solutions, or Salesforce mobile app

Back at Bright Sound Guitars, Hanna Snyder, the project architect, has brought a proposal to the governance team for her project's mobile application. The business has decided to provide its sales team with a mobile app so they can be more efficient when on the road selling.

Hanna presents the basic principle of what she wants her project to deliver. Hanna talks the governance team through her mobile solution architecture. She's looking to develop a native application that will be downloadable from the Apple App Store and the Google Play Store. She wants to target both iOS and Android mobile devices.

Her strategy is to have two teams develop native applications, one focused on using Apple's Swift development system, while the other uses Google's Android Studio development system. Each team will be fed the same requirements, and basically will try to follow the same "look and feel," as Hanna puts it.

Hanna talks through the basic functionality that she expects the mobile application to provide the team of users. These are sales people, and they will need access to their opportunities, accounts, and contacts while on the road.

Hanna introduces Ranveer Shah to talk through at a high level how they expect to achieve this.

Ranveer mentions that they will use offline storage to store the data relevant to the user that has authenticated with the mobile application, which will provide the data that is most important to that user—mainly the account, contact, and any opportunities. Ranveer will integrate with the Salesforce platform through the Salesforce mobile SDK.

Having listened to Hanna and Ranveer, the governance team questions why the need for a native application. Hanna was not aware that there was an alternative approach, and asks for more details. The governance team mentions that the functionality that Hanna has described as the requirements could be achieved using the Salesforce mobile app. This app would more than likely over deliver on the functionality that Hanna is looking to deliver. Additionally, no development teams would be required, and the project could deploy the mobile application almost overnight, compared to the lengthy process of developing a native application and then the relevant app-store processes to publish the application for the sales team to download.

Hanna thanks the governance team and takes back their comments to the business to discuss further.

Summary

There are a few options to consider when looking to deliver a mobile app solution that integrates with the Salesforce platform. One of the key principles is to clearly understand your business' requirements, and then select the appropriate solution that delivers just that. This is an area that can also evolve. Your project may find using the Salesforce mobile app a perfect solution in the short term, with a view to move to a more complex solution over time.

Phase H tackles the governance of your mobile solution architecture, focusing on the possible options to build and execute data sharing, visibility, and security that are required for a mobile solution.

During this phase you have highlighted to your project team the areas of concern and provided feedback as to what needs to be done to bring the mobile solution architecture within an acceptable level to pass governance.

CHAPTER 10

Development Lifecycle & Deployment: Phase I

This phase of the Salesforce Platform Governance Method focuses on the development lifecycle and deployment of your project's application and/or configuration.

Overview

The Salesforce platform differs from other SaaS solutions because it provides the means to perform development and testing outside your production environment. Most other SaaS solutions assume you do all your configuration within your production or live environment.

The Salesforce platform provides a "route to live" capability because it offers far more flexibility in terms of configuration than most other Software as a Service (SaaS) solutions on the market. The Salesforce platform is known as a customer relationship management (CRM) platform, but in reality it is more akin to a Platform as a Service (PaaS) solution, as you can develop applications either declaratively or programmatically and deploy them to the Salesforce platform, applications that in theory could have little to do with customers.

With this level of flexibility, Salesforce needed to deliver a robust set of tools and capabilities that allowed their customers to create on the platform without breaking things for their end users.

If your company is mature in its use of the Salesforce platform, it is likely that you already have in place the rigor needed to make changes and deploy those changes with little to no disruption to your end users. This phase of the Salesforce Platform Governance Method focuses on governing your development lifecycle so that

© Lee Harding and Lee Bayliss 2022
L. Harding and L. Bayliss, *Salesforce Platform Governance Method*,
https://doi.org/10.1007/978-1-4842-7404-0_10

multiple projects can co-exist and successfully deploy while working to some degree independently. As always, this phase is broken down into sub-phases to simplify the governance process and focus, as shown in Figure 10-1.

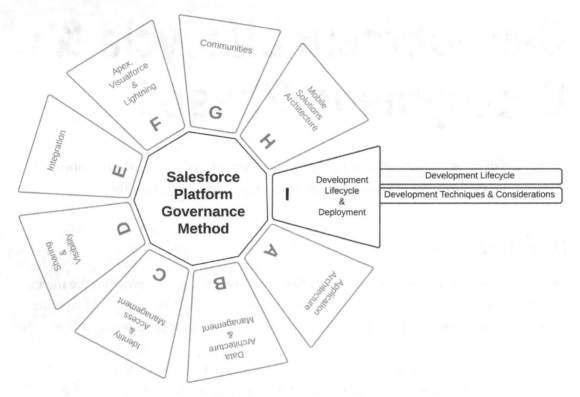

Figure 10-1. *The Salesforce Platform Governance Method: Phase I*

As with previous phases, let us start by defining what we mean by development lifecycle and deployment so that we are clear about what we are governing. The Salesforce platform does not really differ from any other software development processes, so for the context of the Salesforce Platform Governance Method, we will use the Gartner definition for software development:

> *"Project management, specifications, design, programming, testing, installation and training associated with a specific application development project of any size."*

> —Gartner[1]

---

[1] https://www.gartner.com/en/information-technology/glossary/software-development

We will also use the Gartner definition for deployment to complete the definition of what this phase is focused on:

"Deployment services support the implementation and rollout of new applications or infrastructure. Activities may include hardware or software procurement, configuration, tuning, staging, installation and interoperability testing."

—Gartner[2]

Regardless of the size of your company and scale of your development activities, your project should be looking to formalize your development lifecycle. For smaller companies, you may decide to keep things "light" and implement just enough process and formality to be confident that you can deploy something to your end users that is stable and meets their requirements. For the larger implementations, you may have dedicated teams that own their own processes and tooling to facilitate the development lifecycle.

The main areas of focus as suggested by the Gartner definitions are the following:

- Solution requirements. It is good practice to document the basic requirements of what it is your business wants your project to construct. This helps drive focus into your activities and allows everyone to measure the success of the project, in that you have delivered against all of the requirements that have been documented.

- Solution design. At some point you will require your developers or other technical staff to decide how best to deliver the solution requirements, what Salesforce features will be involved, and how you will go about meeting the requirements.

- Solution development. Once your project team has decided how they are going to go about delivering the requirements, your development resources can commence with the work to build. This is usually an iterative processes, working through the requirements, using the design until the work is done.

---

[2] https://www.gartner.com/en/information-technology/glossary/deployment

- Solution testing. Once all the construction has been completed, you will need resources to test what has been built by your development teams against the requirements that have been documented. Any features that do not meet the requirements are returned to development for further work.

- Solution deployment. Once all the testing has completed and everything has been deemed as meeting the requirements and basically works, your project team will want to deploy those changes so that your end users can utilize the new features you have delivered.

- Solution training. It may be that your end users require training on the new features that have been developed.

Of course, this is a very simplified view of what really happens during the development of an application or customization on the Salesforce platform, but it provides the foundation of what your governance team is interested in assuring. Your project will no doubt have some level of project management across off of these areas, providing the "when" things will be done.

Your governance team will not be involved in the actual delivery of the areas previously mentioned, but will be looking to confirm that the project team has introduced enough rigor into the development lifecycle to be confident that what is deployed as a result of that work will not bring the entire Salesforce implementation to a standstill. However, if your company is running a number of projects your governance team may need to expand to provide a platform team capability.

The platform team is a small team that is the custodian of the Salesforce platform and assures that all projects adhere to the standards, and that their resulting Salesforce platform changes all work together in harmony with other projects and pre-existing configuration. In smaller organizations, it may be possible that your project team can also take on this role.

Tip   The platform team is a key part of any Salesforce platform implementation. It is this team that protects existing projects running within the Salesforce platform when new projects come along. It is unusual for a project to take on the work of checking that other projects' work is unaffected by their changes, especially when modifying enterprise objects.

Development Lifecycle

As shown in Figure 10-2, development lifecycle is the first sub-phase for your governance team to focus on.

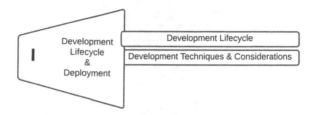

Figure 10-2. *Phase I: development lifecycle & deployment - development lifecycle*

Govern the development and release of applications on the Salesforce platform

All development work, whether declarative or non-declarative, will take a specific route to your production Salesforce platform. This will involve a few stages to ensure quality is met and standards are adhered to. The route to production effectively forms a significant part of your governance process and if done correctly can aid your governance processes to become more efficient and easier to execute.

Fundamental to the route to production are the environments in which the various quality assurance tasks will be undertaken, and governance will play a major role in determining how far along the route a project can go. The basic route to production could look as shown in Figure 10-3.

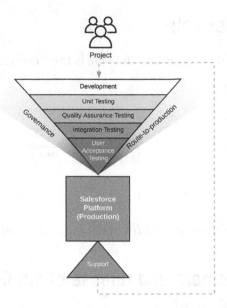

Figure 10-3. *Route to the Salesforce production org*

The route to production introduces a number of environments that will help your project team move its application closer to the production Salesforce platform. These environments, as an example, are shown in Table 10-1.

Table 10-1. *Development Environments*

Environment	Description
Development	An environment in which development, either declarative or non-declarative, takes place. A development environment can be personal to a developer or used by a team and is dependent on specific project requirements.
Unit Testing	An environment in which testing occurs on specific developed units. A unit testing environment can be personal to a developer or used by a team and is dependent on specific project requirements.
Quality Assurance	An environment in which project/product quality assurance testing is undertaken. This environment can be used to system test, or perform early integration-type testing, where components developed by multiple developers can come together.

(continued)

Table 10-1. (*continued*)

Environment	Description
Integration	An environment in which all components internal or external to a project/product come together to make sure everything functions as expected. Within this environment multiple projects may come together to prove that they can co-exist without any conflicts or issues.
User Acceptance Testing	An environment in which all components are brought together prior to release into the live environment. The user acceptance testing environment is used to test the deployment of components, projects, and products. This environment is the final point at which issues can be captured and rectified and requires all stakeholders to approve.
Support	An environment in which troubleshooting takes place. Issues in the live environment are not always easy to remedy in situ; therefore, the support environment provides the ideal place for debugging and other support activities. The support environment will be accessed by multiple teams depending on the nature of the problems being investigated.

Your company may have other environments, but those suggested provide a good starting position for the context of our governance phase. The Salesforce platform supports a number of environment types (known as sandboxes). Each sandbox provides a specific capability (and potentially additional costs to your company) and therefore is suitable for specific environment purposes, as shown in Figure 10-4.

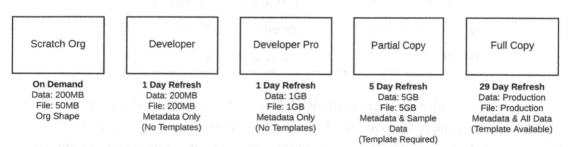

Figure 10-4. *Salesforce sandbox types*

As well as the standard sandboxes, Salesforce introduced the concept of scratch orgs a few years ago. These could be considered lightweight sandboxes that are created and destroyed as and when they are needed, making them perfect for development. Your project should be aware of the limits around scratch org creation, which is controlled by your Salesforce platform edition, as shown in Table 10-2.

Table 10-2. *Scratch Org Limits*

Edition	Active Scratch Orgs	Daily Scratch Orgs
Developer Edition or Trial	3	6
Enterprise Edition	40	80
Unlimited Edition	100	200
Performance Edition	100	200

Given the preceding description for each sandbox type, Table 10-3 shows what could be the appropriate sandbox foreach environment.

Table 10-3. *Environment Sandbox Types*

Environment	Sandbox Type
Development	Developer / Scratch Org
Unit Testing	Developer / Developer Pro
Quality Assurance	Developer Pro / Partial Copy
Integration	Developer Pro / Partial Copy
User Acceptance Testing	Partial Copy / Full Copy
Support	Partial Copy / Full Copy

In only the simplest implementations of the Salesforce platform does the responsibility for the route to production reside with only one team, usually the project team. Therefore, it is a requirement that, given the environments just detailed, responsibility resides with a different team. Core to this requirement is the platform team. The platform team is a central team that owns the governance process and manages the environments that are "closest" to your production Salesforce platform, as shown in Figure 10-5.

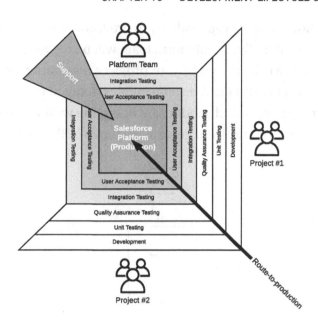

Figure 10-5. *Environment responsibilities*

As illustrated, the platform team controls four environments, while the other environments remain in the control of the projects or teams that are producing components and applications that are targeted for the production environment, the production environment being any Salesforce instance used to support the business (there could be more than one).

The environment responsibilities are shown in Table 10-4.

Table 10-4. *Environment Responsibilities*

Environment	Responsibility
Development	Project Team
Unit Testing	Project Team
Quality Assurance	Project Team
Integration	Platform Team
User Acceptance Testing	Platform Team
Support	Platform Team

It will be the platform team's responsibility to provision the environments for use by your project teams. Additionally, the platform team will be responsible for the refresh of all environments, which will be driven by your project's requirements.

Given the environments and team responsibilities detailed here, the situation where multiple teams, projects, and vendors are operating within one single Salesforce instance becomes easier to control and govern, as shown in Figure 10-6.

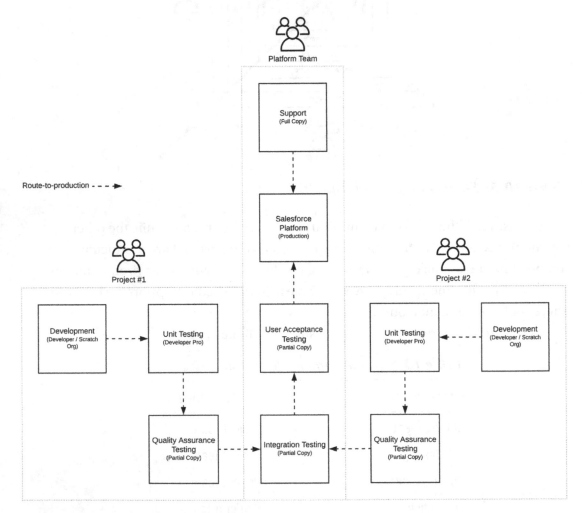

Figure 10-6. *Multiple project teams*

With multiple project teams working in parallel, the route to production converges at the integration testing environment, which is controlled by the platform team, and it is here that the platform team takes control of the movement of projects into the Salesforce platform's production environment. It is likely that the project owners will be involved in this process because they will need to "approve" that their application or configuration is functioning correctly within each environment, something that the platform team may not be able to determine without a standardized way of testing each project automatically.

To facilitate the governance process and to simplify the implementation of governance as much as possible, the tooling and processes to move application components through all of the environments will be critical. The standard approach for implementing this is to use a continuous integration and continuous deployment (CI/CD) pipeline. There are many views on what a CI/CD pipeline should look like, and your company may already have one in place, but for the purposes of this governance phase, let us define a conceptual pipeline as shown in Figure 10-7.

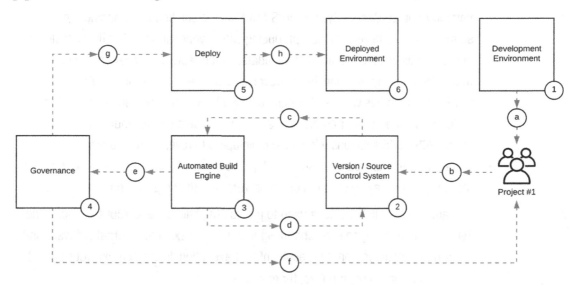

Figure 10-7. *Conceptual continuous integration and continuous deployment solution*

The conceptual CI/CD pipeline has a number of building blocks denoted by the numbers within the circle, and these building blocks are connected together as denoted by the letters in circles to form the pipeline. Let us take a look at the main components, as detailed in Table 10-5.

Table 10-5. *Conceptual CI/CD Pipeline Components*

Component	Description
1	The development environment is basically the sandbox or scratch org that your project's developer will use daily. Depending on how you want to configure your projects, you may have one sandbox per development, or one sandbox per team of developers. This will very much be driven by the development required and the way your project team wants to work. If you have multiple developers using a single sandbox, it is good practice to have one of those developers be responsible for understanding that code base (i.e., what is it that will be pushed to other environments?).
2	Version / Source Control System (VCS / SCS) is the solution to managing the source that your developers are producing within your sandbox. For the Salesforce platform, this will be significantly metadata, which represents changes you have made declaratively. Additionally, however, if your project is developing Apex classes or triggers, then this will also be included. Your VCS / SCS solution will provide a historical view of all your changes based on the code commits your developers make. VCS / SCS solutions allow your developers to revert to previous versions of metadata with ease, but also store multiple releases of your Salesforce platform so that they can always revert to a previous version if things go wrong.
3	The automated build engine is used to provide the backbone to your CI/CD pipeline. Typically, a build engine is a scheduling tool that can execute external software and determine outcomes from the results of that execution. In our context, your project can use this for a few purposes; for example: • Automatically attempt to deploy any code committed to the VCS / SCS into a downstream sandbox • Automatically execute test scripts written in a testing tool • Automatically perform Apex code quality analysis using a code analysis tool • Automatically perform quality checks on declarative metadata, such as checking that all fields have a description and help text

(continued)

Table 10-5. (*continued*)

Component	Description
4	The governance process becomes simpler with the CI/CD pipeline in place because your governance team is looking at the outputs of your automated build engine. Your platform team could automate this also by providing a pass/fail, for example on code quality analysis, which could automatically be fed back to the project team's developers. However, it is likely that some manual review will be required to focus on reuse and the use of enterprise objects.
5	Once the build and governance have completed, you are left with effectively something that is good to be deployed. Your deployment process will take your project's application or configuration and deploy it into the next logical environment in the pipeline. Failure of the deployment is reported back to the relevant team, which will largely depend on what environment was next in the pipeline.
6	Your environment will now be built, either a project environment or a platform team environment, depending on where you are in your release cycle within your pipeline. This environment can now be used to engage the business for verification that the project team has built what was asked of them.

The conceptual CI/CD pipeline components just described are flattened for simplicity, but you can imagine this pipeline would be operating across all of the environments discussed in Table 10-1, development environments and multiple projects and multiple features that are being developed.

Each of the components in our conceptual CI/CD pipeline Each is interconnected to demonstrate a flow of an artifact. A component basically acts upon something it is given, and these flows are described in Table 10-6.

Table 10-6. *Conceptual CI/CD Pipeline Component Interconnections*

Component	Description
a	Your project developers will be making changes within their development sandboxes, either declaratively using the Salesforce platform's admin (Setup) tools or using an integrated development environment (IDE), in the case of developing Apex code. An IDE is not a requirement as the developer console is still available within the Salesforce platform; however, an IDE is recommended. Your project developers will more than likely being working on a specific feature, and once they are happy with their work they will want to use the VCS / SCS system to store those changes.
b	Once your project's developers have completed their feature development, they will push their metadata and Apex code to the VCS / SCS solution. Typically they will working in a feature branch and will commit their code to this branch and push that branch to your remote VCS / SCS repository. It is that commit and push that could trigger the automated build engine.
c	The automated build engine is responsible for performing the tasks required to essentially deliver the needs of the project while also delivering against your governance requirements. The build engine will trigger the governance processes, which could also include automated testing, but fundamentally will extract what is required to the downstream processes from the VCS / SCS solution.
d	A feedback loop that highlights any issues with the downstream processes that the automated build process is controlling, such as governance and deployment. This effectively supports the need to do something about errors and issues that may arise; for example, conflicts in metadata.

(*continued*)

Table 10-6. (*continued*)

Component	Description
e	The automated build process will trigger your automated governance processes, or perhaps wait for a manual governance check, depending on the maturity of your CI/CD pipeline. Automated checks could be static code analysis for quality or using XPath rules on your metadata to determine whether your developers have given every custom object and field a description. You could also automatically produce documentation about the release from this information if desired to effectively provide a release note. Additionally, if you are managing an object library that captures the custom objects and fields within your Salesforce platform to determine which project owns which configuration, this could also be updated automatically. Governance could also perform automated testing so that your platform team (if the release is targeted for the integration testing environment) can ensure that the project's release co-exists with the existing Salesforce platform configuration.
f	Another feedback loop that provides your projects' development teams with any issues around the governance processes; for example, a list of custom fields that have no description provided.
g	Once governance has been completed and everything has passed, or acceptable warning have been provided, your automated build engine will attempt a deploy. The deploy component is responsible for performing all the tasks required to deploy the metadata into a Salesforce sandbox or even the production org.
h	Finally, you should be left with a sandbox or production org that reflects the development lifecycle stage your CI/CD pipeline was delivering. This could be the user acceptance testing environment, for example, and your automated build engine could inform your testing team that their environment has been successfully built and is ready for them to commence testing (automated or otherwise).

The conceptual CI/CD pipelines touch on the basic principles of a CI/CD pipeline. It is more than likely that your pipeline will have more or less functionality depending on your requirements and levels of automation you wish to achieve within your company. Typically, automating a CI/CD pipeline is a large up front investment for your company, but can make massive difference a few years in the future when you are releasing changes to your business in days rather than months.

Of course, there are a number of tools available to automate the majority of the processes just outlined; the resource base section of this book will highlight those most commonly used.

During the CI/CD discussion, branches were mentioned within the VCS/SCS solution. Branches are independent lines of work that stem from a single central code base. Depending on the VCS/SCS, the main branch may be referred to as the `main`, `master`, `default`, `mainline`, or `trunk`. Developers can create their own branches from the main code line and work independently along with it.

Branching enables teams of developers to easily connect with one another inside a single central code base. When a developer creates a branch, the VCS/SCS creates a copy of the code base at that point in time.

Developers can easily integrate changes from other developers to sync up with new features and ensure their private branch does not stray too far from the `main` branch. Any changes a developer makes to their branch will not have an impact on the work of other developers on the team who are working in other branches. This is an advantage because the features under development can create volatility, which can impact all the work if it happens on the `main` code line. To enable the CI/CD pipeline, we need to have a branching strategy. For the purposes of demonstrating this in the context of this phase of the Salesforce Platform Governance Process, let us consider Table 10-7 as a baseline.

Table 10-7. *Branching Strategy*

Branch	Description
Hot Fix	The breakdown of hot fixes or issues should be controlled within an issue tracker. Issues then become the project team's central point of contact for that piece of work. Issue branching directly connects those issues with the source code. Each issue is implemented on its own branch, with the name of the issue key included in the branch name. This way it will be easy to identify a particular issue the code implements. With this level of transparency, it is easier to apply focused changes to the `main` or any longer lasting release branches.
	Since agile pivots around user stories, task branches sync up well with agile development. Each user story (bug fix) lives within its own branch, making it easy to view the issues in progress and those that are ready for release.
Develop	The develop branch is used as an area in which your project's feature branches come together. You may have several development teams working on numerous features that must all ultimately come together into a release. The `develop` branch provides a convenient place for testing the integration of changes at the project level.
Feature	The feature branch keeps all the changes for a particular feature intact inside the branch. After the automated or manual tests fully test and validate the feature, the branch is then merged into the main or developer main branch (to support release branching).
Release	A release is contained entirely within a branch. This means that later in the development cycle, the release manager will create a branch from the main (for instance, a 1.1 development branch). All changes for the 1.1 release must be applied twice: first to the 1.1 developer branch and later to the main code line.
	Release branching is an important part of supporting versioned releases. A single product may have multiple release branches (e.g., 1.1, 1.5, 2.0) to support sustained development. Changes in previous versions (i.e., 1.1) may have to be merged with later release branches (i.e., 1.5, 2.0); for example, if a bug is found in production that must be fixed immediately.

Your governance team may have a branching strategy already in place, and the Salesforce platform should be able to use whichever branching strategy you are familiar with. Figure 10-8 shows a visual representation of the branches mentioned and how the Salesforce metadata flows between them.

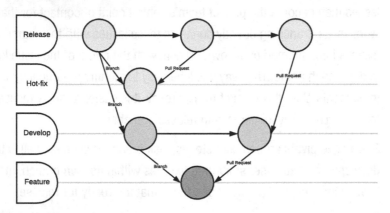

Figure 10-8. *Example branching strategy*

The figure demonstrates the multiple branches working together. Your branching strategy might be more complicated and will certainly contain more releases and features than this simplified example.

Your governance team is looking to ensure that your project has this in place and is using it. If a pre-existing solution is already in place, this will make life much easier for your project team. If this is not already in place, it is well worth the investment of creating it if you intend to develop more than one project on the Salesforce platform.

Tip   Your governance team may have to evangelize an existing CI/CD pipeline to new teams, especially if those teams are made up of Salesforce developers who have not yet embraced a source-driven approach to the Salesforce platform.

Govern the testing strategies and test plan

Your governance team, now identified as needing to manage the Salesforce platform centrally for situations where multiple projects are delivering into the platform, will need to engage the project teams regarding their testing strategies and plan.

In the simplest of implementations, testing is normally carried out by one or two people as they "poke around" in a sandbox into which a developer or app builder has built some changes. This may work perfectly well for very small projects and limited changes targeted for your Salesforce platform. However, in the main you will be looking to have some sort of test strategy in place so that your governance team and by extension your platform team can be confident that every new release of changes to the Salesforce platform will not break the previous release of changes.

With this is mind, your company has two options with regard to a testing strategy. You have the environments defined previously, and your project teams could be engaged to manually test their configuration in every environment before deployment to production is possible. There is an issue with this, however: who will test the pre-existing projects that are already live? Can you ask every project that is already live to come back and retest their application because someone else wants to deploy? This could be a difficult situation to manage. The other approach would be to ask each project team to provide automated test scripts that validate that their project is still fully operational. This would allow regression testing to commence without their involvement. If a failure occurs on a project that has already gone live during a subsequent test trigger by a different project, that project is responsible for solving the issue.

Your governance team will look for assurance that your projects have provided enough validation testing to perform a successful regression testing process for every release into the Salesforce platform.

Your project teams' tests scripts should be managed just like any other source, using the VCS/SCS solution. Mature organizations can use these test scripts as part of their CI/CD pipeline to perform automated testing as part of the build engine's responsibility, again aiding the automation of your governance processes.

Caution   You will no doubt hit massive resistance to developing automated test scripts if this is not part of your company's development culture. Mostly, project teams see this as additional work that provides no business benefit. Your governance team might have to help the business understand the benefits, which will probably be easy after the first time their project stops working in production due to a new configuration's being deployed.

Deployment Techniques and Considerations

As shown in Figure 10-9, deployment techniques and considerations is the next sub-phase on which your governance team should focus.

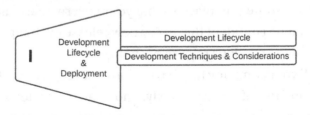

Figure 10-9. *Phase I: development lifecycle & deployment - deployment techniques and considerations*

Govern the deployment strategy and the platform tools, use cases, limitations, and best practices for environment management and data migration strategy

Your governance team will be looking to the project team to understand how it intends to deploy its application, and what (if any) business impact this will have. In some cases, a significant amount of business change happens alongside a Salesforce implementation, and as such your governance team will want to know that this is well under way to coincide with the deployment of your project team's application. The last thing anyone wants is a disgruntled business because they have had their legacy systems' access removed in favor of using the Salesforce platform, which they know little about.

In the previous section, the CI/CD pipeline was discussed; this is a major benefit when it comes to deploying your Salesforce application into the production org. However, not everything is deployable via metadata. Salesforce has a few areas that are still not exported as part of the metadata your project teams have created. However, with every release Salesforce is closing the gap on what is left that requires manual configuration directly within the product org.

Your governance team will be looking to understand if the project is affected by this manual configuration requirement, which Salesforce maintains as its metadata coverage.

Tip   Check the Salesforce webpage `https://developer.salesforce.com/docs/metadata-coverage/52` for details on what exactly is covered by the metadata API.

Salesforce provides a few tools for deploying metadata into a sandbox or production instance. For the CI/CD pipeline discussed earlier, the assumption would be to use Salesforce DX.

Salesforce DX (SFDX) is a Salesforce product that allows users to develop and manage Salesforce apps throughout the entire platform in a more direct and efficient way. SFDX, used primarily by developers, allows users to have true version control over their metadata. SFDX is a command-line tool that is integrated into IDEs such as Microsoft's Visual Studio Code.

Alternatively, if your company has not embarked on moving to SFDX, you may be looking to continue to use the ANT migration tool. Or maybe you are still working with change sets through the admin console.

Your governance team will want to standardize the use of a particular set of tools rather than have every project pick its own. Of course, the Salesforce-provided tools generally have no cost as they are part of the platform. However, there are a number of third-party tools that provide the complete CI/CD pipeline tailored specifically for the Salesforce platform.

Where a platform team has been implemented, it will be their role to define the toolset and instructions for use. Additionally, sandboxes must reflect the current state of the Salesforce platform in production. Your project teams will not want to develop against a configuration that is several months out of date. Having a source-driven development methodology puts less reliance on sandbox refresh strategies because a sandbox can be built from the VCS/SCS, which is one of the most powerful aspects of using this approach. However, your governance team will want to validate that your project team has been developing against the latest metadata before the platform team is handed the package for ongoing deployment to the shared environments.

If your project is re-engineering an existing application onto the Salesforce platform, it is likely that there will be a data migration requirement. Data held in the legacy system that is being re-engineered will need to be migrated. This typically takes the form of an extract, transform, and load (ETL) process. Your governance team will be looking to understand how the project has tackled the ETL and what testing has taken place.

The project team will need to be ready to discuss the "T" part of their ETL process, because it is the translation of data from your legacy application to the re-engineered application that will be important.

Govern the tools (source control and continuous integration for release management)

Your governance team will be looking to assure the tooling that is being used, especially if this is something that has not been done before. It would not be efficient for every project team to implement its own tooling independent of every other project. Not only would the costs be a lot higher, but your resources would also lose a level of mobility between projects. Additionally, supporting these tools is typically a full-time job for someone, so the more tools you have, the more resources you will need to support them.

Today, there is a lot written about the optimum tooling for the Salesforce platform, but fundamentally your governance team will be looking to see the following basics are in place:

- A version/source control system (VCS/SCS) to manage project repositories, branching, and source control

- A deployment system to manage extracting source from the VCS/SCS and deploying it into a sandbox or production org

- A development environment in which Salesforce developers can create the applications your business desires.

Your company can find a solution to all of these with little or no costs. Some will require degrees of manual intervention, while investing more and buying dedicated tools may remove manual intervention and optimize your route to production.

Lastly, your governance team will want to understand the release cadence that is in place. It is not desirable to have multiple projects trying to all go live on the same day. Your governance team will be looking to understand this so that everyone is aware of a release schedule.

Method

Governing the development lifecycle and deployment of applications on the Salesforce platform has two aspects. The first is making sure that a sufficient solution is in place to industrialize the process or release to the production org. In that solution, governance can be implemented that reduces the governance burden in the longer term. The second is the on-going governance required to make sure things are maintained and changes, whether to a project's application or to the release process, are thought through and sensible.

This phase of the Salesforce Platform Governance Method is probably one of the most complex to implement because it relies upon a desire to create a centralized model for managing environments and the CI/CD pipeline outside of a project. Of course if your business is expecting to have just the one project for the foreseeable future, then this responsibility will lie within that project.

Given that, the areas that will be assessed during this phase are as follows:

- Development Lifecycle
- Deployment Techniques and Considerations

Approach

The development lifecycle should be well defined in terms of the environments and tooling and the "route to production" that an application will take before a project starts developing. The purpose of this phase is to have a means of governing the route to production. In the main, this should not change regularly, but it is not unimaginable that additional Salesforce instances may arise within the enterprise, or that external parties are engaged. In these scenarios, the organization will want to determine whether these situations are adhering to the standards.

Additionally, over time, tooling and testing strategies may change, especially as an organization matures in its usage of the Salesforce platform. Therefore, this phase is also used to manage the evolution of the development lifecycle, as well as the tooling and techniques used.

The phase could employ programmatic solutions to governance to implement automated governance, such as code quality, or remain purely as a subjective review. However, there should be standards regarding product selection, such as a development tool change or the use of a configuration management tool, so that a fair and unbiased view can be drawn to determine suitability.

Inputs

For the governance process to be a success, the project must have a few artifacts available to the governance team for review. Suggested artifacts for Phase I of the Salesforce Platform Governance Method are as follows:

- Environment strategy

- Continuous integration and continuous deployment

- Development tooling

- Test strategy and test plan

Steps

The steps to govern your development lifecycle and deployment will help the project team deliver to the business consistently. No one likes a failed deployment, especially when the business is all set to receive a new application or a major update to their existing application. This phase is focused on avoiding deployment failures or destabilizing the existing applications already in use.

Ultimately, the goal is for your project teams to consistently deliver their configuration and code into the production Salesforce platform correctly the first time, but also at speed. The ability to rapidly deploy changes to your production Salesforce platform will reduce the scale of the change as smaller changes can be deployed regularly.

Development Lifecycle

1. Govern the development and release of applications on the Salesforce platform.

2. Govern the testing strategies and test plan.

Deployment Techniques and Considerations

1. Govern the deployment strategy and the platform tools, use cases, limitations, and best practices for environment management and data migration strategy.

Outputs

Once all the steps have been assessed, the outputs to Phase I are as follows:

- Not Applicable – This phase in the Salesforce Platform Governance Method is not applicable to the project.

- Remediate – The governance team requests that the project team remediate its design to accommodate the issues raised during the governance review.

- Pass – The governance team has found no issues or concerns with the project team's proposal and therefore the project has passed this governance phase.

- Review – The governance team has found the inputs cannot be objectively measured and therefore a subjective view has been made, which will lead to a discussion with the project team to reach consensus. Although undesirable, this could be a consequence of unclear standards/policies.

Scenario

For our scenario we are going to focus on one of the steps from the Deployment Techniques and Considerations section of the Development Lifecycle and Deployment Phase I method. This step is as follows:

- Govern the deployment strategy and the platform tools, use cases, limitations, and best practices for environment management and data migration strategy

Hanna Snyder, the project architect from our company Bright Sound Guitars, is now at the point where she needs to think about deployment of her application. She has her requirements and the business funding to develop her application, and she's ready to start her development work, having gotten through a number of the governance phases. Hanna presents to the governance team her ideas around deployment. As Bright Sound Guitars is a small company, it does not have a platform team as part of the governance team, so her project team will take care of things.

Hanna talks through her deployment strategy. She has spoken to her Salesforce administrator, Fenella Owen, about the best approach to deployment to the production Salesforce platform. Fenella has been in the Salesforce ecosystem for many years and has spent a significant portion of that time using the original Salesforce user interface, today referred to as Classic.

Fenella presents to the governance board that she is looking to have one sandbox that all the development takes place in. They have two developers at Bright Sound Guitars, Ranveer Shah and Caitlyn Horton, and they both have separate areas in which they are working so they should not conflict in one sandbox.

Fenella mentions that Ranveer has spoken about Salesforce DX a number of times, but she has not had the time to investigate this tool. Fenella feels that sticking to the traditional change sets will be good enough. Fenella therefore suggests that she will create a change set from the developer sandbox to the production Salesforce platform and deploy that way.

Once a deployment has taken place, she suggests refreshing the sandbox just to make sure it reflects the production Salesforce platform. However, she doubts that will be much of an issue as they are the only development team working on the platform as far as she knows.

The governance team thanks Fenella for her overview. The first point they make is that Bright Sound Guitars has another project that is just starting up, which will deliver a bespoke application for the manufacturing department. With that, the governance team mentions that Hanna's team will no longer be the only project team looking to deploy to the production Salesforce platform.

As part of the justification to build the new application, the governance team has secured the budget for tooling and resources to construct a CI/CD pipeline, which is going to be a minimum viable product approach, but it does mean that they would like Hanna's team and Fenella to review their tooling and deployment approach to work alongside the platform team's CI/CD pipeline implementation.

The governance team mentions that they will be creating a number of processes to automate some of the code checking governance that is part of Phase F of the Salesforce Platform Governance Method. They feel that there are some quick wins that can be implemented with very little effort, especially around code quality analysis, having just invested in the SonarQube product, which has an Apex extension available. Additionally, they will be implementing a number of XPath rules to check that the developers have completed descriptions against all custom fields and objects. Also, they want to implement name-spacing using a prefix on custom objects and fields. They feel this can be easily checked also.

The consequence of this is that the governance team would like Hanna to review her tooling to work toward implementing the standard toolset defined by the platform team, which will include source control.

Hanna is excited that Bright Sound Guitars is taking development on the Salesforce platform to a new level, and wants to return to her project to discuss how they can work with these new tools and the impact of doing so.

Summary

Building a route to production is an investment that is sometimes frowned upon. It does take time and is often seen as not really achieving very much for the business. However, the initial investment becomes very worthwhile once your project teams have made multiple deployments because of business requirement changes or new functionality.

As with any project, it is best to start out with a minimum viable product, tackling perhaps the "quick wins" that your governance team and project teams need.

Summary

CHAPTER 11

Resource Base Introduction

Welcome to the Salesforce Platform Governance Method (SPGM) resource base. This chapter signifies the start of the second half of this book. The first half was focused on all matters governance by architecture domain, as depicted in the SPGM cycle shown in Figure 11-1.

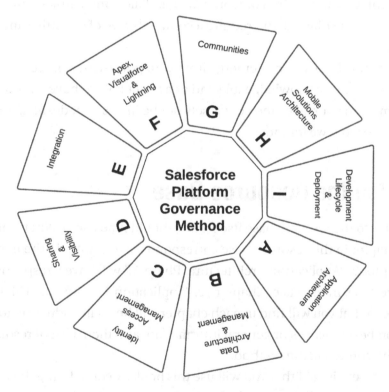

Figure 11-1. *Salesforce Platform Governance Method cycle*

L. Harding and L. Bayliss, *Salesforce Platform Governance Method*,
https://doi.org/10.1007/978-1-4842-7404-0_11

As you know by now, those guys down at Bright Sound Guitars have really been put through the mill by their governance team. As part of the governance process, they have had to consider an awful lot of detail, such as general architecture concerns, sharing best practices, data architecture, and worries about integration. Let's not even mention Apex and SOQL. The BSG team has really done a great job. And that's exactly what we would like for you as well. Success!

Success is a big deal in the Salesforce ecosystem, and we want all Salesforce implementations to be a hit. Whether your organization is a first-time Salesforce consumer or you have been a Salesforce customer for many years, the governance process for all your projects should be completed in a similar way. But to reinforce your ability to successfully govern your Salesforce implementation, you need to have a good understanding of the platform's capabilities at various levels. Therefore, the main objective of the resource base is to achieve exactly that: give you a leg up, provide you with a list of specifically chosen resources that will be informative and educational, and assist you in achieving the desired outcome for your Salesforce implementation. After all, these topics can be difficult and require a certain degree of expertise and a lot of consideration.

If by reading this book you can emerge from your governance process and Salesforce implementation far more knowledgeable and as a result able to have "tranquil dreams" with a huge smile on your face, and conversely not be in a "sea of despair," then I think we have achieved what we intended.

How to Use the Resource Base

Ok, so let's get into the resource base itself. How should it be used? What you will find is that each chapter in this resource base corresponds to a chapter in the method. For example, Chapter 2, "Application Architecture: Phase A," will have a respective chapter in the resource base. In this case, Chapter 12, "Application Architecture (Phase A) Resource Base." What you will find in each chapter will be an introduction to the topic, some words on best practices or general information, and then a list of resources that are pertinent to the content in the method.

Now, we have envisaged that you will use this book by considering the content by domain rather than by starting at the beginning and reading through to the end, although of course you are very welcome to do that if you so wish! However, if data architecture is your primary concern right now, then the corresponding data architecture resource base Chapter 13 should be read in unison so that while you are learning the method, you can also review the technical concepts as part of the same exercise. To this end, you may find some repetitive rhetoric as part of the introductory detail for each chapter in the resource base. That's by design based on how we expect this book to be used. Let's look at how the resource base chapters are structured.

The Resource Base Structure

Each chapter in the resource base is structured in the following way.

- Introduction – A few words on the topic in question

- Guidelines and Best Practices – Contextual information regarding the resources provided; here you will find the link to the GitHub repository where you will find all the markdown files that contain all the URLs to the resources we've added.

- Topic Introduction – This section will provide some explanatory notes on the topic and some important considerations for you to ponder. Remember, this book has not been written to provide you with an exhaustive description of every facet of the Salesforce platform.

- The Resource Base Table – This is where the good stuff is. Here you will find reference details for all the resources, including a synopsis for each resource. Some of the information you find in these tables may be enough to answer a question or lead your thinking to a more appropriate area for research. That's great and is also our intention. First, you will see the "Artifact." This is the actual name of the resource online. Next is the "GitHub Ref" text. This text will directly correspond to the text provided in the GitHub repo markdown files. Therefore, you should be able to find the information you are looking for without any frustrating searching for the detail you need. Finally, the "Description." This provides a short description of each resource that should be informative and help you to decide if this resource deserves further investigation, depending on the context of your interest. Table 11-1 is an example of the information that you will see.

Table 11-1. *Resource Table Example*

Artifact	GitHub Ref	Description
The official title for the resource **For example:** Integration Patterns and Practices	**The searchable reference in the GitHub repo for the URL resource** **For example:** Integrations Patterns	**The synopsis for the resource in context** **For example:** This Salesforce guide offers a detailed description of the patterns or strategies for many common integration scenarios. After reading this resource, you will be aware of approaches you could take using the pattern selection guide, and have a better understanding of the terms used that relate to integration.

- Standards – This section of the resource base provides you with information that we consider to be important as it will either assist you as you navigate through the governance process or is considered best practice; for example, naming conventions for fields, Apex classes, flows, etc.

- Checklist – Finally, as you review the method(s) you will see a logical breakup of the topic into succinct areas for the control and consideration of your governance process. To help you prepare and ensure that you are covering all bases, we have provided a checklist that can be used to ensure that you have considered all areas of the method.

Tip   You do not need to use this resource base as a strict method or process. The idea is that this will give you a good indication of what you should be taking into consideration. The expectation is that you will use this as a guide and then build upon it as you navigate the Salesforce ecosystem.

The GitHub Repository

As explained earlier, we have created a GitHub repository that includes any code snippets, example material, and of course the markdown files for each chapter that contain the resource links for you to get to the details.

The URL for the repo is as follows: `github.com/salesforceplatformgovernancemethod`

We recommend you bookmark this link as the content will be maintained going forward as we aim to keep the content relevant and aligned to new products and updates as released by Salesforce as part of their three yearly product releases.

A Final Word

Before you begin your perusal of the resource chapters, a final word on the content that you will find. While we have tried to be thorough and provide you with as many resources as possible pertinent to the topic at hand, there are bound to be other resources across the internet that may also give you what you are looking for. That's awesome and expected.

This book is not written to be a definitive technical guide for each platform configuration item across the entire spectrum of setup. Rather, the collection of resources we have assembled is there to be more of a springboard of discovery to help you to get a good grounding of knowledge so you can learn what you need or decide whether you need to further your understanding with additional research and study. Regardless, we wish you well on your Salesforce journey and hope these resources that you will review as part of your voyage of discovery will serve you well.

CHAPTER 12

Application Architecture (Phase A) Resource Base

This chapter contains the resources required to govern Phase A of the Salesforce Platform Governance Method. These resources should be considered a starting point and can therefore be tailored to your exact requirements. However, we have made every effort to capture the main topics that have appeared throughout our Salesforce engagements and experience.

Tip You do not need to use this resource base as a strict method or process. The idea is that this will give you a good indication of what you should be taking into consideration. The expectation is that you will use this as a guide and then build upon it as you navigate the Salesforce ecosystem.

Guidelines and Best Practices

This section contains the guidance and best practices that are available from Salesforce, as well as other resources that we have determined will be valuable. This section should serve to provide a good set of guidelines that can be reviewed by anyone delivering the governance function within your organization.

© Lee Harding and Lee Bayliss 2022
L. Harding and L. Bayliss, *Salesforce Platform Governance Method*,
https://doi.org/10.1007/978-1-4842-7404-0_12

We know there is an infinite number of resources available on the Web, and although some are better than others, this resource base will provide you with a good selection of resources that we recommend. We do not intend to go into low-level detail for each item as, this book would be huge and weigh an absolute ton. So, we focus on pointing you to the detail or explaining the high-level concepts, expecting you to then follow up with additional reading where necessary.

General Architecture

As you should be aware by now, this resource base complements the context of the governance method described in Chapter 2, "Application Architecture." To begin we have provided Table 12-1 to supply resource links to the content that's discussed.

When we consider general architecture, we are referring to the building blocks that make your application run smoothly. We are concerned with the performance, since if the application doesn't perform well your users will avoid using it. We also look at scalability, for as your user base grows the platform should scale with it. For capacity management, do you have enough resources available for the app to operate, and more important, have you considered the "cost" of growth over time?

Table 12-1. *General Architecture Resource Links*

Artifact	GitHub Ref	Description
Apex Code Best Practices: Force.com Multi-Tenant Architecture	Multi-Tenant Architecture	Force.com's foundation is a metadata-driven software architecture that enables multi-tenant applications. This paper explains the technology that makes the Force.com platform fast, scalable, and secure for any type of application while allowing multiple tenants or Salesforce instances to co-exist. This is an important foundational concept to understand and serves to explain why platform limits are such an important part of your design.

(continued)

Table 12-1. (*continued*)

Artifact	GitHub Ref	Description
Data and File Storage Allocations	Storage Capacity	Capacity management is sometimes overlooked when governing a Salesforce implementation. Salesforce splits storage into two main areas: data storage and file storage. Both are calculated for you based on the org edition and the number of user licenses you purchase. Use this guide to understand what storage you will be provided based on the org capacity required. Understanding, how your application usage will grow over time will allow you to build your capacity plan. Pay attention to the edition, as this will certainly impact your allocated storage. Once you have a good idea of your growth (number of records over time by month, for example) you can plan ahead and include the cost of additional storage in your resource model. Using a spreadsheet to calculate your storage needs is a really good way to plan for any future financial outlay.
Lightning Console Technical Requirements	Lightning Console Performance	This is great place to start when considering where to begin with assessing Lightning performance requirements. This is an important factor of your Salesforce implementation. How the application will respond in a browser will set the scene for your end-user experience and could therefore affect user adoption. If your Octane score is within the prescribed limits, then you know that the JavaScript engine's performance is running well. Also review EPT, Experienced Page Time, which measures the time it takes to download and load the entire contents of a Web page.
Salesforce Developer Limits and Allocations Quick Reference	Salesforce Limits	To ensure that the Salesforce platform can operate its multi-tenant environment, all transactions must have available resources in order to execute. The way this is governed is through the application of governor limits. These limits are in place to ensure that Salesforce transactions have access to the resources they need to execute—well, as long as you are within the limits defined in the platform. Limits are there to control resource availability for all the Salesforce applications vying for processing power.

(continued)

Table 12-1. (*continued*)

Artifact	GitHub Ref	Description
Improve Inefficient Related Lists	Related List Performance	If you have detail pages that have a large number of related list records, you might be experiencing page load performance and usability issues. Read this article for suggestions on how to improve your pages and provide the right kind of related list information while being performant.
Declarative vs. Programmatic	Declarative vs. Programmatic	When thinking about your application and how to develop it, as a Salesforce Admin / Developer, you'll be weighing using a declarative development option versus using code to build your application. Use this resource and the associated links to help you make this decision about the right way to go. It is possible to use declarative development options and build great apps without writing a single line of code. The emphasis is on having GUI-driven app creation that can be easily maintained and supported. The key decisions here will mainly center on the following: Cost: If the app is developed using declarative methods, this should be far more cost efficient than using code. Time: Time to build using declarative options is more advantageous than the code alternative. Maintenance and Support: Using code to develop your applications will also mean that on-going support and maintenance may well require a certain skillset to further develop and resolve any related issues to the app over time. This can also impact costs for the same reasons. Do you have staff in your organization that can support this codebase, or will you need to go to market to bring these skills in?

(*continued*)

Table 12-1. (*continued*)

Artifact	GitHub Ref	Description
Developer Beginner	Developer Beginner – Trailhead	Here you'll find a broad introduction to many of the key concepts and features you'll need to understand before you begin designing and architecting apps that leverage the unique power of the Force.com cloud application development platform. (Welcome to Trailhead—we love this educational learning platform.) This is delivered as a "Trailmix," a collection of individual trails that will give you a firm grasp of basic development and platform-specific learnings designed to get you creating fantastic applications on the Salesforce Force.com platform.
Enterprise Architecture: Single-org versus Multi-org Strategy	Salesforce Org Strategy	Here is a fantastic resource to help you really delve into the question that every Salesforce professional will have to deal with at some point on their Salesforce journey: Should we use a single-org or multi-org strategy to serve our application needs? Use this resource to learn about the pros and cons of multi- vs. single-org Salesforce architectures. Use these detailed criteria to help you select your company's strategy. This is particularly useful where the environment already has multiple orgs and the requirement is to consolidate. It all comes down to fundamental topics that must be considered carefully. Cost is the obvious one. The more orgs you support, the more financial impact you are going to have. But aside from cost (and as the method suggests), the issues will be about the app requirements themselves and how the application architecture will enable co-existence, the use of a common data model, and also the use of a security model that's not prohibitive against the original intent of the application's use case.

(*continued*)

Table 12-1. (*continued*)

Artifact	GitHub Ref	Description
Licenses Overview	Licenses Overview	This is a huge topic, but it's at the heart of your Salesforce implementation. If you don't consider the most appropriate license type to serve your requirements, you may find that you do not have access to the features and functionality that you need in order to be successful. For example, for Salesforce communities or Experience Cloud, if you have complex sharing and access requirements you will need to use customer community plus licenses over the standard customer community license. So, the lesson here is to enable specific Salesforce functionality for your users; you must choose the most appropriate user license for each user. To enable additional functionality, you can assign permission set licenses and feature licenses to your users or purchase usage-based entitlements for your organization.
Salesforce Features and Edition Allocations	Salesforce Features by Edition	There are many resources available that provide an overview of the Salesforce org limits. This reference provides a general overview of the limits for Salesforce features by edition. Keep this link in your favorites. It's likely that you will need to refer to this regularly. There is an awful lot of detail to consider here, so take some time to review it, as it will undoubtedly reveal some interesting and relevant detail that you either hadn't previously considered or were already acutely aware of.

(continued)

Table 12-1. (*continued*)

Artifact	GitHub Ref	Description
Data Model – Object Relationship Overview	Object Relationships	When you are considering how data elements will relate to other data elements and therefore construct the overall Salesforce data model, look at this overview, which provides detail on all the relationship types that Salesforce has to offer. The object relationships in your data model will be a key part of your data model design. You need to decide if a lookup relationship will serve your needs, or perhaps a many-to-many relationship will be more appropriate; for example, you can use master–detail relationships to model many-to-many relationships between any two objects. A many-to-many relationship allows each record of one object to be linked to multiple records from another object and vice versa. This will all depend on the requirements and how the data will be represented in your model. Remember, it's good practice to document your data model clearly and create a data model dictionary. This document will prove vital for good data model governance. Best practice would be to add clear descriptions for all objects and fields that you add. When other resources come to view the fields available in the model, they will understand the intention for creating the element and can decide if it suits their requirement or business purpose.
Considerations for Relationships	Considerations for Relationships	Now that you have a good understanding of the types of relationships on offer, review the following considerations before creating relationships between your objects.
Salesforce Naming Conventions	Naming Conventions	How to name your objects is all part of designing a data model that not only is fit for the purpose at hand but also follows a defined standard that's enforced across your organization. Review this Salesforce Quip document, where you will find the recommended conventions for all Salesforce data elements from Apex classes and process builders to objects and fields.

(*continued*)

Table 12-1. (*continued*)

Artifact	GitHub Ref	Description
Designing Dashboards and Reports for Force.com Implementations with Large Data Volumes	Reports & Dashboards for LDV	This link provides an overview of how to design reports for large data volumes (LDVs). There's a lot to consider here. Firstly, what is an LDV? Well, you would consider any org that has over 5 million records an LDV. So why is it important? If you have an LDV in your org then when it comes to reports and dashboards you have to consider how the data model is designed to provide optimal performance. We will cover this in more detail in the next phase, data architecture. Just be aware that if you expect your org to have millions of records across multiple objects and a complex relationship model, then creating performant reports and dashboards will be another key consideration.
Improve Report Performance: Best Practices	Improve Report Performance	Many factors can cause a report to perform poorly or to time out. The details in this link will provide a comprehensive guide for applying best practices for report performance. Concepts such as using efficient filtering, which controls how many records are returned, can increase report performance considerably.
Integration Patterns and Practices	Integration Patterns and Practices	This document describes strategies (in the form of patterns) for common integration scenarios. Each pattern describes the design and approach for a particular scenario rather than a specific implementation.
Salesforce Connect	Salesforce Connect	Salesforce Connect provides seamless integration of data across system boundaries by letting your users view, search, and modify data that's stored outside your Salesforce org.

Localization / Global Deployments

In this section of the resource base, we focus on the resources available that cover design aspects for the end user; rather, how we ensure the Salesforce platform is accessible and useable for all end users, customers, and partners that will be using the solution.

To be successful, we need to focus on the aspect of the solution where language and currency influence application design. For example, if your solution will support multiple languages, how will you support every language from a UI and data model perspective? What can you do to make adoption of multiple languages and currencies a simpler task to achieve? The resources in this section should provide a useful reference and put you on the path to success (Table 12-2).

Table 12-2. *Localization / Global Deployments Resource Links*

Artifact	GitHub Ref	Description
Setting up the Translation Workbench	Translation Workbench	The translation workbench lets you specify the languages you want to translate, assign translators to languages, create translations for customizations you've made to your Salesforce organization, and override labels and translations from managed packages. You can also consider the use of custom labels to simplify how you reference translated text in code. You can then create reusable elements in your code that will always display the correct language of the user. This provides a very efficient way to present text in your application's UI.
International Organizations: Using Multiple Currencies	Using Multiple Currencies	Review this guide if your solution will require the use of multiple currencies.

Workflow & Processes

Automation is what makes the Salesforce platform an extremely powerful application. There are many types of automation tools available with which you can turbo charge your application and business processes. Workflow rules, process builders, Salesforce

Flow, triggers, and actions are all examples of automation tools that can be applied. The issue that you will have is deciding which automation tool is the most appropriate for the application that you are designing.

As with all automation tools there are pros and cons for each, and you will need to decide which will best serve the needs of your application. However, you need to be aware of not only what the automation method will provide, but also what the limitations and considerations are for each. And if you mix automation methods together, what does it mean over the longer term as the complexity of your environment increases? For example, if you have multiple applications or projects running in a single Salesforce org implementation, it would not be unreasonable to assume that each project could have a case object process builder to cover its individual project needs. Let's also say that your projects have defined separate "before insert" triggers on the case objects as well–things could get a bit messy.

Let's consider this for a moment. Each project has a trigger component that fires the process builder when certain conditions are met. When you consider the Salesforce order of execution, you cannot guarantee the order in which the triggers will fire, which may impact any dependency that you have defined in a subsequent process builder, which could ultimately cause the business process to fail. Worse still, you could inadvertently create recursive behavior, which means that your automation logic performs badly and gives the application users a really bad experience.

So, best practices for automation should not be overlooked, nor should it be assumed that it will be taken care of by the platform. Time needs to be taken to consider the order of execution of your logic in the context of the business requirement you are trying to resolve. Best practices will dictate how to implement triggers properly with a trigger framework, and ideally there should be only one process builder per object.

Review the resources in Table 12-3 to make sure that you have all the information you need to design and define your automation solution.

Table 12-3. *Localization / Global Deployments Resource Links*

Artifact	GitHub Ref	Description
Which Automation Tool Do I Use	Which Automation Tool	Salesforce provides multiple tools to automate your organization's repetitive business processes: approvals, process builders, workflows, and visual workflows
Process Automation Cheatsheet	Process Automation Cheatsheet	A process flow chart and comparative tables make it easy to figure out which tool is best for any particular use case.
Getting Started with Approval Processes: Approval Process Checklist	Approval Process Checklist	This resource provides a checklist for preparing the appropriate information before creating your approval process.
Automate Your Business Processes: Workflow Limits	Workflow Limits	This resource provides guidance on the limits that apply to rules that are applied to objects in the platform.
Cloud Flow Designer Guide	Cloud Flow Designer Guide	Before you begin building and distributing flows, understand the best practices in the Cloud Flow Designer Guide. In addition, when designing, managing, and running flows, consider the permissions, use limits, and data issues.
Extend Salesforce with Clicks, Not Code: Quick Actions	Quick Actions	Actions enable users to do more in Salesforce and in the Salesforce mobile app. For example, you can let users create or update records and log calls directly in their Chatter feed or from their mobile device.

(*continued*)

Table 12-3. (*continued*)

Artifact	GitHub Ref	Description
Automate Your Business Processes: Process Builder	Process Builder	Many of the tasks you assign, emails you send, and other record updates are vital parts of your standard processes. Instead of doing this repetitive work manually, you can configure processes to do it automatically. Process Builder helps you automate your business processes and gives you a graphical representation as you build it.
Automate Your Business Processes: Process, Limits, and Considerations	Process, Limits, and Considerations	Before you start creating, managing, and activating processes, understand the limits and considerations.

Formulas

Use formulas to take values from fields in either your custom or standard objects to perform a calculation or execute defined logic to automatically populate a field. There are formula field data types that we can define, and there are numerous data elements that we can use in logic to ensure that the data returned is the data that we expect. We can also use formula fields (via cross-object formulas) to reference data that reside in other objects. Cross-object formulas could be up to 10 relationships away. However, careful attention must be given so as to ensure that you are not presenting data to users to which they would otherwise not have access.

Review the following table to find all the resources that cover formula fields, including where and how we use them.

Table 12-4. *Localization / Global Deployments Resource Links*

Artifact	GitHub Ref	Description
Extend Salesforce with Clicks, Not Code: Calculate Field Values with Formulas	Calculate Field Values with Formulas	Formula fields are a great way to derive a field value by performing a calculation from other fields in an object. This resource explains how they work.
Formulas Cheatsheet	Formulas Cheatsheet	Use this resource to quickly see what operators, expressions, and functions you can use with formula fields.
Extend Salesforce with Clicks, Not Code: Common Formula Errors	Common Formula Errors	Review common errors that can occur with formulas and learn how to fix them.
Extend Salesforce with Clicks, Not Code: Tips for Building Formulas	Tips for Building Formulas	This resource provides many tips for building formula fields with a plethora of different use cases.

Files and Social

When we discussed the general architecture resources, we covered concepts related to the capacity planning aspect of your Salesforce solutions. In this resource, we provide more depth specific to the files aspect of your solution. Knowing the data requirements from a file storage perspective will ensure that you do not have unused expensive storage allocated to your org that you don't need.

This resource base also covers the social aspect of your Salesforce solution. There are no guarantees that Salesforce will support social media platforms in the future, so make sure that before you implement any integration with a social media platform you use this resource to ensure that all considerations are understood.

Table 12-5. *Localization / Global Deployments Resource Links*

Artifact	GitHub Ref	Description
Differences Between Files, Salesforce CRM Content, Salesforce Knowledge, Documents, and Attachments	Differences Between Files, Knowledge, Documents, and Attachments	Explore the differences between various ways to manage your files and content. Using this resource, you will see all the various options and a clear description of the differences between them.
Set Up and Maintain Collaboration Tools: The Files Connect Setup Process	Files Connect Setup Process	The setup process for Files Connect differs for cloud-based and on-premises external data sources.
Sales Productivity: Guidelines for Using Social Accounts, Contacts, and Leads	Guidelines for Using Social	Review guidelines for using social accounts, contacts, and leads, including privacy and security details and which social networks are available by record and user experience.

Phase A Standards
General

As much as possible, we want to ensure that your Salesforce org is self-documented. All description fields are required to be completed in line with the following description standards.

Aside from loop iterators such as i, j, and k, variable names, object names, class names, and method names should always be descriptive. Single-letter names are not acceptable. Object names should use `CapitalizedCamelCase`. Method or function names should use `lowerCamelCase`. Constants should be `CAPITALIZED_WITH_UNDERSCORES`.

Note   In fact, this is just an example of what is advised in the "Naming Conventions" link in Table 12-1.

Underscores should not be used for any variable name, object name, class name, or method name except as an application prefix. Overriding standard tabs, objects, and standard names should not be allowed without first seeking approval from your central governance team.

Names must be meaningful. Abbreviated names must be avoided; for example:

Good	Bad
computeAverage()	CompAvg()
boolean isError	boolean isNoError

Similarly, avoid the use of static variables wherever possible. Salesforce keywords cannot be used as class variables, and naming of individual metadata elements must conform to the following standards, including prefixes where specified.

Managed packages are not within the control of the individual project teams. Where a managed package is used it is expected that the use of the package is documented and approval has been sought from the central governance team.

Objects

Salesforce has three types of objects: standard, custom, and external. For our governance requirements, objects are further considered to be split into the following two categories:

- Enterprise Object - Objects that are used by more than one business area; all Salesforce standard objects fall into this category. Any custom objects that are used across multiple business areas also fall into this category.

- Project Object - Objects that are specific to a single project or business area; all custom objects initially fall into this category.

A central governance team will determine which entities are of which type during the engagement via regular architectural reviews. Creation of and/or changes to project objects are permitted by the project team only.

The central governance team may promote project objects to enterprise objects.

Changes may not be made to enterprise objects without the agreement of the central governance team.

All Salesforce standard objects are enterprise objects.

Project objects may not duplicate existing enterprise objects.

Projects may not duplicate classes/approval processes/pages/etc. that function upon enterprise objects.

Projects that need to create/update functionality that interacts with enterprise objects are responsible for engaging with the central governance team for review and risk management.

The naming of project objects must have a unique prefix relating to the business area and project.

Descriptions

Description fields for all objects, fields, and other metadata should be populated where provided and must conform to the following:

- Descriptions must be written in English.

- Start with the business area and product acronym where they are used.

- Include a useful contextual description that is meaningful for others reviewing this piece of metadata at a later date. Descriptions must be updated whenever the metadata changes or is used elsewhere.

Help

Help text for all objects, fields, and other metadata should be populated where provided and must conform to the following:

- Descriptions must be written in English.

- It must contain a useful contextual description that is meaningful for others reviewing this piece of metadata at a later date. Descriptions must be updated whenever the metadata changes or is used elsewhere.

Objects

Generally speaking, objects represent database tables that contain your organization's information. For example, the central object in the Salesforce data model represents accounts–companies and organizations involved with your business, such as customers, partners, and competitors. The term *record* describes a particular occurrence of an object (such as a specific account like "IBM" or "United Airlines" that is represented by an Account object). A record is analogous to a row in a database table.

Objects already created for you by Salesforce are called standard objects. Objects you create in your organization are called custom objects. Objects you create that map to data stored outside your organization are called external objects.

Object names must start with a capital letter and may include a prefix as outlined here.

Enterprise Object

Format	Example
[ObjectName]__c	If your company manufactured guitars, you may want a customer object called Guitar__c.

Project Object

Format	Example
[BusinessArea] [Project]_ [ObjectName]__c	If your company has a business area called Sales and Marketing, and they have a project to develop a custom configuration on the Salesforce platform called Accelerate, your custom object might be called SMACC_Guitar__c where SM refers to "Sales and Marketing" while ACC refers to the project Accelerate.

[Project] is mandatory and must be populated; [BusinessArea] is optional and only needs populating if not limited to a single business area.

> **Note**   The transition of a project object to an enterprise object must go through the central governance team given the potential impact on existing reports, sharing, workflows, and triggers. The promotion of a project object to an enterprise object **WILL** require effort.

Fields

Capture your unique business data by storing it in custom fields. When you create a custom field, you configure where you want it to appear and optionally control security at the field level.

Custom field names should have words delimited by an underscore. Whole words should be used, and the use of acronyms and abbreviations should be avoided. The API field name must meet the convention shown here.

Enterprise Fields (Global, Reusable)

Format	Example
[FieldName]__c	If a new field was created to define a guitar part, such as, Jazz Neck the example would look like Jazz_Neck

Project-Specific Fields

Format	Example
[BusinessArea][Project]_[FieldName]__c	Taking the example above further, SMACC_Jazz_Neck__c where SM refers to "Sales and Marketing" while ACC refers to the project Accelerate.

> **Note**   [Project] is optional and only needs populating if not generic across all business areas.

Workflow

Workflow lets you automate standard internal procedures and processes to save time across your org. A workflow rule is the main container for a set of workflow instructions. These instructions can always be summed up in an if/then statement.

Names should be capitalized clear text, with the event clearly identifiable. The API name must meet the convention as follows.

Enterprise Workflows

Format	Example
[BusinessArea]_[WorkflowName]	Your Sales function may have a requirement to update customer details and therefore a good example could be SM_Update_Customer_Contact_Details.

Project-Specific Workflows

Format	Example
[BusinessArea][Project]_[WorkflowName]	Following on from the previous example, SM_ACC_Customer_Contact_Details.

Workflow field updates, email alerts, and so forth will follow the preceding naming convention.

Lightning Process Builder

Many of the tasks you assign, the emails you send, and other record updates you perform are vital parts of your standard processes. Instead of doing this repetitive work manually, you can configure processes to do it automatically. Process Builder helps you automate your business processes and gives you a graphical representation as you build it.

Names should be capitalized clear text, with the event clearly identifiable. The API name must meet the convention.

Enterprise Process Builders

Format	Example
[BusinessArea]_ [ProcessBuilderName]	A good example might be SM_CASE_Rejection_Process. Notice that CASE has been added to clearly define the Object the Process Builder relates to.

Project-Specific Process Builders

Format	Example
[Business Area][Project]_[ProcessBuilderName]	With the Project added, SM_ACC_ CASE_Rejection_Process.

Workflow field updates, email alerts, and so forth will follow the preceding naming convention.

Flows

Flows are the part of Lightning flow that collects data and performs actions in your Salesforce org or an external system. Lightning Flow provides two types of flow: screen flows and autolaunched flows.

Names should be capitalized clear text, with the event clearly identifiable. The API name must meet the convention.

Enterprise Flows

Format	Example
[BusinessArea]_[FlowName]	SM_Create_New_Service_Record.

Project-Specific Flows

Format	Example
[BusinessArea][Project]_[FlowName]	SM_ACC_Create_New_Service_Record.

Workflow field updates, email alerts, and so forth will follow the preceding naming convention.

Validation Rules

Validation rules verify that the data a user enters in a record meets the specified standards before the user can save the record. A validation rule can contain a formula or expression that evaluates the data in one or more fields and returns a value of "True" or "False."

Names should be camel case, with the field and rule clearly identifiable. The API name must meet the convention.

Enterprise Validation Rules (Global, Reusable)

Format	Example
[BusinessArea]_[ValidationRuleName]	An example of a Validation Rule could be SM_Telephone_Number_Required.

Product-Specific Validations

Format	Example
[BusinessArea][Project]_[ValidationRuleName]	SM_ACC_Telephone_Number_Required.

Labels

Custom labels enable developers to create multilingual applications by automatically presenting information (for example, help text or error messages) in a user's native language. Custom labels are custom text values that can be accessed from Apex classes, Visualforce pages, or Lightning components. The values can be translated into any language Salesforce supports.

Rather than name labels in relation to a business area or project, categories must be added to each label. There must be a category for the business to which it relates.

Format	Example
[Category]_LabelName	Survey_CustomerSurvey_Question_1.

Lightning Components

The Lightning component framework is a UI framework for developing single-page applications for mobile and desktop devices.

As of Spring 2019 (API version 45.0), you can build Lightning components using two programming models: the Lightning Web Components model, and the original Aura Components model. Lightning Web components are custom HTML elements built using HTML and modern JavaScript. Lightning Web components and Aura components can coexist and interoperate on a page.

The Lightning component should be named using camel case and Lightning Web Components as pascal case as shown here.

Format	Example
`[BusinessArea][Project]_ComponentName`	Lightning Components (Aura) `AccountLookupCmp` and for Lightning Web Components use `accountLookupCmp` where Cmp denotes a component.

Profiles

Profiles define how users access objects and data, and what they can do within the application. When you create users, you assign a profile to each one.

As profile names are used by business users, to avoid confusion the business area will be used in full rather than the acronym.

Format	Example
`[BusinessArea]ProfileName`	For example, Sales and Marketing Community User

Permission Sets

A permission set is a collection of settings and permissions that give users access to various tools and functions. The settings and permissions in permission sets are also found in profiles, but permission sets extend users' functional access without changing their profiles.

Where a Permission Set is specific to a Business Area

Format	Example
[BusinessArea]_PermissionSetName	An example API name for a Permission set is SM_Accounting_Approvals

Record Types

Record types let you offer different business processes, picklist values, and page layouts to different users. You might create record types to differentiate your regular sales deals from your professional services engagements, offering different picklist values for each. Or you might display different page layouts for your customer support cases versus your billing cases.

Format	Example
[BusinessArea]_[RecordTypeName]	For example, SM_Chat_live_Agent or Chat_Live_Agent where the Record Type is generic across the business.

Page Layouts

Page layouts control the layout and organization of buttons, fields, s-controls, Visualforce, custom links, and related lists on object record pages. They also help determine which fields are visible, read-only, and required. Use page layouts to customize the content of record pages for your users.

To avoid conflicts across multiple projects, or even if to begin with only one project exists within your Salesforce organization, it is good practice to name your page layouts according to the format shown here.

Format	Example
[BusinessArea]_[Object]	For example, Sales and Marketing_Account Layout

Roles

Salesforce offers a user role hierarchy that you can use with sharing settings to determine the levels of access that users have to your Salesforce org's data. Roles within the hierarchy affect access to key components such as records and reports.

Format	Example
[BusinessArea] - Role Name	Sales - Regional Managers

Custom Settings

Custom settings are similar to custom objects in that they let you customize org data. Unlike custom objects, which have records based on them, custom settings let you utilize custom data sets across your org. Custom settings also let you distinguish particular users or profiles based on custom criteria.

Format	Example
[BusinessArea][Project]_CustomSetting	For example, SM_ACC_Billing_Data__c.

Static Resources

Static resources allow you to upload content that you can reference in a Visualforce page, including archives (such as .zip and .jar files), images, style sheets, JavaScript, and other files.

Format	Example
[BusinessArea][Project]_StaticResource	For example, SM_ACC_Billing_Data__c

Duplication Rules

A duplication rule defines what happens when a user views a record with duplicates or starts creating a duplicate record. Salesforce provides standard duplication rules for business and person accounts, contacts, and leads. You can also create duplication rules.

Format	Example
`[BusinessArea][Project]_DuplicationRule`	For example, Sales ACC Duplicate Contact Rule

Matching Rules

A matching rule defines how duplicate records are identified in duplication rules and duplicate jobs. Salesforce provides standard matching rules for business and person accounts, contacts, and leads. You can also create custom matching rules.

Format	Example
`[BusinessArea][Project]_MatchingRule`	Sales ACC Matching Contact Rule

Checklists

The phase checklist simply tracks that each step and sub-step within the phase is governed correctly and completely. Each sub-step may have several subject areas to form complete coverage from a governance perspective.

Governance Step	
Govern the General Architecture	**Pass / Fail**
Govern the solution for optimal performance, scalability, usability, and maintenance.	
Govern the appropriate use of declarative and programmatic functionality used.	
Govern the considerations for a single-org or dedicated org strategy.	
Govern the usage of license types (capabilities and constraints).	
Govern the data modeling concepts and implications of database design.	
Govern the usage of reports and analytics (platform considerations and tradeoffs).	
Govern the usage of external applications (Salesforce AppExchange and Application Integration).	

(continued)

Governance Step	
Localization / Global Deployments	**Pass/Fail**
Govern the usage of the platform's internationalization functionality (multiple currencies, translations and languages)	
Govern the Use of Process Automation	**Pass/Fail**
Govern the use of workflow capabilities (rules, tasks, emails, field updates, and approvals) within the solution.	
Govern the use of visual workflow taking into account the limitations and considerations of a visual workflow solution.	
Govern the capabilities and limitations of Salesforce actions.	
Govern the use of Lightning Process Builder, taking into account the limitations.	
Govern the Use of Formulas	**Pass/Fail**
Govern the use of advanced formula features (VLOOKUP, roll-up summary, image, x-object), check against limitations.	
Govern the use of hierarchical custom settings in a declarative solution.	
Files and Social	**Pass/Fail**
Govern the application's usage of files and content, including Chatter files, attachments, content, and knowledge.	
Govern the integration with social capabilities of the platform.	

CHAPTER 13

Data Architecture & Management (Phase B) Resource Base

This chapter contains the resources required to govern Phase B of the Salesforce Platform Governance Method. These resources should be considered a starting point and can therefore be tailored depending on your project and governance requirements. However, we have made every effort to capture the main topics that have appeared throughout our Salesforce engagements and experience, so these should serve as a good reference in relation to the method.

Tip   You do not need to use this resource base as a strict method or process. The idea is that this will give you a good indication of what you should be taking into consideration. The expectation is that you will use this as a guide and then build upon it as you navigate the Salesforce ecosystem.

Guidelines and Best Practices

This section contains the guidance and best practices that are available from Salesforce, as well as other resources that we have determined will be valuable. This section should serve to provide a good set of guidelines that can be reviewed by anyone delivering the governance function within your organization.

© Lee Harding and Lee Bayliss 2022
L. Harding and L. Bayliss, *Salesforce Platform Governance Method*,
https://doi.org/10.1007/978-1-4842-7404-0_13

We know there is an infinite number of resources available on the Web, and although some are better than others, this resource base will provide you with a good selection that we recommend you review. As per all the resource base documentation in this book, we do not intend to go into low-level detail for each item, as we should not consume any more paper than absolutely necessary. Instead, we focus on pointing you to the details or explaining the high-level concepts for you to then follow on with additional reading where necessary.

As is the case with all the resource base chapters in this book, the links to the resources will be managed in the Salesforce Platform Governance Method GitHub account. The URL for this account is as follows: `github.com/salesforceplatformgovernancemethod`.

Design & Optimization

Needless to mention, this resource base complements the context of the governance method described in Chapter 3, "Data Architecture & Management." To begin, we have provided Table 13-1 to supply resource links to the content that's discussed.

Data architecture and design and optimization are critical parts of your Salesforce org, and how you optimize your data model will undoubtedly have a direct impact on the success of your application. In this resource base you will find references to the concepts and technical considerations that will help you to ensure that your Salesforce data architecture design is fit for its purpose and has considered the controls and limitations that should govern the overall design. We have tried to cover the scenarios that you will for sure find yourself seeking guidance on, or a deeper level of understanding. As with all Salesforce concepts, there is a mountain of information, discussion topics, views, and opinions from other professionals in the industry available to you for review. However, this resource base provides you with a comprehensive list of concepts that we recommend you review in the context of data architecture and management design.

Table 13-1. *Data Optimization Resources*

Artifact	GitHub Ref	Description
SFDC Data Modeling Introduction	Data Modeling	This Trailhead module is a great introduction to Salesforce data modeling concepts, including simple object relationships, standard and custom objects, and the schema builder. If you are new to the Salesforce ecosystem, this would be a great place to start your data modeling journey.
Data Model – Object Relationship Overview	Data Model Object Relationships	The next resource is the object relationships, or rather, what object relationships are available and how they work. Remember that object relationships in your data model will be a key part of your data model design. You need to decide if a lookup relationship will serve your needs, or perhaps a master–detail relationship would be more appropriate. Finally, it's good practice to document your data model clearly and create a data model dictionary. This document will prove vital for good data model governance. Best practice would be to add clear descriptions for all objects and fields that you add. When other resources come to view the fields available in the model, they will understand the intention for creating the element and can decide if it suits their requirement or business purpose.
Considerations for Relationships	Data Model Relationship Considerations	Review this resource for data model relationship considerations before creating relationships between your objects. If you have reviewed the previous resource base, this will serve as a good reminder for the options Salesforce has to offer.

(*continued*)

Table 13-1. (*continued*)

Artifact	GitHub Ref	Description
External Data Access	Define External Objects with Salesforce Connect	With Salesforce, you can access external data sources and view data as if it resides on the Salesforce platform. There are many ways in which this can be achieved, and this resource covers this concept using Salesforce Connect and the associated adaptors; for example, cross-org, OData (2.0, 4.0), or custom Apex adaptors.
Things to Consider using External Objects or Data Sources	Salesforce Connect Considerations for all Adaptors	Salesforce Connect, although useful, does have some special behaviors and limitations that should be considered in your solution. For example, not all object relationship types are available, and of course if the external data source is unavailable or suffering a degradation in performance it could directly impact your application performance in relation to loading external data views.
What Are Custom Metadata types	Custom Metadata Types	We know Salesforce and we know what metadata is (data about data), but with custom metadata types we can define data in our apps as metadata. This gives us the control we need to manage application data (metadata) via the Metadata API, package this data up as managed or un-managed packages, and even build logic using validation rules to validate data entered by users to standards that you define. The main benefit of using custom metadata types is having the ability to deploy app data from one environment to another. If we consider a custom setting, for example, you can only move the metadata from environment to environment. So any values you specify in the custom setting cannot be managed in the same way as data defined in a custom metadata type. The reason is that the data defined in your custom metadata type IS metadata, so when you are migrating custom metadata types from one environment to another, the values are treated not as data, but as metadata. You can even define relationships between custom metadata types. We use this feature to create relationships with other metadata types or custom objects and fields and static resources.

(*continued*)

Table 13-1. (*continued*)

Artifact	GitHub Ref	Description
Custom Settings Description and Examples	Custom Settings	Custom settings are like custom objects. They allow you to create custom data sets across your org. The main benefit of custom settings is that the data is available in the application cache; therefore, when you need to access this data you can do so efficiently as you will not need multiple queries to the database. However, there are limitations that you should note, the main one being that you cannot easily move custom settings data from one environment to another. This is because, unlike custom metadata, custom settings values are classed as data. A good use case for defining a custom setting would be if your application has a need to list country codes for all countries used in an application. You can therefore easily access this data without expensive database queries.
Picklist Limitations	Picklists vs. Custom Objects and associated Limitations	As discussed in the method, part of your governance process should look at the data granularity and how normalized your data model design is. All of these things will contribute to your app performance, so you need to be aware of how certain decisions you make impact your application overall. For example, it is ideal to have less than 1,000 values in your picklist. Any more than this and a custom object would be more appropriate. There are other limits that should also be top of mind when considering options. This resource should provide some guidance on limits and their performance implications.
Data Management Strategy	Data Management Best Practice Guides	Use this resource to really challenge your thinking and approach to data management. The integrity of your data must always be the single most important thing when you consider your data integrations and how and where data is mastered. These resources will help you to think about best practices and to consider how your application integration methods could affect data integrity, as well as to consider the overall strategy you adopt to control how data flows in and out of your Salesforce implementation.

(*continued*)

Table 13-1. (*continued*)

Artifact	GitHub Ref	Description
Large Data Volumes	Introduction to Large Data Volume Concepts	Salesforce enables customers to easily scale their applications up from small to large volumes of data. This resource provides you with an introduction to large data volume (LDV) concepts, such as search options and the use of skinny tables. LDV is a term used to describe an org where typically there are tens of millions of records, hundreds of gigabytes of data, or where an object has in excess of 5 million records. This resource provides a good starting point to grasp the fundamentals before exploring deeper technical reference material. For example, consider the impact to performance as your data scales. We must assume that as data volumes increase, the time required for certain operations, such as search, may also increase. So, the ways in which architects design and configure data structures and operations can have a significant impact on the expected performance of an application.
LDV Best Practices	Best Practices for Deployments with Large Data Volumes	This definitive Salesforce resource provides you with a very comprehensive guide to large data volumes, search architecture, optimization techniques, skinny tables, and the associated best practice recommendations. Things like making queries selective or using techniques to reduce the data stored in Salesforce will all be key to understanding and controlling how the volume of data impacts your application characteristics, performance, and the design decisions you make.
Query Plan Tool	Query Plan Tool	It might be a good idea to use the query plan tool in the Salesforce developer console to check the query plan for any SOQL queries that are slow and inefficient. The tool will basically help you to understand how efficient your query is and how to make the query more performant.

(*continued*)

Table 13-1. (*continued*)

Artifact	GitHub Ref	Description
Custom Indexes	Custom Indexes	Within this resource, you will learn that the best query is a selective query, but if you are have issues and need to specify additional indexes, then a custom index could be the right approach. Review this resource to learn more about how custom indexes can be applied to your specific use case.
Skinny Tables	Skinny Tables	Looking deeper into the topic of LDV, we meet the concept of skinny tables. This is something we advise you to consider when your query performance is causing production issues and you are sure that you've performed all due diligence on your query design, explored custom indexes, and reviewed the issues with Salesforce customer support (where applicable). Having done all that, there is still something that can be done to improve query performance, and that's to implement skinny tables. Salesforce will have to do this for you, as this is not something that you can configure on the platform yourself. A skinny table is a custom table that contains a subset of fields from the source object. The basic idea is that with a skinny table you define the fields that are required by your business case. Then when your query executes, the scan process should be able to return more rows of data (due to the reduced number of fields in your table), as query throughput is significantly increased. So for queries on objects with millions of rows of data, a skinny table could be just the ticket for a performant solution.

(*continued*)

Table 13-1. (*continued*)

Artifact	GitHub Ref	Description
Big Objects – Trailhead, Implementation Guide	Salesforce Big Object Reference	For applications that have huge data requirements—for example, where the purpose of the Salesforce application is to retire a legacy system—it may be necessary to use a big object on the Salesforce platform. If the legacy app has hundreds of millions of records or perhaps even more volumes of records (say more than a billion), then to maintain application performance you'll need to focus on using a big object. However, there are several considerations that must be reviewed so that it's clear how big objects work, how they are used, how you interact with them, and other limitations that could influence your decision to use them for your use case. Bear in mind that the main use cases for big objects are for archiving huge amounts of data or where you have the requirement to bring in large data sets from an external data source or legacy application. This resource covers all the basic concepts of big objects and will also provide guidance for increasing the limits should this be a consideration for your use case.
Query Performance	Maximizing the Performance of Force.com SOQL, Reports, and List Views	Query performance is key when designing Salesforce applications. Think about it: Your app could have a great UI that's way superior to that of your competitors, but this will pale into insignificance if the performance of your application is hindered by bad search and query design. The time it takes to request data from the database for presentation will ultimately dictate if your application "just works" rather than playing a pivotal part in your application's being a success and delighting your customers. Having responsive and selective queries is therefore a vital part of the overall architecture. Review this set of resources to ensure that your queries are optimal and follow the guidelines for selectivity.

(*continued*)

Table 13-1. (*continued*)

Artifact	GitHub Ref	Description
Selective SOQL Queries	Make SOQL Query Selective	Now we know that selectivity for our queries is the key to having a fast, responsive query set. But what do we really mean by selectivity? Well, it all comes down to using a query that makes appropriate use of the WHERE clause (as well as others) to narrow down the data set returned using index fields. And this is the key to selectivity: using indexed fields in the query and also keeping the number of returned rows within a system-defined threshold.
Large SOQL Queries	Working with Very Large SOQL Queries	In the resources that cover this topic, you will find additional examples that require further consideration when working with very large SOQL queries where the defined heap limit has been reached and you've hit an error.
Search and Query Optimization	Salesforce Query Search Optimization Cheat Sheet	Using this resource, you should be able to quickly understand if your query is selective in nature. This resource will give you all the information you need to understand the thresholds that govern how many records you can return in your data set while maintaining a level of performance. Given what we have already covered in this resource base, having this knowledge and applying its rhetoric to your design will be a huge factor for performance.

Data Movement

In this section of the resource base, the focus is on data– more specifically, the movement of data. You will undoubtedly have many requirements throughout your Salesforce career to either migrate, archive, back up, load, remove, create external data integrations, or perform many other actions that all revolve around the management and security of the data that powers your Salesforce applications.

There are several topics and resources that, as a result of the requirement to control the data flow, we should be aware of, especially when we need to apply our governance method to be successful. For example, loading data into the Salesforce platform should be a relatively simple task, and it is; however, you need to prepare and understand the impact of what loading huge data volumes actually has on your production service. We'll cover this and more in the resources provided in Table 13-2.

Table 13-2. *Data Optimization Resources*

Artifact	GitHub Ref	Description
Data Load Resources	Data Load – Importing Data into Salesforce Choosing a Method for Importing Data	Loading data into Salesforce can be a simple task. But that depends on several factors or characteristics of the data that you are trying to load into Salesforce; for example, the number of records you wish to upload will play a significant part in the decision as to which tool you use. The first thing to consider will be the storage limits of your Salesforce org. Trying to import more data than your storage allocation seems like an obvious point to consider, but it's best that you start with this type of mindset from the start. Then you will need to consider the load order of the records. Which records should you load first? General rule of thumb will dictate that the load order be users then accounts and then opportunities, as an example. You can see the chain of record dependency here that predicates the order. Then you need to look at the tool that you intend to use, a choice largely driven by the number of records that you wish to load. But first, review the resources in this section as they will provide you with the guidance and information you need to get informed.
Data Import Tools	Choosing a Method for Importing Data	One choice you will need to make is the data load tool that is most appropriate for your requirement. The main consideration is the number of records. This resource provides a table that will help you to derive the correct tool to use.

(continued)

Table 13-2. (*continued*)

Artifact	GitHub Ref	Description
Bulk Data Loads	Bulk API 2.0 and Bulk API Developer Guide	With Data Loader you can choose to load your records using the Bulk API. The Bulk API allows you to load your records by creating a job that contains one or more batches. This is a very useful and important tool that you have at your disposal to load very large sets of records. Using Bulk API, you could effectively load up to 150,000,000 records in a 24-hour period. That's specifying 15,000 batches that each have up to 10,000 records. However, there are a number of factors that you will need to consider in order to use the Bulk API effectively. This resource will provide you with all the information you need and serve as a good reference point in the future. For example, one of the common issues with loading data using the Bulk API involves lock contention (also see granular locking). This is where your load fails due to multiple batches' trying to update the same account record at the same time when using Bulk in parallel mode. An issue like this might force you to load the records using serial mode. The downside to this is that it will increase the execution time significantly. Other things to consider are things like how you will bypass any object automations that you have configured—process builders or triggers, for example. These will need to be bypassed for the duration of the data load. If you do not do this, your data load will most certainly fail or will take an inordinate amount of time to execute. So, in review, the number of records, automation bypass, database locking, time of execution, batch size, operational impact, data load plan, and choice of load tool are all examples of what you must consider when thinking about loading data into Salesforce. Something else that is often overlooked is the prospect of data skew, which we consider next.

(*continued*)

Table 13-2. (*continued*)

Artifact	GitHub Ref	Description
Data Skew	Designing Record Access for Enterprise ScaleManaging Lookup Skew	There are three types of data skew that we should be concerned about when either moving or importing data into Salesforce or managing large data volumes As previously discussed, these are account, data ownership, and lookup skew. Data skew can essentially be described as the effect of having 10,000 child records associated with a single parent record. This can cause application performance issues and record locking when performing DML (Data Manipulation Language) actions. Use these resources to learn more about skew, the effect it has on your implementation, and how to avoid falling foul of this silent application performance killer.
Granular Locking — Group Membership Locking	Granular Locking	This has been touched on already (and will be detailed in the Sharing & Visibility chapter), but one thing you need to be aware of is the potential for lock errors. This can occur when two processes are trying to write to the same database table at the same time, causing the write to fail due to the table's being locked by the first process. In Salesforce, this occurs when you are updating the role hierarchy or when making changes to the group membership. Review this resource in order to note the impact of locking and how granular locking helps you to avoid errors.

(*continued*)

Table 13-2. (*continued*)

Artifact	GitHub Ref	Description
Data Backup & Restore	Data Backup	I don't think you need to read this book to understand why you need to protect the data that you store in your Salesforce implementation. It's your data, and this data is what you rely on to provide your customers or your business function a service. You must ask yourself, what would be the impact if suddenly the data that underpins my business function became unavailable? How would we get the data back? To what point in time and how long would it take? These are all common questions that IT organizations have been asking ever since the dawn of the data revolution. But this is cloud—why do I need to worry about backup? While Salesforce will provide you with a platform to propel your business to stratospheric heights, up to now it has not provided you with an automatic data backup service out of the box. Well, this is all about to change. During Summer 2021, Salesforce began the backup and restore services pilot with the product going GA in November 2021. You can still utilize all the AppExchange partner solutions for backup and restore, and there is the option to contact Salesforce support to perform data restoration.

Phase B Standards

As described in the resource base for application architecture, as much as possible we want to ensure that your Salesforce org is self-documented. There are many resources in the Phase A "Standards" section that also apply here for the control and management of data architecture components. So, we must reiterate the importance of documenting the overall data model and object relationships. We also underline the importance of following naming standards to make it easier to identify objects, either by the type or the projects to which they belong. All description fields are required to be completed in line with the description standards that follow.

Aside from loop iterators such as i, j, and k, variable names, object names, class names, and method names should always be descriptive. Single-letter names are not acceptable. Object names should use `CapitalizedCamelCase`. Method or function names should use `lowerCamelCase`. Constants should be `CAPITALIZED_WITH_UNDERSCORES`.

Note   In fact, this is just an example of what is advised in the "Naming Conventions" link in Table 12-1 from the Phase A resource base.

Underscores should not be used for any variable name, object name, class name, or method name except as an application prefix. Overriding standard tabs, objects, and standard names should not be allowed without first seeking approval from your central governance team.

Names must be meaningful. Abbreviated names must be avoided; for example:

Good	Bad
`computeAverage()`	`CompAvg()`
`boolean isError`	`boolean isNoError`

Data Model Definition

When we define our data model, it's best practice to document the model using some form of tool. Remember, your data model describes the data entities, relationships, and associated attributes, and will be reviewed by the governance team in order to understand how the solution data all hangs together.

The data model should provide all the metadata (data about data) for each object that you define. So, for example, the model should be structured in such a way that not only is the object naming clear, but all the related fields are defined, including the type of field and attributes such as type and description. This is what makes a well-defined data model easy to understand; all resources on a project will use it as part of the solution development. There are three models that you potentially will need to create: physical, conceptual, and logical. A conceptual model provides a high-level view of data, the logical model depicts the model with separation from the data's physical storage, and, finally, the physical model shows the lowest level or physical representation of how data is stored in the database. There are many ways that we can provide a physical view of our data model. The most common is to provide a physical diagram that shows the relationships, which is usually accompanied by a spreadsheet or a data dictionary where the low-level descriptive data for each object is defined.

As an example, you could document the Business Contact object for our Bright Sound Guitars business as follows:

Object Label	BSG Business Contact				
Object API	BSG_Business_Contact__c				

Label	API	Type	Reference	Attributes	Description
Business	Business__c	Lookup	Account		Lookup to Account Record
Business Contact Name	Name	Text(80)			Name of Business
Contact	Contact__c	Lookup	Contact		Lookup to Contact Record
Key	Key__c	Text(255)		Unique, Case insensitive	Unique Identifier
First Time User	First_Time_User__c	Checkbox		Boolean	Denotes New Customer Eligibility Status
View Contact	View_Contact__c	Lookup	Contact		Dynamic contact ownership field used to drive sharing

This method of documenting your data model is good practice and will be an important artifact in your project's documentation. Each object in the model should have its own tab, and every field should have as much information as possible defined.

Objects

Remember, objects represent database tables that contain your organization's information. For example, the central object in the Salesforce data model represents accounts–companies and organizations involved with your business, such as customers, partners, and competitors. The term *record* describes a particular occurrence of an object (such as a specific account like IBM or United Airlines that is represented by an Account object). A record is analogous to a row in a database table.

Objects already created for you by Salesforce are called standard objects. Objects you create in your organization are called custom objects. Objects you create that map to data stored outside your organization are called external objects.

Object names will start with a capital letter and may include a prefix, as outlined here:

Enterprise Object

Format	Example
[ObjectName]__c	If your company manufactured guitars, you may want a customer object called Guitar__c.

Project Object

Format	Example
[BusinessArea] [Project]_ [ObjectName]__c	If your company has a business area called Sales and Marketing, and they have a project to develop a custom configuration on the Salesforce platform called Accelerate, your custom object might be called SMACC_Guitar__c where SM refers to "Sales and Marketing," while ACC refers to the project "Accelerate."

[Project] is mandatory and must be populated, [BusinessArea] is optional and only needs populating if not limited to a single business area.

Note   The transition of a project object to an enterprise object must go through the central governance team given the potential impact on existing reports, sharing, workflows, and triggers, etc. Promotion of a project object to an enterprise object **WILL** require effort.

Fields

Capture your unique business data by storing it in custom fields. When you create a custom field, you configure where you want it to appear and optionally control security at the field level.

Custom field names should have words delimited by an underscore. Whole words should be used, and the use of acronyms and abbreviations should be avoided. The API field name must meet the following convention:

Enterprise Fields (Global, Reusable)

Format	Example
`[FieldName]__c`	If a new field was created to define a Customer's Secondary Email Address, the example would look like `Secondary_Email_Address__c`

Project-Specific Fields

Format	Example
`[BusinessArea][Project]_[FieldName]__c`	A project specific field could look as follows, `SMACC_Secondary_Email_Address__c`

Note   `[Project]` is optional and only needs populating if not generic across all business areas.

Custom Settings

Custom settings are similar to custom objects in that they let you customize org data. Unlike custom objects, which have records based on them, custom settings let you utilize custom data sets across your org. Custom settings also let you distinguish a particular set of users or profiles based on custom criteria.

Format	Example
[BusinessArea][Project]_CustomSetting	For example, SM_ACC_Billing_Data__c

Checklists

The phase checklist simply tracks that each step and sub-step within the phase is governed correctly and completely. Each sub-step may have several subject areas to form complete coverage from a governance perspective.

Governance Step	
Govern Design & Optimization	**Pass / Fail**
Govern the solution for optimal performance, scalability, usability, and maintenance	
Govern the appropriate use of declarative and programmatic functionality used	
Govern the considerations for a single org or dedicated org strategy	
Govern the usage of license types (capabilities and constraints)	
Govern the data modeling concepts and implications of database design	
Govern the usage of reports and analytics (platform considerations and trade-offs)	
Govern the usage of external applications (Salesforce AppExchange and Application Integration)	
Data Movement	**Pass/Fail**
Govern the usage of the platform's internationalization functionality (multiple currencies, translations, and languages)	
Govern the use of visual workflow, taking into account the limitations and considerations of a visual workflow solution	
Govern the capabilities and limitations of Salesforce actions	
Govern the integration with social capabilities of the platform	

CHAPTER 14

Identity & Access Management (Phase C) Resource Base

This chapter contains the resources required to govern Phase C of the Salesforce Platform Governance Method. If you've been reading this book and using these resources, you'll know that although we have tried to cover all the major areas relating to this topic, you should always do additional research into the subject matter. The areas covered in this resource base have been meticulously chosen to reflect the method, set you up for success, and help you to govern your project implementation.

Tip You do not need to use this resource base as a strict method or process. The idea is that this will give you a good indication of what you should be taking into consideration. The expectation is that you will use this as a guide and then build upon it as you navigate the Salesforce ecosystem.

Guidelines and Best Practices

This section contains the guidance and best practices that are available from Salesforce, as well as other resources that we have determined will be valuable. This section should serve to provide a good set of guidelines that can be reviewed by anyone delivering the governance function within your organization.

We know there is an infinite number of resources available on the Web, and although some are better than others, this resource base will provide you with a good selection of

© Lee Harding and Lee Bayliss 2022
L. Harding and L. Bayliss, *Salesforce Platform Governance Method*,
https://doi.org/10.1007/978-1-4842-7404-0_14

resources that we recommend you review. As per all the resource base documentation in this book, giving you the complete technical definition for every aspect of identity and access management is not the objective; if we did, the book would be as thick as a medieval wall, which if you didn't know could be up to five meters thick. The resource base is divided into two main sections: the resources themselves and then related standards, and finally there is a supporting checklist.

As is the case with all the resource base chapters in this book, the links to the resources will be managed in the Salesforce Platform Governance Method GitHub account. The URL for this account is as follows: `github.com/salesforceplatformgovernancemethod`.

Salesforce Identity & Single Sign-On (SSO)

Given that you have arrived at the resource base, we must assume that you have been reading the content in the governance method described in Chapter 4, "Identity & Access Management," and to get you on the right track we have provided Table 14-1 to provide resource links to the content that's discussed.

Table 14-1. *Single Sign-On Resources*

Artifact	GitHub Ref	Description
Salesforce Identity Implementation Guide	Identity Implementation Guide	This resource is where you should focus your initial attention. It answers the questions relating to what identity is and how Salesforce natively provides support for access to resources via SSO. Whether Salesforce is the IdP (Identity Provider) or your solution opts for an external IdP, this resource explains all the key concepts to consider.
Single Sign-On Reference	Single Sign-On	Review this resource to understand more about the SSO use cases and related terminology for SAML and OpenID Connect–based SSO implementations and FAQs. There is a lot to learn regarding this topic, but these resources are well written and explain the concepts extremely well.

(continued)

Table 14-1. (*continued*)

Artifact	GitHub Ref	Description
Understanding More about Authentication	Understanding Authentication	Use this resource to learn more about how you can use the OAuth protocol to access resources without having to expose user access credentials. Salesforce supports numerous authentication flows, some of which are described here.
SSO Strategy	Choosing an SSO Strategy – SAML vs. OAuth2	This resource covers the basic principles of both SAML and OAuth. The basic flows are described, and the attributes of both options are discussed in detail. To provide a user with a single sign-on experience, a developer needs to implement an SSO solution, but which one? This resource helps to provide some guidance as well as a comparison between SAML and OAuth2.
Connected Apps	Connected App	A connected app is used to enable access to your Salesforce application—either API access or by using numerous protocols, such as SAML, OAuth, and OpenID Connect. Review this resource to understand the part a connected app plays and how you can use this platform feature to drive authentication to Salesforce resources.
Learning Connected Apps with Trailhead	Connected App Trailhead Resources	For additional learning for connected apps, review this Trailhead learning resource. This will provide a good overview of how external applications can integrate with your Salesforce application.

(*continued*)

Table 14-1. (*continued*)

Artifact	GitHub Ref	Description
SSO with SAML	SAML SSO Covers IDP and Service Provider Enablement	SAML (Security Assertion Markup Language) is an open authentication standard that allows IdPs and service providers to securely exchange user information to enable user authentication. This resource explains how you can use SAML in your SSO solution and how to configure it, with example flows. Here you will find resources that cover SAML as the service provider and as the identity provider. In addition, with SAML you can add support for JIT (Just-In-Time) user provisioning, and this resource covers how to achieve this in your solution.
Using OpenID Connect	Configure an Auth Provider using OpenID Connect	You may want to use a third-party authentication provider that uses OpenID Connect. Once authenticated to Salesforce, users are authorized to access Salesforce-protected resources. If this is your use case, then this resource will provide useful insights on how this can be achieved.
OAuth Tokens and Scopes	OAuth Tokens and Scopes in Detail	If you intend to use OAuth as part of your authorization flow, you need to get familiar with all the terminology and token definitions used in this resource, how they are used, and what information they must contain. Additionally, this resource defines the OAuth scopes or Salesforce API resources that your application is authorized to access.

(*continued*)

Table 14-1. (*continued*)

Artifact	GitHub Ref	Description
OAuth Flows	OAuth Authorization Flows	If you decide to use OAuth and OpenID Connect as part of your identity solution, there are several different flows that will need to be considered. This resource details each one that could be applicable to your use case. Whether your app is a Web app, mobile app, or a server-to-server integration, all the applicable auth flows are detailed. For server-to-server integration, for example, you will need to create a JSON Web Token (JWT) that's supplied from one server to another and signed with a trusted certificate. This enables access to a resource without interactively logging in.
Salesforce Authentication Provider	Configure a Salesforce Authentication Provider	This resource covers the requirement to add a Salesforce authentication provider, which allows users to login to an external web application using their Salesforce credentials.
SSO FAQs	Single Sign-On FAQs	Review the Salesforce SSO FAQs page for some best practice tips that may prove to be useful as part of your solution design. Things like MFA adoption, testing SSO, and login configuration are all covered in this resource.
Coding SSO Securely	SSO Secure Coding	If you are a developer, this wiki resource is a must read that will inform on techniques used to protect a user's session ID (SID, the authentication token that's akin to a username and password). This resource describes the vulnerability and provides the reader with a set of instructions on how to test and validate if your application is vulnerable.

(*continued*)

Table 14-1. (*continued*)

Artifact	GitHub Ref	Description
Identity Training with Trailhead	Identity Trailhead Learning Resource	This Trailmix provides you with a good overview of Salesforce identity and how to use this feature to give users access to resources. Here you will find learning resources for Salesforce Identity Connect, My Domain, identity for mobile, and user authentication.
Salesforce My Domain	My Domain	This resource introduces the My Domain feature in Salesforce. My Domain is a feature that allows you to create a subdomain for your Salesforce org, which is essential if you want a URL that reflects your company name. It's also essential to consider this feature in your design as many Salesforce features depend on this being configured. Plus, with My Domain you can take advantage of branding your login experience, set up authentication providers such as Google or Facebook, and enable custom login policies that determine how users are authenticated. You will need My Domain if you intend to use SSO, so this really cannot be overlooked.
App Launcher	Configure and Use the App Launcher	The Salesforce App Launcher is what your users will use to switch between applications in your Salesforce environment. This feature is available to all Lightning users by default. However, if your Salesforce environment is on the classic-based UI, then there are some additional things you will need to consider as part of your application design. This resource provides details on how to configure the App Launcher feature for your users.

(continued)

Table 14-1. (*continued*)

Artifact	GitHub Ref	Description
SSO for Mobile Apps	Set up SSO and Access for Mobile Apps	This resource covers the configuration required for setting up your mobile applications to work with SSO. This resource section also demonstrates how SSO is integrated with mobile applications with Salesforce identity.
Login Flows	Salesforce Custom Login Flows	As part of your solution, you may want to direct your users through a login process that's used to capture end user information or to conduct additional security checks before access to a resource is granted. A good use case for this could be to apply a custom MFA-based solution using TOTP (Time-based One-Time Password). Another example could be to fulfill a requirement for new users to accept service terms and conditions before system access is provided. Use this resource for examples of login flows and how to implement them.
Multi-factor Authentication	MFA	By now, two-factor authentication, or 2FA, should be widely understood as this is commonplace in most organizations. This is based on a principal of your providing two pieces of information in order to complete the login process, namely something you have and something you know. MFA takes this one step further in that you can increase the number of factors required in the login process to be more than two if required. This resource details what you can achieve with Salesforce; be aware that from February 2022 MFA will become a platform requirement.

So, how important is identity and access management to the success of your project? The answer to this is quite simple: extremely. This is how you, as the custodian of the keys to your castle (sticking with the medieval theme), define the solution pattern your users and your customers will use to access the application resources. We're talking specifically about authentication and authorization. In this section we cover the concept of authentication services, SSO (or single sign-on), and other important identity-based services that you will need to know to successfully build and expose your application to your customer base. So, what is identity management in the context of Salesforce? Identity defines how we manage the users in the Salesforce org and how those users connect to the resources and services available to or exposed by an application. SSO is essentially the technology solution that enables users to gain access to the application using a set of credentials that are trusted across multiple services.

The good news is that Salesforce supports SSO natively, and there is a plethora of resources available to you to ensure that you get this designed correctly while adhering to your company's security standards and policies. SSO provides a convenient authentication model that should be secure, protect your resources, and enable access to your applications and systems where the user is privileged to do so. When designing your application, the auth requirements should be your guide for how the solution needs to be architected. Understanding how Salesforce offers authentication and authorization services will be key to the success of the project. Review the following resources to help guide you through these technologies and understand how the various elements work together.

Phase C Standards

For this chapter, the main message is to consider how you document or define your authentication solution. It might seem obvious, but as part of your governance process, you will be in constant review meetings with various stakeholders going over how the auth process will support the requirements for the project, and there will be many iterations of design that will undoubtedly be discussed.

So how can we make the process of reviewing the approach for auth easier to describe, not just for the internal teams, but also for any third-party provider that has a vested interest. For example, you may be working with an external IdP using OAuth 2.0 and OpenID Connect. In this scenario, you will need to have a clearly defined requirements document that describes exactly how the data interaction will flow from one element to another. One option that we would recommend for bringing your authenticating flow to life is to use a sequence diagram.

A sequence diagram is a great way to model the logic flow of a business process or to illustrate how objects or solution elements interact with each other for a specific use case. In the context of the authentication flow, a sequence diagram is a powerful way to illustrate all the actors in the process and highlight all the interactions and ultimately where certain responsibilities lie. If you use a sequence diagram, there are plenty of tools on the Web that use the UML (Unified Modeling Language), which can be used to easily model your process logic.

See Figure 14-1 for an example of how a sequence diagram can be used to describe a process, the actors (browser and Salesforce, in this example), and where the steps in the process are executed.

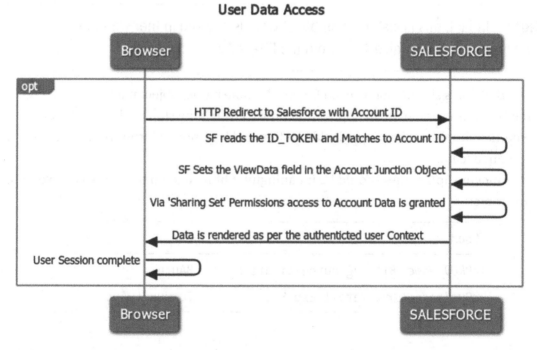

Figure 14-1. *Sequence diagram example*

In this example, the browser is passing an account ID to Salesforce within an ID token. Salesforce then matches the account ID value to an account in Salesforce and sets a field value that controls whether data can be accessed by an external user. We know that the user in this context is accessing the records via an experience site, as access is granted via a sharing set. Sharing sets are a special sharing mechanism that can be used in Salesforce to grant access to records for external users. Of course, this just an example, but you can see the value of using sequence diagrams as all the steps are clearly defined.

Other standards to consider are the naming standards used in your connected apps. It's good practice to use names that make it easy to identify the application and project that the connected app is related to. There will be apps in your app manager that are created as part of a managed package, but for applications that are created internally by a project, the connected app name must first be unique in the org, contain the namespace of the project, and be descriptive enough to be clear what the connected app is for. The description field should always be used and give a full description of the connected app's intended use.

Other naming considerations are as follows. Single-letter names are not acceptable. App names should use CapitalizedCamelCase.

Note   In fact, this is just an example of what is advised in the "Naming Conventions" link in Table 12-1 from the Phase A resource base.

Underscores should not be used for any variable name, object name, class name, or method name except as an application prefix. Overriding standard tabs, objects, and names should not be allowed without first seeking approval from your central governance team.

Connected app names should be meaningful. Abbreviated names must be avoided, for example:

Good	Bad
<PROJ_Name> Billing Authentication	BAuth
<Business_Line> Retail Exp Site	CommunityApp

Checklists

The phase checklist simply tracks that each step and sub-step within the phase is governed correctly and completely. Each sub-step may have several subject areas to form complete coverage from a governance perspective.

Governance Step	
Single Sign-On	**Pass / Fail**
Govern that the correct SSO components have been used in the overall application (OAuth, connected app)	
Govern SSO configuration and components (SAML configuration, MyDomain, Scope Parameter Values, OpenID)	
Govern any App Launcher changes	
Govern mobile SSO requests	
Govern OAuth integrating to an external platform	
Govern SAML integrating to an external platform	
Govern any multi-factor authentication requirements	
Identity Management	**Pass/Fail**
Govern any customizations of user authentication (login flows)	
Govern any changes to user provisioning, syncing, and de-provisioning	

CHAPTER 15

Sharing & Visibility (Phase D) Resource Base

This chapter contains the resources required to govern Phase D of the Salesforce Platform Governance Method. The approach we have taken is to assemble the most relevant resources that align with the corresponding governance method. Since you've been working through the book and using these resources, you'll know that although we have tried to cover all the major areas relating to this topic, completing your own research in addition to examining the resources we have provided will really set you up for success.

Tip   You do not need to use this resource base as a strict method or process. The idea is that this will give you a good indication of what you should be taking into consideration. The expectation is that you will use this as a guide and then build upon it as you navigate the Salesforce ecosystem.

Guidelines and Best Practices

This section contains guidance and best practices available from Salesforce, as well as other resources that we have determined will be valuable. This section should serve to provide a good set of guidelines that can be reviewed by anyone delivering the governance function within your organization.

We know there is an infinite number of resources available on the Web, and although some are better than others, this resource base will provide you with a good selection of resources that we recommend you review. As per all the resource base documentation in this book, providing the complete technical definition for every aspect of sharing

© Lee Harding and Lee Bayliss 2022
L. Harding and L. Bayliss, *Salesforce Platform Governance Method*,
https://doi.org/10.1007/978-1-4842-7404-0_15

and visibility is not the objective; if it were, I think we could devote the entire book to this topic alone. The resource base is divided into two main sections: the resources themselves and related standards, and finally the supporting governance checklist.

As is the case with all the resource base chapters in this book, the links to the resources will be managed in the Salesforce Platform Governance Method GitHub account. The URL for this account is as follows: `github.com/salesforceplatformgovernancemethod`.

Sharing & Visibility

Given that you have arrived at the resource base, we must assume that you have been reading the content in the governance method described in Chapter 5, "Sharing & Visibility." To get you on the right track, we have offered Table 15-1 to provide resource links to the content that's discussed.

I think it's fair to say that the importance of how we secure our data cannot be understated in any context. Data is at the center of everything we do. If we cannot secure our data appropriately, then the ramifications for our business could be catastrophic. As a business, we have a duty of care for our customers to ensure that business data is secured and only shared with those that need to access it. In Chapter 5, the concept of least privilege was discussed; this is a security principle that all CISOs (Chief Information Security Officer) and security organizations within an enterprise will be expecting to be implemented as standard policy. This ensures that data is only shared when there is a specific requirement to do so and with specific resources, be it user (internal or external), other business processes, systems, or tools.

Tip   Internal users are the users within your organization who consume a Salesforce license and log in directly to the Salesforce platform. External users are the Experience Cloud customer users or users who do not log in directly to the platform.

The Salesforce sharing model has been specifically designed to give you a flexible and robust framework via which to share platform data. Org-wide defaults, role hierarchy, implicit sharing, manual sharing, programmatic sharing, field-level sharing, teams, profiles, permission sets, sharing rules, and sharing sets are all sharing methods you can use within the Salesforce platform to share records with your users. However, you must be sure that you are applying the correct sharing method and ensure that you are not inadvertently sharing a record with users to whom you did not intend to give access. In this case you need to be aware of the relationship types you opt for in your data model, as this could impact how records are shared. For example, where you have a master–detail relationship, detail records will always inherit the security settings and permissions from their parent. Therefore, if you share the master record, the detail or child records will also be shared.

In all scenarios, it's best practice to plan your sharing model carefully. Decisions you make on how to share and give access to your Salesforce resources must be carefully considered, as you want to make sure that the sharing choices made will enable business success not just for your initial implementation, but also for future data access. The resources discussed here will help you on this journey. Reviewing all the available sharing methods and having a good understanding of the types of sharing available, along with sharing use cases, will set you on the right track and should also help to make the governance process far simpler. Being able to explain why a specific sharing method is used over another will be a crucial aspect of the governance and sign-off process that you will need to present to the governance control board.

Declarative Sharing Resources

In Salesforce the term *declarative* is used to define the notion that we can build powerful applications without writing a single line of code. Rather, we use the platform's user interface to build the apps and define our metadata as required. In the context of record access, there are many resources that give us the ability to share records with users using the declarative capability of the platform. This part of the resource base covers many of these features, many of which you will certainly be using to provide access to business data.

Table 15-1. *Sharing & Visibility – Declarative Resources*

Artifact	GitHub Ref	Description
Salesforce Security Guide	Salesforce Security Guide	This is the definitive guide to the Salesforce platform security. This guide covers the basics of Salesforce security, from health check, authentication, data access and sharing to shield encryption and real-time monitoring.
A Guide to Sharing Architecture	Salesforce Sharing Architecture	For lighter reading, you may wish to review the Salesforce resource titled "A Guide to Sharing Architecture." This guide provides all the concepts of sharing in a more concise package.
Control Who Sees What	Who Sees What	If you are new to the subject of Salesforce security, we recommend this resource, as it provides a good overview of the various sharing methods available in Salesforce. Additionally, the video series for Who Sees provides a demonstrative aspect of how the basics of Salesforce sharing works.
Who Can See My File?	Who Can See My File	There are different ways that files can be shared in Salesforce: private to you, privately shared, or visible to your entire company. This resource helps you to learn how to identify file-sharing settings and how to change them.
Organization-Wide Sharing Defaults	Org-Wide Defaults	In Salesforce in Setup / Sharing Settings, you will find the org-wide defaults. This provides you with the default security definition for your org. Essentially, the OWDs (org-wide defaults) define the level of access that the users in your org have to each other's data. It is important to set the most restrictive security here. Then use the sharing methods to open access to data as per the data access requirements for your business.

(continued)

Table 15-1. (*continued*)

Artifact	GitHub Ref	Description
Profiles	User Profiles	In Salesforce we assign users to profiles; in fact we have to. When you create a new user, you must also assign a profile. Profiles are used to control how users access objects. We also use profiles to manage several different facets of access that define what users can do in applications. This resource will give you a deeper understanding of how profiles are used to control what users can do and also how they are used to control the user's environment: password policies, IP login hours, field-level security, and access to page layouts, to name a few.
Permission Sets	Permission Sets	Permission sets are used as an extension to profiles. Remember that users can only be assigned to a single profile. With permission sets you can extend the access configuration and assign the permission set to a group of users. Additionally, you can assign multiple permission sets to a user, giving you a very flexible way to provide additional access. There are also several different types of permission sets, so depending on your requirement, a specific permission set may be more suitable than another.
Developers Blog: Behind the Scenes of Record Ownership in Salesforce	Record Ownership	For a detailed and comprehensive view on how record ownership works within the Salesforce platform, review this resource. Here the record sharing architecture is described in enough detail to be easily understood. It also describes the process or sequence of events that occurs when a record is accessed.

(*continued*)

Table 15-1. (*continued*)

Artifact	GitHub Ref	Description
Custom Permissions	Custom Permissions	In Salesforce, you may have a special use case where you have to assign a permission to a user in support of your business process or app that is custom in nature. In other words, your requirement cannot be achieved with standard permission built-in options. Review this resource to learn more about custom permissions and how they can be used.
Manual Sharing	Manual Sharing	Manual sharing is really what it sounds like. With manual sharing a user can share a record that they own, or a user can share a record where the user sharing is higher in the role hierarchy than the owner of the record. This method satisfies a sharing requirement that is ad hoc, or when a user wishes to share a specific record.
Controlling Access Using Hierarchies	Role Hierarchy	In Salesforce you can control access to records using hierarchies that apply to roles. Using this method, you can provide users access to records that they do not own. Essentially, the configuration "Grant Access Using Hierarchies" will grant access to records owned by all subordinates in the hierarchy. This resource explains how hierarchies work, how to set them up, and how to use them successfully.
Developers Blog: Locking Down Record Access in Salesforce	Locking Down Record Access in Salesforce	Following on from the previous resource, this resource provides further context on the sharing configuration "Grant Access Using Hierarchies."

(*continued*)

Table 15-1. (*continued*)

Artifact	GitHub Ref	Description
Team Resources	Salesforce Teams	Salesforce provides you the ability to organize users that work together on a sales opportunity, account record or case record. As a record owner, you can assemble a team that can work collaboratively on specific records. This resource covers each use case and the associated considerations that you should review. For example, you can use opportunity teams, where users work together and mange how revenue credit is shared among the team members using opportunity splits.
Queue Resource	Salesforce Queues	In Salesforce, every record must be owned by either a user or a queue. With queues, you can organize work into a manageable distribution to users who are members of the queue. As an example, you may wish to set up queues as part of an omni-channel configuration to manage how case records are distributed in a service support team.
Sharing Records with Manager Groups	Manager Groups	Manager groups allow you to control how you share records with managers in the management chain in the role hierarchy. You may only want specific managers to be able to see your record instead of the default.
Enhanced Folder Sharing for Reports and Dashboards	Enhanced Folder Sharing	If you have a requirement to have more granular sharing options for reports and dashboards, then enable this feature. Review this resource to understand the differences between legacy and enhanced sharing and to learn what happens when enabled. There are also some practical examples of how enhanced folder sharing works.

(*continued*)

Table 15-1. (*continued*)

Artifact	GitHub Ref	Description
Implicit Sharing	Implicit Sharing	When we refer to implicit sharing, we are referring to sharing behaviors that are built into the platform and require no additional configuration by your awesome admins. For example, if you have access to a parent account record, then you will also by default have access to the account's child records, such as cases or opportunities. Use these resources to understand how implicit sharing works and the associated implications for parent–child data skew, as an example.
Object Relationships Overview	Salesforce Object Relationships and Sharing	In Salesforce, there are several relationship types that can be configured to control how objects relate to each other. Master–detail, lookup, and many-to-many are all examples of how you can model relationships in the platform. Using these resources will serve to reaffirm your understanding of the sharing behavior when considering the object relationship you have configured.
Viewing Which Users Have Access to Your Records in Lightning Experience	Sharing Hierarchy	Since the Summer 2021 release there is a new feature that you can use to easily view which users have access to your records and, more important, why. For accounts, opportunities, cases, contacts, and custom objects, you now have a new menu option in the record's list view action menu to view "Sharing Hierarchy" details. What's great about this is that you can also see the reason why the record was shared, the relationship, and the level of access.

(continued)

Table 15-1. (*continued*)

Artifact	GitHub Ref	Description
Set Up Sharing Sets	Sharing Sets	With sharing sets you can share any record with your Experience site users where the account or contact matches that of the user or via an access mapping defined in a sharing set. Access mappings support indirect lookups from the end user and target record to the account or contact object. Sharing sets provide a useful way to share records without exposing records that you do not intend to share. This resource covers this feature in detail.
Use Share Groups to Share Records Owned by High-Volume Experience Cloud Site Users	Sharing Groups	Use sharing groups to share records that are owned by your high-volume Experience site users with authenticated internal and external users. Use this resource to learn more about sharing groups and how to set them up.
Super User Access	Super User Access	With Experience sites, you may want to provide elevated access to your partner users. When you grant super user access, you give the partner user permission to view other users' data as long as they have the same role (or higher) in the partner role hierarchy. This level of access does not respect sharing rules or org-wide defaults. Review this resource to learn more about super user access and how it could be used to open record access for your partner users.

(*continued*)

Table 15-1. (*continued*)

Artifact	GitHub Ref	Description
Configure an External Account Hierarchy	External Account Hierarchy	Following on from the previous resource, with partner or customer Experience sites you can create an external account hierarchy that gives you similar functionality to role hierarchies, but for your external users. (You need the correct licenses!) There are some limitations for this sharing feature, and this resource covers them in detail. Review this resource if you are planning to use this feature to share records with external users. There is also a Trailhead that's an excellent resource as you build the functionality in a safe environment.
Role and Territory Sharing Groups	Territory Management	First, you need to understand what territories are in the context of Salesforce. Simply put, we use sales territories to define how sales teams manage their accounts (and related contacts and opportunities) across our business or business regions, for example. When we configure territories, we can use them to control how access to these objects is set for users in the territory. Review this resource to learn more about how this works.

Programmatic Sharing

In addition to declarative sharing methods, there is also the more complex programmatic sharing, or Apex (the platform's programming language). As part of your code, in Apex, you can define access to records and ensure that sharing rules are honored based on users' access to records in the class definition. Table 15-2 provides you with a set of resources that will help ensure that you do not inadvertently expose records to users if you need to programmatically control sharing or access to Salesforce data using Apex.

Table 15-2. *Sharing & Visibility – Programmatic Sharing Resources*

Artifact	GitHub Ref	Description
Apex Developer Guide: Apex Security and Sharing	Apex Security and Sharing	All the security resources are included in this guide. If you are looking to review the entire section, then start here. Even if you are not a developer, it's good practice to be aware of the sharing capability as when it comes to governance and reviewing whether the development function has adhered to best practice, this guide will give you the understanding you need to question if your code is using these security features.
Enforcing Sharing Rules	Apex Sharing – Enforcing Sharing Rules	This resource covers the implications of using "with sharing" and "without sharing" in your Apex classes to define security. Apex will by default have full access to the Salesforce database unless the security context is specified in the declaration. From a governance perspective, you do not want to expose data to a user that they do not and should not have access to. This resource explains the differences and security implications.
Enforcing Object and Field Permissions	Apex Sharing – Enforce Object and Field Permissions	This resource is a must read as it explains how DML (Data Manipulation Language) actions (those associated with creating, updating, and deleting database records) can be incorporated with security checks. Basically, the DML action will not execute if the user does not have the required permission to make the change. This resource explains how this can be achieved by calling the sObject describe result methods.

(continued)

313

Table 15-2. (*continued*)

Artifact	GitHub Ref	Description
Enforce Security With the StripInaccessible Method / Filter SOQL Queries Using WITH SECURITY_ ENFORCED	Apex Sharing – SOQL Data Filtering	These resources delve further into the security features available to developers in Apex to enforce security on the platform. In this resource, stripInaccessible and WITH SECURITY_ENFORCED are explained with practical examples of how they are used to enforce the sharing rules for users of the platform.
Class Security	Apex Sharing – Class Security	Depending on your use case, it may be appropriate to control which users can execute Apex classes. This resource explains how to configure this using either profiles or permission sets.
Understanding Apex Managed Sharing	Apex Sharing – Apex Managed Sharing	This resource covers Apex managed sharing. At this point, we probably have a good grasp of the declarative sharing capabilities of the platform. But how this works in the context of code is an important part of the sharing model in Salesforce. This resource covers sharing broadly, how to share a record in Apex, and considerations for recalculating Apex managed sharing.

Sharing & Performance Impacts

As we have discussed in the method, making changes to the sharing model can dramatically impact the performance of the platform. For example, when you make a large number of changes to the Account object, such as activating all your Person Accounts as Partner Accounts and change the portal account ownership, or when making many changes to groups or sharing rules, it can slow things down as the platform attempts to recalculate the sharing model. So, if you know you are going to be making these types of changes to your org, there are some things you can do to speed up the change activity and ensure that your operations complete within your change window and do not impact business operations. The resources in Table 15-3 cover this topic in more detail.

Table 15-3. *Sharing & Visibility – Performance Sharing Resources*

Artifact	GitHub Ref	Description
Defer Sharing Calculations	Defer Sharing Calculations	When performing many configuration changes to groups, account ownership / reparenting, or any change that involves changing users' access rights, sharing recalculations will be inevitable. You can, however, defer sharing calculations. This means temporarily disabling sharing calculations until a more convenient time. Normally this would be when the sharing operation or change being performed is completed. Re-enabling sharing calculations will then process all the updates in the background until complete.
Speed Up Recalculation of Sharing Rules	Sharing rule Recalculation	Aside from deferring sharing calculations, if you run into problems with the impact that sharing recalculation poses then you can look at the other options that are available to you that may help to lessen the effect of changes on your org. You can either opt to manually run the recalculation process via the setup interface, or have asynchronous parallel recalculation switched on for your org. This option runs the recalculation process in the background, and you can track progress via the Background Jobs interface in Setup.

Data Security

This final part of the Sharing and Visibility resource base refers to any data security requirements that cover data encryption requirements. See Table 15-4.

Table 15-4. *Sharing & Visibility – Data Security Resources*

Artifact	GitHub Ref	Description
Strengthen Your Data's Security with Shield Platform Encryption	Shield Platform Encryption	Data encryption is a business and, in some cases, regulatory imperative in today's enterprise environment. Modern business operational standards demand that any user's private data that is stored in a remote platform, be it cloud hosted or on-premises, should always be securely stored and therefore not be susceptible to unauthorized access. In addition, data should be encrypted wherever possible during transit and at rest. The Salesforce solution for encrypting data at rest is Shield Platform Encryption. There is a classic-based alternative, but this resource covers platform encryption in its entirety.
Classic vs. Platform Encryption	Encryption Types – Classic vs. Platform Encryption	Salesforce Platform Encryption is a feature add-on product and therefore requires an additional license. Classic encryption is an option but does not provide the same level of functionality. This resource provides the information required to understand the differences between the two encryption methods on offer from the Salesforce platform.

Phase D Standards

As we have read, in this chapter the main message is how to use the platform to secure business and user data. This is an important part of your architecture and solution design. Security breeds consumer trust, and trust will enable your business to grow and therefore increase your customer base. Exposing users' data inappropriately or not securing data sufficiently could have a detrimental impact to user adoption of your services, and ultimately you'll see your market share diminish over time. Therefore, the importance of data security cannot be understated in any capacity.

In support of the governance process, you may need to find simpler ways to show the sharing model for your application than showing your team the platform interface itself. Depending on the audience, a simple spreadsheet that defines the sharing (CRUD) assigned to a profile / permission set for each object should be sufficient way to convey how permissions have been applied. Similarly, it's good practice to document the role hierarchy in the same way.

Other standards to consider are the naming standards used for your permission sets, groups, and roles. It's good practice to use names that make it easy to identify the application and project to which the sharing element is related. In addition to documenting the sharing model as described, making sure that any additional custom security you enable is named appropriately will help other admins find and understand what the security group or permission set is for. The description field should always be used and give a full description detailing what the permission set or group is intended for.

Other naming considerations are as follows: single-letter names are not acceptable; app names should use `CapitalizedCamelCase`.

Note   In fact, this is just an example of what is advised in the "Naming Conventions" link in Table 12-1 from the Phase A resource base.

Underscores should not be used for any variable name, object name, class name, or method name except as an application prefix. Overriding standard tabs for object and standard names should not be allowed without first seeking approval from your central governance team.

Security configuration names should be meaningful. Abbreviated names must be avoided; for example:

Good	Bad
Permission Sets `<PROJ_Name>` Or `<PROFILE_NAME>` `<Purpose>` Example: Standard User Access to `<Custom Object>`	UserAccess
Group `<Business_Process>` Retail User Group	Grp1

Checklists

The phase checklist simply tracks that each step and sub-step within the phase is governed correctly and completely. Each sub-step may have several subject areas to form complete coverage from a governance perspective.

Governance Step	
Declarative Sharing	**Pass / Fail**
Govern the core declarative platform features that are used to meet record-level, object, and field sharing requirements	
Govern the use of team functionality to meet business requirements	
Govern list view, report folder, and dashboard folder security	
Govern implicit sharing within the platform	
Govern the appropriate sharing design for the various community user types	
Govern the application of territory management	
Programmatic Sharing	**Pass/Fail**
Govern the core programmatic platform security features that have been used to meet sharing requirements	
Govern the security risks in programmatic customizations relative to data visibility; focus on difference in capabilities between programmatic sharing for standard vs. custom objects	
Performance	**Pass/Fail**
Govern that the solution is scalable and maintainable to enterprise levels	
Data Security	**Pass/Fail**
Govern any specific secured data implementation on the Salesforce platform	

CHAPTER 16

Integration (Phase E) Resource Base

This chapter contains the resources required to govern Phase E of the Salesforce Platform Governance Method. As per all phases in this resource guide, the approach we have taken is to assemble the most relevant resources that align with the corresponding governance method. Since you've been working through the book and using these resources, you'll know that although we have tried to cover all the major areas relating to this topic, completing your own research in addition to the resources we have provided will really set you up for success.

Tip   You do not need to use this resource base as a strict method or process. The idea is that this will give you a good indication of what you should be taking into consideration. The expectation is that you will use this as a guide and then build upon it as you navigate the Salesforce ecosystem.

Guidelines and Best Practices

This section contains the guidance and best practices that are available from Salesforce, as well as other resources that we have determined will be valuable. This section should serve to provide a good set of guidelines that can be reviewed by anyone delivering the governance function within your organization.

We know there is an infinite number of resources available on the Web, and although some are better than others, this resource base will provide you with a good selection of resources that we recommend you review. As per all the resource base documentation in this book, providing the complete technical definition of every aspect of Salesforce

© Lee Harding and Lee Bayliss 2022
L. Harding and L. Bayliss, *Salesforce Platform Governance Method*,
https://doi.org/10.1007/978-1-4842-7404-0_16

integration is not the objective; if it were, I doubt the book would ever be complete due to the complexity and breadth of this topic. The resource base is divided into three main sections: the resources themselves, related standards, and finally the supporting governance checklist.

As is the case with all the resource base chapters in this book, the links to the resources will be managed in the Salesforce Platform Governance Method GitHub account. The URL for this account is as follows: `github.com/salesforceplatformgovernancemethod`.

Salesforce Integration

Given that you have arrived at the integration resource base, we must assume that you have been reading the content in Chapter 6, "Integration." To get you going, we have provided a table of resources to help guide you in relation to the content covered in the method.

More than ever, we find the requirement to blend data from one or many systems in support of our applications a business imperative. As the Salesforce platform builds its prevalence in the marketplace, awesome admins across the entire ecosystem are finding new and innovative ways to utilize the power of the Salesforce platform to bring disparate data systems together. It should therefore be of little surprise that Salesforce integration is yet another critical part of your Salesforce implementation. Integrating business data is key to building applications that can revolutionize the way we do business both internally and externally for our customers. Whether it's enriching Salesforce data with external data or the other way round, there are many different use cases that drive how and why system integration is a key part of our architecture. For example, we've already discussed the use case where we integrate with external data sources, but Salesforce is very flexible and supports a broad scope of integration possibilities. But let's think differently about integration and consider telephony integration with Open CTI or, more recently, Service Cloud Voice with AWS. The latter of these two examples is a very powerful integration solution that utilizes the power of AWS Connect to bring relevant call data (IVR data, call transcription, and voice recording, to name a few) into Salesforce in real-time to enhance the end-user experience. This applies the power of the platform, Einstein's next best actions, Salesforce knowledge, and your service center experience for the user, which together results in the service your customers experience being completely transformed.

However, integration doesn't have to be as complex as SCV; it could also be a process defined to load data into Salesforce via data loader. This is also a valid example of integration on the Salesforce platform.

Regardless of your use case, the point here is that having the capability to integrate with other systems will undoubtedly enable your business to develop and grow significantly. This does not come without many considerations and risks. As described in the method, you should be integrating systems in line with defined integration patterns that your organization has agreed to support. Then, where the integration requirement means that the solution will deviate from the supported pattern, the governance process should be enforced to approve any addition to the supported integration solution. Remember, the risks of integration need to be managed, security controls and data security must always be maintained, and the user experience and application performance should always be a primary focus point for all projects throughout the delivery process.

The resources in this chapter will help you to understand Salesforce integrations in detail. It's important to be able to document your solutions in such a way that the governance process runs smoothly and does not add significant time to the overall project lifecycle. Either way, your governance team should understand what integration patterns are approved, and the project team should be able to clearly articulate any solution deviations, along with solid reasons why it is necessary. Reviewing all the available integration options in this resource base will set you on the right track and should also help to make the governance process far simpler.

Integration Resources

In this section of the resource base, we focus on general Salesforce integration topics, the tools that we have at our disposal for documenting and testing our integrations, the integration patterns that are supported, as well as the associated APIs, the impact integrations can have on Salesforce limits, and a multitude of other resources that should prove to be essential reading if the integration solution for your project/implementation is a critical part of your role. See Table 16-1.

Table 16-1. *Integration*

Artifact	GitHub Ref	Description
Integration Patterns and Practices	Integrations Patterns	This Salesforce guide offers a detailed description of the patterns or strategies for many common integration scenarios. After reading this resource, you will be aware of approaches you could take using the pattern selection guide, and have a better understanding of the terms used that relate to integration.
UML 2 Sequence Diagrams: An Agile Introduction	Sequence Diagrams	In a previous chapter, "Identity & Access Management," we discussed how sequence diagrams can be used to show the logic flow of your application or system design. We can use sequence diagrams for both analysis and design purposes, depending on the outcome required. Sequence diagrams are the most popular UML (unified modeling language) artifact for dynamic modeling, which focuses on identifying the behavior within your system.
Catalog of Patterns of Enterprise Application Architecture	EA Architecture Patterns	This resource provides an overview of the patterns that are covered in the fantastic reference book *Patterns of Enterprise Architecture*. Although the book was written some time ago, the patterns covered are just as relevant today for any developer working on modern-day applications. It's a book of resources (hmm, seems familiar) that will prove to be useful to any integration architect working in the Salesforce ecosystem. In addition, we have added a resource that covers the topic of enterprise integration patterns more generally. This includes other reference material (articles, books, and patterns) that would also be good to review.
An Introduction: Integrating with the Salesforce Force.com Platform	Integrating with the Salesforce Platform	This article is a good read for when the integration requirement is based on Web services. Is the requirement a straightforward data integration or is there business logic that must be taken into consideration as well? This resource helps to define if SOAP API or Apex callouts using REST-based APIs are most appropriate.

(continued)

Table 16-1. (*continued*)

Artifact	GitHub Ref	Description
Integration Architecture for the Salesforce Platform	Salesforce Integration Architecture	This resource provides valuable insight from a Salesforce architect as part of the Salesforce developer's blog series. This article reinforces the need for integration standards to be defined and therefore available for project teams in your organization. In addition, the author takes a deep dive look at a Salesforce integration reference architecture that should prove to be thought provoking and should assist in the approach taken.
Video Series – API Integration	Integration API Overview – Video Series	These video resources are a must watch for anyone wanting to understand more about what APIs actually are and how they are used in Salesforce. The focus is on REST and SOAP as these are the most used API types in Salesforce integrations.
APIs and Integration	APIs and Integration	This is a great resource that you can use as a launch pad of discovery for the plethora of integration options that Salesforce offers. This resource also provides you with learning resources that will be essential if Salesforce integration is your problem to solve. The video series included may also prove to be a good reference, as will the trailhead resource available. There is also a tools section that provides a resource for how you can use Postman; see the next resource.
Which API Do I use?	Which API Do I Use?	This resource gives you fantastic "When to use …" views of each API type available in Salesforce.
Explore the Salesforce APIs with a Postman Collection	Testing with Postman	Postman is a tool that can be used to test and troubleshoot the APIs that you develop in support of your application. Postman is a desktop application that lets you configure and call HTTP-based APIs like REST and SOAP; therefore, this is a tool any Salesforce professional working on integration projects can utilize to test and prove integration solutions.

(*continued*)

Table 16-1. (*continued*)

Artifact	GitHub Ref	Description
Salesforce to Salesforce	Salesforce to Salesforce	This resource covers the integration method Salesforce to Salesforce. With this integration option you can connect orgs for the purposes of sharing data between them. You can publish objects and fields for which subscribing orgs can see the data published. A good use case for this type of integration could be when your requirement is to share Salesforce data with your partner networks.
Salesforce Developer Limits and Allocations Quick Reference Guide	Salesforce Developer Limits – Quick Reference	This resource covers the most critical limits that you should be considering when developing applications in Salesforce. Especially useful when considering the limit implications on HTTP callouts, for example, or SOQL query runtime limits.
Using Mashups	Mashups	Mashups are used to bring external data (external to Salesforce) via callouts or via an embedded UI element so that from a UX perspective the data is all presented via Salesforce. This resource introduces this concept, which can be used to reduce the amount of data stored in the platform.
Canvas Developer Guide: Introducing Canvas	Introducing Canvas	Another integration method is to use a Canvas app. Canvas allows you to integrate or expose a third-party application into Salesforce so that you can create a seamless experience for your users. This resource covers this integration method in detail, including the various use cases and how Canvas apps are built.
Salesforce Open CTI	Salesforce Open CTI	This resource covers the Open CTI integration for Salesforce Call Center. Open CTI allows you to integrate your Salesforce org in such a way that you can receive and make calls directly from Salesforce. There are many configuration options that can be used, and there is a supporting Open CTI developer guide.

(*continued*)

Table 16-1. (*continued*)

Artifact	GitHub Ref	Description
Service Cloud Voice	Service Cloud Voice	Service Cloud Voice (SCV) is another telephony integration option. The difference with SCV is that it seamlessly integrates with your omni-channel setup so that you can manage call distribution to the best agent for a particular call. With call transcription in real-time, the customer experience delivers a more professional and personalized service. There are two main SCV offerings for service cloud voice: the native product that provides all the functionality powered by AWS connect, and a BYOT (Bring Your Own Telephony) service that uses a third-party adapter to drive similar functionality. This resource covers SCV and the various options and is a must read if this is your requirement.
Introducing the SOAP API	SOAP API	This resource is part of the SOAP API developer guide and focuses on SOAP (Simple Object Access Protocol). The SOAP API is XML based and can be used for many different use cases. This resource covers all the possibilities using SOAP, including how to make calls, perform searches, security considerations, and many others.
Understanding Outbound Messaging	Outbound Messaging	With the SOAP API, you can use outbound messaging that is triggered via a workflow rule or flow when there has been a change to a field in Salesforce, which then sends a message to an external endpoint. This resource covers this topic in detail. Note: Salesforce has announced that Process Builder and Workflow rules will be deprecated in the winter 2023 release. Salesforce Flow can be used to trigger the outbound message.

(*continued*)

Table 16-1. (*continued*)

Artifact	GitHub Ref	Description
Best Practices to Avoid Excessive SOAP and REST API DML	SOAP and REST API Best Practices	This resource covers the best practice recommendations for using SOAP and RESTful APIs to avoid unnecessary DML (Data Manipulation Language) database changes. This is about making your code as efficient as possible. Techniques such as bulkification (process updates in batches) and being aware of what object automation has been configured on fields will be key elements of design you should be considering as part of your governance. This resource offers other guidelines to ensure that performance is not adversely affected.
Differences between Salesforce-Provided WSDL files	Salesforce WSDL: Differences	When considering the use of the SOAP API, there are two types of WSDL that can be used" Enterprise WSDL and Partner WSDL. This resource covers the differences.
Introducing Lightning Platform REST API	REST API	This resource introduces the Lightning platform REST API. With REST you can perform CRUD DML actions to update the Salesforce database as well as a host of other functions. This resource, being a developer guide, covers the use of REST in detail.
Apex Developer Guide: JSON Support	JSON Basics & Support	This resource covers in detail how JSON (Java Script Notation Language) is supported in Apex. Serialization and deserialization, JSON generation, and parsing are all areas discussed. In addition, a link to JSON basics is provided that explains what JSON is and how it's used.
Bulk API 2.0 and BULK API Developer Guide	Bulk API	The Bulk API can be used to asynchronously perform DML actions. This resource explains the Bulk API in detail: the differences between Bulk API and Bulk 2.0 API, the associated limits, and a "how to"–style guide for using the Bulk API with practical examples.

(*continued*)

Table 16-1. (*continued*)

Artifact	GitHub Ref	Description
Connect REST API Developer Guide	Connect REST API	This resource covers the Connect REST API and gives multiple examples of why you would use it. With the Connect REST API data is structured so that it will render on websites and mobile applications; it returns localized data specific to a user. Use this resource to delve deeper into these use cases and learn more about how the Connect API is used.
Streaming API Developer Guide: Streaming API	Streaming API	The Streaming API is used to steam or publish events generated in Salesforce to all subscribing clients. This resource covers the multitude of scenarios where the Streaming API could be used. Clients will only receive the notification if the client subscribes to the channel. This improves performance and reduces the number of calls made that return an empty payload.
Chat REST API Developer Guide	Chat REST API	If your organization uses chat-based channels to interact with your customers, the Chat REST API can help you to extend the functionality of your chat windows and enable you to build custom windows within your iOS, Android, or other Web applications.
REST API Developer Guide: Composite API	Composite API	When using the Salesforce REST API you can make composite requests that basically bundle all of a series of REST API requests into a single call. This resource provides details for the request and response body and describes the format of the call using subrequests. The advantage of using composite requests is that the entire series of requests count as a single call toward your API limits.

(*continued*)

Table 16-1. (*continued*)

Artifact	GitHub Ref	Description
Tooling API	Tooling API	This resource details the Salesforce Tooling API. This API can be used to build custom development tools or apps for Lightning platform applications. One of the advantages of using the Tooling API to retrieve fine-grained metadata from your org is performance. Using this API rather than the Metadata API will result in fewer retrieves, which in turn means better performance, especially when making SOQL queries.
Getting Started with Salesforce Integration patterns using MuleSoft	MuleSoft Integration Patterns	Your organization may decide that a middleware approach to integration is a good fit for your integration requirement, especially where you are looking to connect your Salesforce data to other third-party data sources and vice versa. MuleSoft provides many integration connectors out of the box that will support your integration requirements using a declarative approach. This resource introduces these concepts and provides details on the common Salesforce / MuleSoft integration patterns.
Configure Remote Site Settings	Remote Site Settings	This resource covers an important topic on why you need to configure remote site settings for any Visualforce page, Apex callout, or JavaScript code using XMLHttpRequest. If you do not register the remote site, the callout will fail. This resource provides the details for exactly what you need to do to avoid this issue.
Named Credentials	Named Credentials	Name credentials are a standard Salesforce feature that can be used to store a URL endpoint and credentials for internal users that can be used to make authenticated callouts to external services. There are numerous benefits of using named credentials to manage how callouts are made in your solution. This resource goes into detail on all these topics, including the supported protocols, authentication types, and how named credentials can be added to your code.

Phase E Standards

Any integration aspect of your project will have a huge impact on the success of your overall solution. Choosing the right integration pattern for your project will ensure a successful outcome. The main focus for your integration will be security and of course performance. In a scenario where you are integrating with an external system or third-party data provider, you will need to ensure that you are able to authenticate and share data securely, but you will also need to use the third parties' API documentation to make successful callouts without error. Similarly, where a third party is consuming an API that you are exposing, you will need to document your API clearly so that API calls made to your application will return the correct payload.

This may all seem obvious, but API documentation is so important. Best practice would recommend that any API that you consume be documented by the project as part of the standard document deliverables matrix. It will be important for your governance team to understand the purpose of the API, what it will be used for, what data elements will be retrieved and stored, and data mappings between the external objects and the Salesforce objects that you intend to store data. Similarly, the authentication method will be equally as important to document as the data. As part of the API documentation, the Auth protocol should be described along with a sequence diagram that shows the authentication flow and the data exchange between the relevant components.

Note   The document deliverables matrix is essentially a list of all the documents that a project will publish in support of the solution. This should include but is not limited to high-level design, low-level design, requirements, API documentation, and security (SSO, authentication).

The same rule applies for any APIs exposed by the project. In this scenario, the recommendation would be to document the API interface so that any consuming service will be able to use your API successfully. The example in Table 16-2 provides a simplified API interface specification.

Table 16-2. *API Interface Specification Example*

Title	Submit Guitar Wood Export request
	This REST API is to submit a request for exporting all guitar woods in stock for a given date range and status
API URL	***Bright Sound Guitars URL***/services/apexrest/BSG/v1/dataExportWood
API Method	The request type
	POST
Query Parameters	Wood Status <string> – Optional
Header	Authorization: Bearer <Access Token>,
	Content-Type: application/json,
	Signature: Signed using a cert
Data Params	```{```
	``` "startDate": ISO Standards Date,```
	``` "endDate": ISO Standards Date,```
	``` "woodStatus": "Semi colon separated string of list of```
	``` statuses"```
	```}```
Success Response	HTTP Response Code:
	200 – OK

(*continued*)

Table 16-2. (*continued*)

Error Response	API will respond with HTTP response code ranging between 400 – 500 for various error scenarios. Response Code: 400 to 500 Header: Content-Type: application/json Body:

```
{
    "errors": [
        {
            "code": "ErrorCode",
            "source": "Error Source",
            "title": "Error Type",
            "detail": "Error Message"
        },
        {
            "code": "ErrorCode",
            "source": "Error Source",
            "title": "Error Type",
            "detail": "Error Message"
        },
    ]
}
```

Error codes should be documented in an appendix to the specification

(*continued*)

Table 16-2. (*continued*)

Example Call	Example call to API endpoint ($.ajax call or a curl request)

```
header: {
    "Content-Type": "application/json",
    "Authorization": "Bearer <JWT Details>",
    "signature":" "
},
Data: {
    "startDate": ISO Standards Date,
    "endDate": ISO Standards Date,
    "woodStatus": "Dried;Planed;"
}
method : "POST"
```

Additional Notes	Interface specifications:

Expected return format: JSON

The following are the required body parameters:

```
{
    "startDate": "ISO Standards Date",
    "endDate": "ISO Standards Date",
    "woodStatus": "Semi colon list of status"
}
```

Security:

1. Consumer to acquire Oauth2 token before making call to this REST API using JWT.
2. Access token to be added in every REST API call made to Salesforce using bearer token in the header.
3. JSON Validation: Salesforce to validate the JSON structure and convert all the escape characters before processing the JSON.

Documenting your APIs in this way will be essential for any consuming service to successfully call out and get the desired response from your API. Additionally, when you update, extend, or redesign your API, having documentation like this will inform any developers taking future responsibility to enhance an existing API specification.

Checklists

The phase checklist simply tracks that each step and sub-step within the phase are governed correctly and completely. Each sub-step may have several subject areas to form the complete coverage from a governance perspective.

Governance Step

Technologies & Overall Integration Strategies	**Pass / Fail**

Govern the enterprise integration landscape and overall integration strategy, with associated risks, trade-offs, and business and technical considerations

Govern the data backup/archiving/data warehousing integration strategies

Govern that the appropriate integration strategy and standard integration patterns have been used

Govern the integration components involved in a flow and consider transaction management and error and exception handling

Integration Solution Tools	**Pass/Fail**

Govern that the appropriate platform-specific integration technology is used to integrate with external systems

Govern the usage of the Lightning platform integration APIs and features and determine whether they have been appropriately used

Security	**Pass/Fail**

Govern how security requirements are met at each of the integration layers

---

CHAPTER 17

Apex, Visualforce & Lightning (Phase F) Resource Base

This chapter contains the resources required to govern Phase F of the Salesforce Platform Governance Method. As per all phases in this resource guide, the approach we have taken is to assemble the most relevant resources that align with the corresponding governance method. Since you've been working through the book and using these resources, you'll know that although we have tried to cover all the major areas relating to this topic, completing your own research in addition to examining the resources we have provided will really set you up for greatness!

Tip You do not need to use this resource base as a strict method or process. The idea is that this will give you a good indication of what you should be taking into consideration. The expectation is that you will use this as a guide and then build upon it as you navigate the Salesforce ecosystem.

Guidelines and Best Practices

This section contains the guidance and best practices that are available from Salesforce, as well as other resources that we have determined will be valuable. This section should serve to provide a good set of guidelines that can be reviewed by anyone delivering the governance function within your organization.

© Lee Harding and Lee Bayliss 2022
L. Harding and L. Bayliss, *Salesforce Platform Governance Method*,
https://doi.org/10.1007/978-1-4842-7404-0_17

We know there is an infinite number of resources available on the Web, and although some are better than others, this resource base will provide you with a good selection of resources that we recommend you review. As per all the resource base documentation in this book, providing the complete technical definition for every aspect of code not clicks (can you see what I did there?) is not the objective. There are many ways in which you can achieve your desired outcomes using code in Salesforce. Therefore, this resource base has been created with reference to the topics covered in the method that you will find informative and relevant. The resource base is divided into three main sections: the resources themselves and then related standards and associated tooling, and finally the supporting governance checklist.

As is the case with all the resource base chapters in this book, the links to the resources will be managed in the Salesforce Platform Governance Method GitHub account. The URL for this account is as follows: `github.com/salesforceplatformgovernancemethod`.

Apex, Visualforce & Lightning

Given that you have arrived at the resource base for programmatic resources, we must assume that you have been reading the content in the governance method described in Chapter 7, "Apex, VisualForce & Lightning." To get you going, we have provided a table of resources to help guide you in relation to the content covered in the method (Table 17-1).

Table 17-1. *Programmatic Resources*

Artifact	GitHub Ref	Description
Salesforce Architects: Development Standards	Development Standards	This resource provides an informative guide into the topic of development standards: what they are, why they are important, and how you create and maintain them in your environment.
Apex Developer Guide: What is Apex	What is Apex	This resource introduces Apex, a strongly typed (meaning that Apex validates references to objects at compile time) object-oriented programming language. Salesforce developers use Apex to revolutionize the way they create on-demand applications. Apex is the first multi-tenant, on-demand programming language for developers interested in building business applications.
Trailhead: Apex Basics a& Database	Apex Basics	This resource provides a basic introduction to Apex and its basic concepts: sObjects, Data Manipulation Language (DML), SOQL, and SOSL. Also review the video resources that provide many tutorials and examples that may prove useful.
Apex Developer Guide: When Should I Use Apex	When Should I Use Apex	This resource provides a guide to answer the question of when Apex should be used. Here you will read about examples of when Apex is appropriate based on your use case and additional context on Lightning components, Visualforce, and SOAP.
Lightning Component Library	Component Library	This resource provides you with a full library of all the Lightning components in the form of a guide. The component library includes both Lightning Web components and Aura components, along with example code that can be used as a base for further development.

(continued)

337

Table 17-1. (*continued*)

Artifact	GitHub Ref	Description
Apex Design Best Practices	Apex Design Best Practices	When coding in Apex, you want to write code that is efficient, scalable, and aligned to best practices. This resource covers some best practice techniques that you can employ in your code to ensure that you are designing your code correctly. Learn about bulkification, efficient SOQL queries, and other best practice principles that you can include in your code.
Visualforce Developer Guide: What is Visualforce	What is Visualforce	This resource introduces the Visualforce concept. Visualforce is a framework that your developers can utilize to build custom UIs (user interfaces) hosted on the platform. This resource explains what Visualforce is and how it is architected.
Visual Development – When to Click Instead of Write Code	Clicks not Code	Writing code is not always the only option. I know this resource base is focused on all things code, but it is good practice to remind ourselves that there are other options, and in some cases this could be a better option. Time, cost, and time to deliver—the project management triangle that we've all seen before.
Visualforce Developer Guide: Standard Controllers	VF Standard Controllers	Learn how to use standard controllers to define what data and behaviors are available to users when they interact with a Visualforce component.
Visualforce Developer Guide: Custom Controllers and Controller Extensions	VF Custom Controllers and Controller Extensions	Use custom controllers when you want your Visualforce page to run entirely in system mode, which does not enforce the permissions and field-level security of the current user.
Visualforce Developer Guide: JavaScript Libraries with Visualforce	JavaScript Libraries with Visualforce	Using JavaScript in Visualforce pages gives you access to a wide range of existing JavaScript functionality, such as JavaScript libraries, and other ways to customize the functionality of your pages; review this resource to learn more.

(*continued*)

Table 17-1. (*continued*)

Artifact	GitHub Ref	Description
Visualforce Developer Guide: When Should I Use Lightning Web Components Instead of Visualforce	LWC or Visualforce	Being a Salesforce developer, you will at some point need to decide if an LWC would be better for your application than a Visualforce alternative. This resource guides you through this process and highlights the benefits that an LWC can offer. Bear in mind also that for all new development, Salesforce will always recommend LWC and Lightning Experience "low-code" tools.
Lightning Web Components Dev Guide: Introducing LWC	LWC Dev Guide	Lightning Web Components (LWCs) are custom HTML elements built using HTML and modern JavaScript. LWCs offer many benefits over Visualforce; for example, namely performance. LWCs use core Web standards for which Salesforce is committed. This resource looks at LWCs in detail, including help on how to set up your development environment, what resources are available on Trailhead (you gotta love Trailhead!), and many examples and technical standards.
Salesforce OmniStudio	Salesforce OmniStudio	Salesforce now offers you a suite of powerful tools that can be used to accelerate the development of digital experiences as part of the OmniStudio tool set. OmniStudio provides a number declarative or low-code options when developing guided experiences in Salesforce and comes as part of Einstein Automate, or as part of your Salesforce Industries license. Use these resources to learn more about this development option and its various components—flex cards, OmniScript, data raptors, and integration procedures—and also the deployment tools that can be used to release functionality.

(*continued*)

Table 17-1. (*continued*)

Artifact	GitHub Ref	Description
Introduction to the Salesforce Lightning Design System	SLDS	The Salesforce Lightning Design System is a styling framework that enables you to build, amongst other things, Experience Sites that share the same look and feel as the Salesforce platform. SLDS allows the development team to focus on application functionality and user experience rather than creating pixel-perfect sites. There is a lot to review regarding this topic, and the resources we have provided reflect that.
Secure Coding Guide: Secure Coding Guidelines	Secure Coding	This informative resource provides a set of guidelines that you should review to ensure that your code is secure. This guide is composed of a set of security issues that Salesforce has identified and therefore should be relevant for your application. This does not, however, cover every security issue that you should code for. Always check the OWASP site for a more thorough view on current Web application security flaws.
The Open Web Application Security Foundation	OWASP	The OWASP foundation's primary focus is to improve the security of software. The OWASP foundation has existed for over 20 years as of 2021, and provides many resources and guides for how to secure the Web. The "OWASP Top 10" provides details for the most critical security concerns for Web application security. This report is created by leading professionals from all over the world.
Apex Design Patterns	Apex Design Patterns	It's already been said that with Apex you can pretty much build any custom solution on the Salesforce platform. This resource covers the more common design patterns and best practices for Apex development.

(*continued*)

Table 17-1. (*continued*)

Artifact	GitHub Ref	Description
Implementing Idempotent Operations with Salesforce	Idempotent Operations	This resource covers the importance of idempotent operation design. Idempotent operations basically make you think about how your code will behave if it were to execute multiple times. Would it matter? If so, what can you do to manage any unwanted side effects while maintaining the performance of the code?
Apex Enterprise Patterns: Service Layer	Apex Ent Pattens	This Trailhead module covers some of the complexities seen when developing applications for the enterprise. Apex is a very flexible language that can accomplish quite a bit with only a few lines of code. This Trailhead module delves deeper into topics such as separation of concerns, service layer, and domain layer, which are all design patterns that you should be aware of.
Developers Blog: 4 Steps to Successful Async Processing	Successful Async Processing	This article introduces asynchronous processing with the Salesforce platform. It is a good resource to review before you move on to more practical or "hands on" resources.
Trailhead: Asynchronous Apex	Asynchronous Apex	This Trailhead module is essential for any developer who wants to learn more about how to write more efficient code with asynchronous processing.
Apex Developer Guide: Future Annotation	Future Annotation	Use the future annotation to identify methods that are executed asynchronously. When you specify future, the method executes when Salesforce has available resources.
Apex Developer Guide: Using Batch Apex	Batch Apex	This resource describes Batch Apex, providing the developer the ability to run complex, long-running processes in chunks across your entire data set. You can run Batch Apex at specific times using the Apex scheduler and fire platform events from Batch Apex.

(*continued*)

Table 17-1. (*continued*)

Artifact	GitHub Ref	Description
Apex Flex Queue: Batch Apex Liberation	Apex Flex Queue	This video resource introduces the Apex flex queue. This is essentially a holding queue for jobs waiting to be processed by the batch job queue when resources become available.
Enhance Salesforce with Code: Monitoring the Apex Flex Queue	Monitoring the Apex Flex Queue	With the Apex flex queue, you can place up to 100 batch jobs in the queue, all waiting for resources to be freed up to process each batch. While batches are in this holding state, you can reorder the jobs in the queue using the FlexQueue class. Review this resource to learn more details.
Apex Developer Guide: Apex. Execution Governors and Limits	Apex Governor Limits	As previously discussed, Salesforce is a multi-tenant environment. Therefore, mechanisms must be in place to ensure that runaway code cannot monopolize platform resources where another Salesforce instance could be adversely impacted. Salesforce achieves this by employing a set of limits, Governor Limits, to protect the platform and ensure that all code can execute. If you breach a given limit your code will throw an exception. This resource provides details for the limits imposed, and therefore this should be reviewed, understood, and put into practice when developing on the Salesforce platform.
Trailhead: App Development Without Limits	App Dev Without Limits	This Trailhead module and developer blog covers the concepts that for a developer will be essential reading. Learning how to code while avoiding the limits enforced by the platform will save a lot of time and headache that would occur should you exceed limits enforced by the platform. The most common limit is concurrency—long-running jobs that take over five seconds to execute. These resources provide insightful and informative details on how to avoid these problems.

(*continued*)

Table 17-1. (*continued*)

Artifact	GitHub Ref	Description
Apex Developer Guide: Triggers	Apex Triggers	Apex triggers can be invoked when certain record actions are performed. There are two types of triggers: before and after triggers. This resource describes how triggers work and provides several considerations that should be reviewed to ensure that they are used properly.
Apex Developer Guide: Triggers and Order of Execution	Order of Execution	To maintain the integrity of the data in Salesforce, for all automation actions performed when you save a record there is an order of execution that occurs. These resources describe this order and why it is important and provide numerus considerations for your review.
Apex Developer Guide: Understand Testing in Apex	Apex Testing	Salesforce cares a great deal about unit testing of code. In fact, it's mandated that at least 75% of your code must be covered by unit tests that complete successfully. Without this, you will not be able to deploy your code into production. To this end, Salesforce is an advocate of test-driven development, where you code your tests at the same time as functional code development. These resources describe how testing in Apex should be done and therefore are essential for all developers to understand and act upon. A video presentation is provided, as well as Trailhead modules and the content provide in the developer guide.
Apex Developer Guide: Testing HTTP Callouts	Testing Apex Callouts	When writing your Apex code, you need to ensure that you have 75% test coverage. This is just as important as the actual code itself. Test methods do not support HTTP callouts, so to get around this limitation, we generate mock HTTP responses in tests. There are two ways that you can achieve this, which are explained in this resource. In addition, the Trailhead modules included in this resource are well worth reviewing, especially if you are a new developer beginning to code in Apex.

(continued)

Table 17-1. (*continued*)

Artifact	GitHub Ref	Description
Apex Developer Guide: Exceptions in Apex	Exceptions in Apex	Debugging your code is a critical part of the development process. You can debug your code using the developer console and debug logs. To make your debug logs more readable, Apex supports exception statements and custom exceptions. This resource explains how exceptions note errors and events that disrupt the flow of code execution and explores other methods of handling errors, including why one method is better than another.
Salesforce Development Tools	Development Tools	There are many tools that you can use for Salesforce development. This resource provides a table of tools and their associated use cases. Tools listed include the developer console, Visual Studio Code, and the Salesforce CLI. Use this resource to choose the environment that works best for you.
Visualforce Performance: Best Practices	VF Performance Best Practice	This resource provides a collection of best practice considerations that can be used to improve the performance of your Visualforce pages.
Enhance Salesforce with Code: Static Resources	Static Resources	Static resources allow you to upload content that you can reference in a Visualforce page, including archives (such as .zip and .jar files), images, style sheets, JavaScript, and other files. Use this resource to learn how to use them, and try it out for yourself using Trailhead.
Developers Blog: A Guide to Application Performance Profiling in Force.com	Application Performance Profiling	When developing your application on the Salesforce platform, you want to know that your application will perform as designed and handle the volumes of data over time. This resource introduces the concept of application performance profiling and provides examples that use the Salesforce tooling to achieve this.

(*continued*)

Table 17-1. (*continued*)

Artifact	GitHub Ref	Description
Developers Blog: Paginating Data for Force.com Applications	Paginating Data	This resource helps to demystify pagination strategies that you could use to achieve peek application performance.
Apex Developer Guide: JSON Support	JSON Support	In Apex you can support JSON serialization and deserialization, generate JSON-encoded content, and parse JSON data such as a response to a Web service callout. This resource provides examples of each, including JSON support considerations.
Enhance Salesforce with Code: Custom Labels	Custom Labels	Custom labels are essential for developers who are creating multilingual applications. We use custom labels to specify custom text values that can be accessed from Apex classes, Visualforce pages, Lightning pages, or Lightning components. The values can be translated into any language Salesforce supports.
Apex Reference Guide: Custom Settings Methods	Custom Settings Methods	We discussed custom settings in Chapter 13, "Data Architecture & Management." This resource builds on your understanding and provides a detailed usage reference for both types of custom setting methods: List and Hierarchy.

As you undoubtedly already know, the big Salesforce technical benefit is that many of your organization's automation requirements can be serviced using the declarative tools available on the platform. However, there are also situations where the declarative option will not give you the outcome that you need; for example, if your requirement is to create a Web service, or if you need to perform complex validation that requires the field values across multiple objects. Other use cases include custom login flows or authentication handlers that require the programmatic approach rather than the declarative alternative.

The programmatic options available in Salesforce are Apex, Visualforce, and Lightning components (Web or Aura). The resources in this chapter aim to provide links to many of the topics that cover the programmatic aspects of each option and associated requirements.

As we know, Salesforce is a multi-tenant environment. This is important to consider, especially when writing code in Apex. There are stipulations that Salesforce enforces on any developed Apex code to ensure the multi-tenant architecture is not compromised by runaway code. Apex governance limits and test coverage requirements are both examples of the rigor Salesforce mandates you to comply with.

Programmatic Resources

The resources in the following table will help you to understand the technical aspects of the Salesforce programmatic environment and to navigate your way through the governance process by paying attention to code quality, security, access control, governor limits, code performance, unit tests, and, finally, the order of execution.

Phase F Standards

Your organization should have well-defined development standards that are used by your dev teams to ensure that all code deployed into your production environments is efficient, secure, well documented, tested, and aligned to the coding principles defined by your governance process. An important part of your development documentation set will be your Software Development Lifecycle (SDLC).

A good SDLC should include a detailed guide as to how you gather requirements, navigate the design phase, articulate the development process, being specific about naming standards, coding styles, and code documentation, and essentially ensuring that your development team develops code that conforms to the blueprint defined for each language used in your organization. Your SDLC will also describe the testing process used by your organization and the tools available for this purpose. Finally, deployment. If you are an organization that operates a multitude of project delivery methodologies, for example, agile or waterfall, then the SDLC should provide detailed definitions for the release process for each methodology employed by your organization.

But why have coding standards? I mean, it's likely that all your developers have been coding since they were in adolescence or are fresh from their training and have all the information top of mind and "know" what they are doing. After all, your developers were hired for a reason; they are talented and valued members of the development team and always deliver code that serves the intended purpose. Having documented coding standards, however, serves to ensure that regardless of how experienced or talented your dev teams are, all code is developed in a uniform way. This makes it much easier for dev teams to improve readability across teams, reduces code complexity, and therefore helps the process of maintaining code in the future. We want to avoid a situation where only specific individuals can manage the code base. Imagine a scenario where your principal software developer has decided to take advantage of other opportunity outside of your organization and the rest of the devolvement team must then try to pick apart existing code to add new functionality, resolve bugs, and so on. This could be costly from a resource perspective and cause unsavory delays to other projects in flight. OK, this is an extreme example, but we wanted to make the point clear.

Having these standards in place should promote a consistent development style that enables you to debug your code, identify reuse opportunities, and build a solid coding practice that's easier to enforce as part of the overall project governance process.

A recurring theme in this book is the importance of naming standards, and now that we are discussing Apex and coding standards, it's appropriate to refer to this topic once more. Table 17-2 provides the naming conventions that we advise be added to your coding standards for your development teams to adhere to.

Table 17-2. *Apex Naming Standards*

Type	Case Type	Naming Convention	Comments	Wrong Examples
Apex Class	PascalCase	<Namespace>_ <Class Name> <Optional Suffix>	Namespace: optional. Short, often an acronym. Use only for classes that are exclusive to a single app/project, and are sure to stay that way over time. Don't confuse this with the namespace as used in packages or dev orgs! Class name: nouns, describing the class's functional purpose. Avoid acronyms and abbreviations. Suffix: indicates common class types - Controller, Extension, Handler, Utilities, TriggerHandler.	CustomerAssessment – Lacks project namespace + suffix; not obvious what it does. SmallBusinessConfigureAnd PricingTool_Customer AssessmentController – Namespace too long. Use acronym instead. SBCPTCustomerAssessment Controller – Where does namespace end and class name start? Use underscore. SBCPT_Customer_ Assessment_Controller – Uses underscores within the class name.
Apex Test Class	PascalCase	<Class Being Tested>_Test		SBCPT_CustomerAssessment ControllerTest – Does not use an underscore before "Test."
Apex Methods	camelCase	<Verb(s)> <(optional) Noun Set>	Verbs: describe the actions being performed: get, save, check, etc. Noun set: describes what the verbs are acting on	parentAccount() – Missing verb. What action is being performed on the parent account? GetParentAccount() – Starts with capital letter.

(continued)

Table 17-1. (*continued*)

Type	Case Type	Naming Convention	Comments	Wrong Examples
Apex Variables	camelCase	\<Short yet meaningful nouns>	Avoid one-letter variable names, except for temporary variables or loop variables.	parAcc – Unclear what this represents. parentAccountSave – Uses a verb. ParentAccount – Starts with a capital letter.
Apex Constants	SNAKE_ CASE	\<Capitalized words>	Should be descriptive of the constant without using too many words.	maxCharacters – Indistinguishable from a variable. MAXIMUM_NUMBER_OF_ CHARACTERS – Too long.

In conclusion, having a well-defined and enforceable development standard in your organization will be an essential part of controlling how successful your software applications will be. To recap, the following list of items should be covered in your SDLC and coding standards:

- How to gather and document business requirements

- What design collateral should be created, reviewed, and governed as part of a "design" package of work in the overall governance process

- Well-defined coding standards: coding tools such as preferred IDEs, naming conventions, how to document code properly, writing efficient and performant code (bulkification, as an example), and coding with a strong focus on security; for example, using "with sharing" by default

- What coding patterns and frameworks are advocated as best practice. A great example is the use of trigger frameworks that control how object automation is processed, being sympathetic to the Salesforce order of execution and preventing recursive operations.

- Having a well-defined testing process with clear outcomes. Firstly, all code has met the testing requirements enforced by the platform, code coverage and test classes written, and tests passed. Your governance process should ensure that only tested code that has passed your quality gates and code scans such as PMD or Veracode should be approved for release to production.

- Release and deployment is another great example of standards that your SDLC should provide. If you have a CI/CD process employed within your overall release process, then the principles and standards enforced by your governance process should be clearly articulated and maintained.

Checklists

The phase checklist simply tracks that each step and sub-step within the phase is governed correctly and completely. Each sub-step may have several subject areas to form complete coverage from a governance perspective.

Governance Step	
Design and Functionality	**Pass / Fail**
Govern the continuum of UI options used against those available on the platform (buttons, mashups, Canvas, Visualforce pages, and Lightning components)	
Govern the sharing and visibility model in code solution	
Govern the code against the security best practices to ensure all Visualforce and Apex code is developed per OWASP standards.	
Govern the object-oriented design principles and design patterns that were adhered to when developing the solution (Singleton, etc.)	
Govern the appropriate use of the Model-View-Controller pattern	
Govern any Apex controllers against the technical standards (extensions to standard controllers and custom controllers)	
Govern the usage of custom settings and synchronous vs. asynchronous patterns, and all the available execution contexts (e.g., batch, trigger, callout, etc.)	

(*continued*)

Governance Step	
Govern the usage of batch Apex and the flex queue	
Govern the Apex / Visualforce solution against the governor limits	
Govern the order of execution of transactions within the platform (specifically against pre-existing triggers)	
Govern the quality of test coverage (required for production deployment, callout testing is a special case)	
Govern the approach to error/exception handling	
Performance and Scalability	**Pass/Fail**
Govern that performance and scalability best practice has been considered within Visualforce pages and Apex code (Performance Profiling, use of static resources)	
Govern the Apex and Visualforce performance to include LDV scenarios (pagination, JavaScript remoting)	
Govern the use of external web technologies and complementary UI technologies.	
Maintainability and Reuse	**Pass/Fail**
Govern multi-language support, determine the appropriate solution has been used to support globalization	
Govern the options and techniques used to make programmatic components maintainable and reusable on the platform (custom settings, skeleton templates, custom metadata types)	

CHAPTER 18

Experience Cloud (Communities) (Phase G) Resource Base

This chapter contains the resources required to govern Phase G of the Salesforce Platform Governance Method. As per all phases in this resource guide, the approach we have taken is to assemble the most relevant resources that align with the corresponding governance method. Since you've been working through the book and using these resources, you'll know that although we have tried to cover all the major areas relating to this topic, as ever, conducting your own research in addition to examining the resources provided will really set you up for awesomeness!

Tip   You do not need to use this resource base as a strict method or process. The idea is that this will give you a good indication of what you should be taking into consideration. The expectation is that you will use this as a guide and then build upon it as you navigate the Salesforce ecosystem.

Guidelines and Best Practices

This chapter provides a collation of resources that brings together guidance and best practices available from Salesforce, as well as other resources that we have determined will be valuable. The objective is to ensure that the information provided in this section will enable you to actively contribute to the governance process in your organization or simply enhance your subject-level expertise.

© Lee Harding and Lee Bayliss 2022
L. Harding and L. Bayliss, *Salesforce Platform Governance Method*,
https://doi.org/10.1007/978-1-4842-7404-0_18

We know there is an infinite number of resources available on the Web, and although some are better than others, this resource base will provide you with a good selection that we recommend you review. As per all the resource base documentation in this book, providing the complete technical definition for every aspect of Salesforce Experience Cloud, (formally Salesforce Communities) is not the objective. Therefore, this resource base has been created with reference to the topics covered in the method that you will find informative and relevant. The resource base is divided into three main sections: the resources themselves and then related standards, associated tooling, and finally the supporting governance checklist.

As is the case with all the resource base chapters in this book, the links to the resources will be managed in the Salesforce Platform Governance Method GitHub account. The URL for this account is as follows: `github.com/salesforceplatformgovernancemethod`.

Salesforce Experience Cloud

Given that you have arrived at the resource base for Communities, or Salesforce Experience Cloud, we must assume that you have been reading the content in the governance method described in Chapter 8, "Communities." To get you going, we have provided a table of resources to guide you in relation to the content covered in the method.

As described in the method, we use Salesforce Experience Cloud to create branded spaces for our employees, partners, and customers. We like to refer to these spaces as "sites," providing digital experiences for users.

If you have been in the Salesforce ecosystem for some time, you will know the terms *Community* or *Communities* and automatically associate them with Salesforce Community Cloud. Well, since the Spring 2022 release this has been rebranded by Salesforce to Experience Cloud, and this is reflected in all the Salesforce documentation.

Salesforce is a great platform for integrating data elements to provide powerful interaction with your data, and with Experience Cloud, integration with your Salesforce apps and CRM data is provided out of the box. This means that you can elevate and extend your business process directly to your consumers using the declarative tools in Experience Builder. Essentially, you can create powerful website experiences by providing your users, partners, and customers direct access to the data in your Salesforce org.

A great example of this is the customer service portal. Using an Experience site, you can easily empower consumers by providing a self-help service, enabling customers to resolve their own issues either by using your knowledge base or by connecting to agents via chat, as an example. Also, customers can use your site to find out the status of a service issue or claim without using any other channel. There are many use cases for sites, and reviewing the resources in this chapter will provide a plethora of information on what Experience Cloud is in detail, its basic features, how to ensure that while using sites as a channel to engage your consumers data is secure and protected, and how to build engaging digital experiences with targeted content for specific audiences.

Experience Cloud Resources

The resources in Table 18-1 will help you to understand the technical aspects of the Salesforce Experience Cloud and give you the knowledge required to support your governance process.

Table 18-1. *Experience Cloud Reources*

Artifact	GitHub Ref	Description
Trailhead: Experience Cloud Basics	Experience Cloud Basics	For Experience Cloud basics we turn to Trailhead. These modules introduce Experience Cloud, giving a basic view of what the product is and how it can be used to engage with customers and partners.
Set Up and Manage Experience Cloud Site: Experience Cloud Overview	Experience Cloud Overview	This resource provides a broader view of Experience Cloud with additional links to some of the resources that you will need to get a good understanding of how you can use sites to engage with your consumers. Some of the topics covered in this resource are also specified in this resource base. This is one to bookmark.
Plan Your Implementation	Plan Your Implementation	When considering how to build your site with Experience Cloud, there are several things that need to be properly considered: what license type should be used, will the site be public facing, and, most important, who are you creating the site for. Lastly, will you use an Experience Builder Site or Salesforce Tabs + Visualforce?

(continued)

Table 18-1. (*continued*)

Artifact	GitHub Ref	Description
Experience Cloud Authentication and Security	Authentication and Security	This resource covers Experience Cloud security in detail. Here, you can learn about the various methods that can be used in your solution to authenticate users. In addition, this resource covers clickjack protection (where users are tricked into clicking a button or link that they believe to be genuine) and many other topics, including encryption, content security policy, and the cookies used by Experience Cloud. In addition, this resource provides detail on social login, or how you can use a third-party account such as LinkedIn to authenticate to your site and other options that you can use to customize the login process.
Set Up and Maintain Your Salesforce Organization: Experience Cloud Users Licenses	Experience Cloud User Licenses	This resource covers the various license types that can be used with Experience Cloud. It's important to review each license type and decide which is most appropriate for your application. For example, if you wish to give external users access to your site, you may need to consider the sharing model, especially where your use case requires the members to view all cases related to an account. This requires advanced sharing and therefore would require a Customer Community Plus license. This resource goes into detail for each license type and explains the differences between member-based and login-based license models.
Developers Blog: How to Provision Salesforce Communities Users	Provision Community Users	This article explains the basic mechanics for provisioning a community user and gives an overview of the different techniques available to provision users, either manually or in an automated fashion.

(*continued*)

Table 18-1. (*continued*)

Artifact	GitHub Ref	Description
Set Up and Manage Experience Cloud Sites: Who Can See What in Communities	Who Sees What in Communities	This resource covers the types of access that the different user types have in a community. This is a useful topic as quite often you will need to know what access a community user will have to specific Salesforce functions. This will prove valuable when you are designing your solution and need to understand the impact on your sharing model of giving access to a resource that isn't available by default.
Sharing Sets and Sharing Groups	Sharing Sets / Sharing Groups	This resource has already been described in Chapter 15, "Sharing & Visibility Resource Base." See this resource base for details regarding sharing sets and sharing groups.
Personalization Using Audience Targeting in Experience Builder Sites	Audiences	One of the great features of Experience Cloud is the ability to configure page variations for pages in your site and then add these to specific users or audiences to create targeted digital experiences for your consumers. This resource explains what audiences are and how to use them, including a Trailhead learning resource, and things that you need to consider when using audiences when presenting content.
Manage Your Site with Experience Workspaces	Workspaces	Experience Workspaces are where you can build, configure, and manage your Salesforce Experience site implementation.
Which Experience Cloud Template Should I Use	Templates	When you build a site in Salesforce using the Experience Builder, you can choose from several Lightning templates to make the whole process much simpler and without code. This resource details all the templates available and how you can customize their components to provide branded, responsive sites for your consumers.

(*continued*)

Table 18-1. (*continued*)

Artifact	GitHub Ref	Description
LWR Sites for Experience Cloud: What is the Build Your Own (LWR) Template	Templates LWR	Within the choices of templates on offer for your Experience Cloud site is the LWR, or Lightning Web Runtime, template. This option is ideal if you want to build super-fast responsive sites using custom LWC components. Using this template means that you can move away from the SDLS (Salesforce Lightning Design System), to create fully customized experiences for your customers. However, there are some limitations that should be considered; for example, many of the standard preconfigured pages such as Knowledge and Account Management are not available with LWR, and these will need to be created from scratch. Review this resource to ensure you are fully informed before selecting this template type.
Customize Sites with Experience Builder	Builder	Once you have chosen the template that you wish to use for your site, you can use the Builder to customize further. Configure role-based access, add style to your site with themes, and configure settings like language support and security. This resource covers all these topics and more, as well as being a practical resource with Trailhead.
Improve Experience Cloud Site Performance	Site Performance	This resource introduces several topics all related to page performance for your Experience Cloud solution. Use the page optimizer to analyze your site and identify issues that require attention or review the Performance and Scale Best Practice guide, or set up a CDN (content delivery network) to reduce page load times. This resource contains lots of information that should be reviewed to avoid performance-related issues.

(*continued*)

Table 18-1. (*continued*)

Artifact	GitHub Ref	Description
The 360 Blog: What is a CMS / Salesforce CMS	CMS	These blog and Salesforce technical articles dive into the details regarding what a content management system (CMS) is and why you would use one and what you can expect from the Salesforce CMS system. In Salesforce, we think of the Salesforce CMS as a hybrid CMS, where content stored in the Salesforce CMS can be presented via the Salesforce WYSIWYG (what-you-see-is-what-you-get) tools, such as Experience Builder. You can also curate content across other channels using the Salesforce CMS Headless APIs. However, the Salesforce CMS solution does not replace your digital asset management (DAM) or enterprise content management (ECM) solutions. Review these resources to learn exactly what functionality can be supported.
Introduction to the Salesforce Lightning Design System	SLDS	The Salesforce Lightning design system (SLDS) is a styling framework that enables you to build, among other things, Experience sites that share the same look and feel as the Salesforce platform. The SLDS allows the development team to focus on application functionality and user experience rather than creating pixel-perfect sites. There is a lot to review regarding this topic, and the resources we have provided reflect that.
Access Experience Cloud Sites in the Salesforce Mobile App	Mobile App	One of your use-case requirements will be to access your site via a mobile app. Much of this topic will be covered in Chapter 19, "Mobile Solutions Architecture (Phase H)." However, this resource introduces the topic in the context of your experience site. Remember, the Salesforce mobile app does not support Experience Builder sites, so this will be an important factor to consider as you architect your solution.

(*continued*)

Table 18-1. (*continued*)

Artifact	GitHub Ref	Description
Mobile Publisher	Mobile Publisher	Mobile Publisher is a feature that Salesforce provides that enables you to create a mobile app container for your branded Salesforce app or Experience Cloud site. Then Salesforce can help you to distribute the app to either the Google Play Store or Apple App Store. This resource describes exactly how this can be achieved: how to build and brand, test, and distribute your app.
Securely Share Your Experience Cloud Sites with Guest Users	Guest User Access	Guest user access to public sites in Experience Cloud is a topic that Salesforce has made some significant changes to recently. This resource details exactly what can and cannot be supported in relation to an unauthenticated session. This is an important topic to review, especially if you intend to create a site that allows a guest user to access resources. Essentially, guest users can only have read access to records and can no longer, from Winter 2021, own any (new) records in Salesforce. Records owned by guest users prior to the changes implemented remain accessible, but you should work to protect these records and change ownership to comply with the wider Salesforce directive. It's important to review what this means for your site's sharing design as this could impact any Apex that you develop in support of your business requirement.

Phase G Standards

Salesforce Experience Cloud enables your organization to build world-class sites that drive your business process. However, how you design your site will largely dictate how successful your site will be. It should seem obvious, but it's not always a simple task, especially when your business process is complex and involved.

It's likely that your organization has established design principles that can guide how to build effective, meaningful experiences that are intuitive and fun for customers to use. This is a key part of your design and arguably is more important than the function the site provides its users. For example, if the site design is not well thought out or easy to use, it's likely that as time goes by user adoption will fade and you will need to redevelop aspects of your solution to try to win back customers. This can be costly and time consuming for your organization.

So, to avoid spending lots of time and effort developing a site that is difficult to use and turns your consumers away rather than engaging them some key principles should be considered. What we are referring to is the importance of having an effective UX (user experience) with an easy-to-use UI (user interface).

Note   UX and UI are two very different things. UX is the user experience, or rather the journey that your consumers will follow to complete the activity end to end using your solution. It also includes branding, support, and how users get the right outcome as intended. The user interface (UI) refers to the features, screens, and components that the user will use as part of that journey.

Table 18-2 provides a list of items that should encourage you to think more deeply about how you can design your sites with UX and UI principles and standards in mind. Ultimately, having a site with a good UX will serve to promote your business and leave users with a feeling of trust. Having the trust of your users will promote loyalty and a greater prospect of repeat business. Let's review these principles now.

Table 18-2. *Design Principles UX/UI*

Principle	Description
Put the user first	The challenge for designers is that there is always a business outcome that must be achieved. If the process to achieve the outcome is complex, it should not be evident in the user experience of your solution. If anything, the UX should be sympathetic to the needs of the user, and therefore the design of the solution should always center on the needs of the user. This is referred to as user-centered design. Firstly, document the business process in a sequence or flow diagram to clearly define the outcome that your solution must achieve. Then apply user empathy and begin to visualize how the user journey will work to achieve the desired outcome.
Conduct user research to elicit feedback and ideas about how to make your site a success	There's no substitute for getting information straight from the source. Why second guess what will work and what won't when you can gauge this from those who know best, the users. Crafting well-thought-out questions to ask users will be key to getting what you need. Also make sure that you choose users who can provide valuable input. Collate the feedback, analyze the results, and use this information to drive design decisions. The outcome of this stage should be a UX that achieves the business process but incorporates the user feedback and provides an easy-to-use UI with everything required to ensure that the user can successfully follow and complete the flow.
Ensure design consistency and ease of use	It's important to ensure that the flow of the solution is consistent across all screens so that your UX feels joined up and connected. It should seem effortless for the user to achieve the objective.

(*continued*)

Table 18-2. (*continued*)

Principle	Description
Always build prototypes and wireframes to showcase your solution	It's good practice that as part of your rigorous testing processes you create a pre-release version of the solution to canvas feedback from a selection of end users. This could be an online image-based prototyping tool like InVision that allows you to create a click-through flow of the solution with mocked-up screens that illustrate the UI design and the end-to-end user experience. Remember to keep the design simple, and do not over engineer the solution. Sometimes less is better, and therefore you should be ready to explain every aspect of the solution and available options in the design as part of your governance review.
Listen to Feedback	At this point it would be a mistake to not listen to the feedback that you have been provided as this could be the key to building not only a successful site that achieves the desired business outcome but also a UX that's well received and enjoyable to use.

Checklists

The phase checklist simply tracks that each step and sub-step within the phase is governed correctly and completely. Each sub-step may have several subject areas to form complete coverage from a governance perspective.

Governance Step	
Design	**Pass / Fail**
Govern the license types associated with the sites and communities	
Govern the sharing usage for partner, customer, and employee community users	
Govern the different UI / UX capabilities to style a community	
Govern the mobile considerations for communities	
Identity Management	**Pass/Fail**
Govern how identity management is handled within communities: provisioning, syncing, and de-provisioning	
Govern the use of external identity (Facebook, Google, etc.) if appropriate	

CHAPTER 19

Mobile Solutions Architecture (Phase H) Resource Base

This chapter contains the resources required to govern Phase H of the Salesforce Platform Governance Method. As with all phases in this resource guide, the approach we have taken is to assemble the most relevant resources that align to the corresponding governance method. Since you've been working through the book and using these resources, you'll know that although we have tried to cover all the major areas relating to this topic, as ever, conducting your own research in addition to examining the resources provided will really set you up for the dizzy heights of greatness!

Tip You do not need to use this resource base as a strict method or process; the idea is that this will give you a good indication of what you should be taking into consideration. The expectation is that you will use this as a guide and then build upon it as you navigate the Salesforce ecosystem.

Guidelines and Best Practices

This chapter provides a collation of resources that brings together guidance and best practices available from Salesforce, as well as other resources that we have determined will be valuable. The objective is to ensure that the information provided in this section will enable you to actively contribute to the governance process in your organization or simply enhance your subject-level expertise.

© Lee Harding and Lee Bayliss 2022
L. Harding and L. Bayliss, *Salesforce Platform Governance Method*,
https://doi.org/10.1007/978-1-4842-7404-0_19

We know there is an infinite number of resources available on the Web, and although some are better than others, this resource base will provide you with a good selection of resources that we recommend you review. As per all the resource base documentation in this book, providing the complete technical definition for every aspect of mobile solutions architecture is not the objective. Therefore, this resource base has been created with reference to the topics covered in the method that you will find informative and relevant. The resource base is divided into three main sections: the resources themselves and then related standards and associated tooling, and finally the supporting governance checklist.

As is the case with all the resource base chapters in this book, the links to the resources will be managed in the Salesforce Platform Governance Method GitHub account. The URL for this account is as follows: `github.com/salesforceplatformgovernancemethod`.

Mobile Solutions Architecture

Given that you have arrived at the resource base for mobile solutions architecture, we must assume that you have read the content in the governance method described in Chapter 9, "Mobile Solutions Architecture," and so the table of resources that follow will help guide you in relation to the content covered in the method.

In this day and age, it goes without saying that mobile applications are important. In fact, we would go as far to say that if your business does not have a mobile presence, then there is a good chance that your business could suffer badly. So, why is this? In the advent of powerful mobile devices' being accessible to just about everyone, the need to rely on your computer to manage your interests aside from normal work are over. The customer of today, rather than use a PC to manage affairs, wants the option to use their mobile device as their principal method of communication, maintaining a social presence, managing finances, and completing the majority, if not all, of all their online interactions.

Of course, generally, choosing to have a mobile app will depend on the type of business and the appropriateness of investing in mobile development given your user base. But for most businesses, it is crucial, in fact imperative, that you provide a mobile application that enables your consumers to interact with your products and services from anywhere at any time.

And now, the challenge we face as mobile app usage increases exponentially is to ensure that as we move to a mobile first way of life, that all our data, interactions, and downloads are secure and private. Our mobile experiences should be optimized, performant, and personalized for us in a way that makes the experience compelling, fun, and easy to use.

Salesforce is no different. For quite some time now Salesforce has been at the bleeding edge for mobile application options that enable Salesforce customers to use the power of the platform "on the go." Whether you are in the airport, in between meetings, or at a show, you should always have the option to respond to your customers, respond to that urgent message, or close that deal.

To enable this, Salesforce provides the Salesforce mobile app. This is the mobile version of the Salesforce platform, providing you access to the desktop apps that you use to propel your business. Salesforce also provides the mobile SDK, which your development team can use to create meaningful mobile applications using your preferred framework, and for your experience sites, it offers Salesforce Mobile Publisher. All of these options for Salesforce mobile applications are provided in the following resources.

Mobile Resources

The resources in Table 19-1 will help you to understand the technical aspects of the Salesforce mobile solution architecture and give you the knowledge required to support your governance process.

Table 19-1. *Mobile Resources*

Artifact	GitHub Ref	Description
Developers Blog: New Mobile Services for the Micro-Moment	Mobile Micro-Moments	This resource gives insight as to why mobile apps are so important to us; the idea that we check our phones on average 150 times a day seems a lot, even by today's standards. But it does raise a strong point, that mobile development and meaningful, beautiful applications are more important and relevant than ever before. This article discusses this topic and the micro-moment concepts as well as the available tools.
Salesforce Mobile App	Salesforce Mobile App	This resource introduces the Salesforce mobile app. The highlight is that you now have access to your Salesforce implementation via this out-of-the-box application. However, there are several limitations that need to be reviewed carefully against your overall business requirements. This may influence the mobile strategy and development framework you use to develop your mobile solution.
Salesforce Developer Centers: Mobile SDK	Mobile SDK	With the mobile SDK you can develop native applications for both Android and iOS; this is referred to as a native app. The Salesforce SDK also supports other development platforms as well, such as HTML5, hybrid apps, and React native. This resource goes into detail for each of the development options.
Trailhead: Develop with the Mobile SDK	Develop with the SDK	We have decided to offer this resource separately from the mobile SDK developer guide as this trail provides practical insight into each development option available with the SDK.
Mobile SDK Development Guide: About Native, HTML5, and Hybrid Development	Custom App Development	In Salesforce you can provide your user base a mobile experience using the Salesforce mobile app or by using a custom-developed mobile application. This resource focus on the custom application development options. Native, HTML5, or hybrid are all development options available to you via the Salesforce mobile SDK.

(continued)

Table 19-1. (*continued*)

Artifact	GitHub Ref	Description
Salesforce Mobile Development Best Practices	SFDC Mobile Dev Best Practice	This resource highlights numerous items that you should consider when developing for the Salesforce mobile app. This is by no means an exhaustive list but serves to cover aspects that relate to developing custom pages.
Mobile Publisher	Mobile Publisher	Mobile Publisher is a feature that Salesforce provides that enables you to create a mobile app container for your branded Salesforce app or Experience Cloud site. Then Salesforce can help you to distribute the app to either the Google Play Store or Apple App Store. This resource describes exactly how this can be achieved—how to build and brand, test, and distribute your app.
Mobile Application Security	Mobile Application Security	This resource delves into the topic of mobile application security, addressing the security concerns that may need to be considered as part of your governance process. Use this resource to understand and answer questions that relate to security for mobile applications. This resource covers many topics, including authentication, mobile device management, and connected apps, and includes best practices and troubleshooting tips.
Mobile Device Management (MDM)	MDM	Mobile device management is worth a mention specifically as many organizations use MDM software to manage, monitor, and secure company-owned mobile devices. MDM software allows you to control many aspects, including the applications that can be installed and basic device configuration settings. This resource covers the prerequisites for MDM for both iOS and Andriod and other aspects of how your MDM software works with the Salesforce mobile app.

(*continued*)

Table 19-1. (*continued*)

Artifact	GitHub Ref	Description
Identify Your Users and Manage Access: Send Mobile Push Notifications	Push Notifications	This resource details how Lightning platform developers can push notifications to users' mobile devices as business events occur. There are several requirements that must be met to support push notifications. These are all detailed in this resource, along with all the requirements for iOS and Android support.
Field Service Mobile App	Field Service Mobile App	If your use case is to support a field service implementation, then this resource is for you. The Field Service mobile app supports both iOS and Android. This resource goes into all the details for field service, including all the limitations—and there are quite a few—that your solution will need to consider.

Phase H Standards

In the previous chapter, we discussed the importance of establishing and applying UX/UI design standards and principles to your Salesforce Experience Cloud site. In this chapter, we again iterate the importance of design principles; however, in this context the focus will be on mobile app design principles.

With any application, you want a design that will keep users coming back to utilize the features your app offers. Considering the mobile aspect of this rhetoric, not only does your app need to look great and reflect the business it serves to promote via branding and styling, but also it needs to be responsive and performant or users will be less likely to return to it.

Performance is a huge factor on which application developers should focus, especially in this age of business consumerism "on the go." Let me explain what we mean by that. Let's say you are a desktop user; chances are that you have booted up your desktop device or laptop to do some work and likely have several applications open at once, and will be switching from one app to another as you go about your business. Although application performance is a critical factor for you as well, the end user may be that be little bit more forgiving as a desktop user should there be any app delays waiting for processes to complete.

However, on a mobile device it's more likely that the end user has opened the device to complete a specific task, and therefore if the experience is poor the level of frustration will be amplified because of this fact. So, the point we are making is that mobile application performance is probably the most critical aspect of your solution design.

Then there is the big question of which development process methodology should be used to produce your app. Let's first consider the Salesforce mobile app. The important thing to note is that the Salesforce mobile app is developed, built, and distributed by Salesforce. This could be a big issue for organizations that want to control how apps are represented and branded in the app store. The benefits, however, include a pre-defined user interface, and it is possible to customize the Salesforce mobile app in many aspects. This makes it an attractive proposition and can enable you to deliver with speed.

However, if you develop a native app using the Salesforce mobile SDK, then you can use multiple platforms and processes to design, build, and manage your app. For example, if you create a custom app, then the following platforms are supported:

- Native iOS

- Native Android

- React Native

- Cordova-based Hybrid

- HTML5 and JavaScript

Table 19-2 provides a comparison of the mobile architecture options available based on some of the common requirements that should be of interest.

Table 19-2. *Architectural Comparison*

Element	Native	HTML5	Hybrid
Graphics	Native APIs	HMTL, Canvas, SVG	HMTL, Canvas, SVG
Performance	Fastest	Fast	Moderately Fast
Look and feel	Native	Emulated	Emulated
Distribution	App store	Web	App Store
Camera	Yes	Browser dependent	Yes
Notifications	Yes	No	Yes
Contacts, calendar	Yes	No	Yes
Offline storage	Secure file system	Not Secure; shared SQL, key–value stores	Secure file system, shared SQL (through Cordova plugins)
Geolocation	Yes	Yes	Yes
Swipe	Yes	Yes	Yes
Pinch, Spread	Yes	Yes	Yes
Connectivity	Online, Offline	Mostly Online	Online, Offline
Development Skills	Swift, Objective-C, Java, Kotlin; JavaScript (React Native only)	HTML5, CSS, JavaScript	HTML5, CSS, JavaScript

Checklist

The Phase H checklist simply tracks that each step and sub-step within the phase are governed correctly and completely. Each sub-step may have several subject areas to form the complete coverage from a governance perspective.

Governance Step	
Mobile Strategy and Design	**Pass / Fail**
Govern the mobile solution for use of the appropriate mobile platform: HTML5, Native (iOS / Android), hybrid solutions, or Salesforce mobile app	
Govern the authentication / authorization (including SSO), offline storage, and sync requirements	
Govern the use of Salesforce mobile app declarative design	
Mobile Security	**Pass/Fail**
Govern how the project has secured the mobile application and its data, including offline data encryption	

CHAPTER 20

Development Lifecycle & Deployment (Phase I) Resource Base

This chapter contains the resources required to govern Phase I of the Salesforce Platform Governance Method. As per all phases in this resource guide, the approach we have taken is to assemble the most relevant resources that align with the corresponding governance method. Since you've been working through the book and using these resources, you'll know that although we have tried to cover all the major areas relating to this topic, as ever, conducting your own research in addition to examining the resources provided will really set you up to bask in the glory of ultimate achievement!

Tip You do not need to use this resource base as a strict method or process. The idea is that this will give you a good indication of what you should be taking into consideration. The expectation is that you will use this as a guide and then build upon it as you navigate the Salesforce ecosystem.

Guidelines and Best Practices

This chapter provides a collation of resources that brings together guidance and best practices available from Salesforce, as well as other resources that we have determined will be valuable. The objective is to ensure that the information provided in this section will enable you to actively contribute to the governance process in your organization or simply enhance your subject-level expertise.

© Lee Harding and Lee Bayliss 2022
L. Harding and L. Bayliss, *Salesforce Platform Governance Method*,
https://doi.org/10.1007/978-1-4842-7404-0_20

We know there is an infinite number of resources available on the web, and although some are better than others, this resource base will provide you with a good selection of resources that we recommend you review. As per all the resource base documentation in this book, providing a complete technical definition for every aspect of how Salesforce development and deployment is achieved is not the objective. Therefore, this resource base has been created with reference to the topics covered in the method that you will find informative and relevant. The resource base is divided into three main sections: the resources themselves and then related standards and associated tooling, and finally the supporting governance checklist.

As is the case with all the resource base chapters in this book, the links to the resources will be managed in the Salesforce Platform Governance Method GitHub account. The URL for this account is as follows: `github.com/salesforceplatformgovernancemethod`.

Development Lifecycle and Deployment

Given that you have arrived at the resource base for development lifecycle and deployment, we must assume that you have been reading the content in the governance method described in Chapter 10, "Development Lifecycle & Deployment." To help with some of the concepts described in the method, we have provided a table of resources that will help guide you in relation to the content covered in the method.

Whether your organization practices a waterfall or agile-based solution to delivery, documenting and understanding the aspirations of the business and translating that vision into a set of requirements is the first real phase of any project lifecycle. However, once this has been completed, the next challenge for the project team will be how the requirements are developed, and then once developed, how they will be deployed or released into the production environment.

Waterfall deployment is the project delivery methodology where each stage of the delivery process must be complete before the next stage can begin. Typically, this would follow the order of requirements gathering, designing, building, testing, and deploying. The resulting outcome for a waterfall-based method is that users can only use the new features once all the steps in the process have completed. Conversely, in an agile-based delivery, the requirements are translated into "user stories" and then added to a development backlog. The development activity is then delivered in short "sprints" or "iterations," which ensures that the end user can take advantage of features and functionality being delivered iteratively throughout the project lifecycle. The premise is that users will receive access to the deliverable early and therefore realize its value quickly. Then, as the remaining sprints deliver new functionality, the user can realize the additional value throughout the process as soon as it's ready. So, agile is a very attractive methodology to adopt, as essentially the sooner your users can take advantage of new features, the sooner the business can reap the economic reward.

This resource base will provide numerous links to resources that will enable you to consider many of the different processes and methods you can employ to tackle some of the challenges associated with development and deployment with Salesforce. Specifically, with development there are many aspects that an organization will need to consider to be successful. For example, which development methodology will you use? In more recent times, the less favorable option has been to release changes via change sets, whereas a more versatile option is package development and SFDX (the Salesforce Developer Experience product) with Microsoft VS Code and possibly scratch orgs.

Similarly, the choice of deployment tools at your disposal will also require consideration. The size of your organization and the rate of change and quite possibly the available funding may be significant factors in the tool you choose to use. For example, if you are an enterprise-sized business, your focus will more than likely be on automated test tooling, not just to handle activities like integration testing but also to manage the issue you will undoubtedly face with regression testing. Regression testing can take a lot of time and resources to process, so automating this part of testing can save a lot of time and allow you to focus your resources on more critical tasks. Then there is the tool or process that you will use to push code or metadata changes through the deployment pipeline to production. Which VCS will you employ, what branching and merging strategy will you use to manage and control multiple facets of change that are at various stages in the end-to-end lifecycle?

Many of the resources discussed in this chapter can help to guide you through the available options and introduce the concepts and topics that are relevant in the Salesforce context. Another example we should mention is environments, or having the right Sandbox strategy to underpin your deployment process based on your organizational requirements.

Development Lifecycle & Deployment Resources

The resources in Table 20-1 will help you to understand the various options and tools that relate to the development lifecycle and deployment topic that are available to you in support of your Salesforce implementation.

Table 20-1. *Development & Deployment*

Artifact	GitHub Ref	Description
Salesforce Architects: Development Standards	Development Standards	This resource is an informative guide into the topic of development standards: what they are, why they are important, and how you create and maintain them in your environment.
Salesforce Extensions for Visual Studio Code: Development Models	Development Models	This resource provides a technical overview and setup process for the two development models available: Org Development Model and Package Development Model. Org Development is used when you work with orgs that do not have source tracking, while Package Development does use source tracking and allows you to create self-contained packages that are deployable as a single package.
Trailhead: Learn Salesforce Agile Practices	Salesforce Agile Practices	This trail provides you with the basic concepts of agile delivery and why Salesforce adopted this methodology. Agile is more about mindset, a way of thinking that enables your development and delivery teams to innovate and respond to an evolving set of deliverables while always putting the customer at the heart of the solution. Review this trail to learn more about agile and how it works with Salesforce.
SDLC Waterfall Model	Waterfall Model	This resource explains the project methodology process known as waterfall. Waterfall delivery is essentially a linear, sequential flow of delivery stages that typically does not yield any value until the end of the project lifecycle. This resource describes each stage in the process and also describes the advantages and disadvantages of this model.
Trail: Build Apps Together with Package Development	Package Development Trail	This resource is a trail from Trailhead that covers the Package Development model. The trail is involved and gives you the basics with practical examples of source-driven development as well as strategies on test and release. The trail also offers training on SFDX and unlocked packages.

(continued)

Table 20-1. (*continued*)

Artifact	GitHub Ref	Description
Sandboxes: Staging Environments for Customizing and Testing	Sandbox Information	Sandboxes are environments that are available to Salesforce customers that enable you to build new applications, customize your org, and test new features without impacting your production environment or users. There are several different types of sandbox, each with its own limitations. It is good practice to have a defined sandbox strategy that defines what each environment is used for. It's also common for sandboxes to be used as part of the overall release pipeline to production. This resource explains the different types available, how to set them up, how to refresh a sandbox, how to manage them, and what resources you should expect in each type.
Salesforce DX Developer Guide	SFDX Developer Guide	This resource provides you a complete reference for how to use the Salesforce DX to develop and manage apps on the Lightning platform. Using this resource, you will learn how to set up a project and create a scratch org and source files, as well learn the entire development lifecycle.
Salesforce DX Developer Guide: Scratch Orgs	Scratch Orgs	A scratch org is an ephemeral Salesforce org environment that is source driven (meaning that it's built from your source control repository with only the required metadata). Once you have your version control system set up and your source organized into packages, you can then create a scratch org. Once created, you can start on your development project. This resource explains all the facets of how to use a scratch org, and how to create and push a source to and from your scratch org.
Change Sets	Change Sets	This resource discusses change sets. A change set is a tool that can be used to send the customizations that you make in one org to another org. One important thing to note is that when using change sets, only the modifications you make via the setup menu are supported. You cannot use change sets to move record data, for example.

(*continued*)

Table 20-1. (*continued*)

Artifact	GitHub Ref	Description
A Guide to Git (and Version Control) for Salesforce Admins	Git & Version Control	It's good practice for development teams to always master their code base in a version control system (VCS). This resource discusses the topic of versioning and using Git to maintain code versions, as well as why this is important in the overall DevOps context. VCS tools allow multiple development streams to occur at the same time using branches while maintaining the integrity of the master code branch or repository. Branching, code commits, and working with pull requests are all concepts discussed in this informative resource.
Git Branching Strategy	Branching Strategy	This resource explains the importance of and functional reasons why adopting a branching and merging strategy to manage and share code promoting collaboration within the development community.
Salesforce CLI Setup Guide	Salesforce CLI	This resource covers the Salesforce CLI, which is a command-line interface that simplifies development and build automation when working with your Salesforce org. You can use the Salesforce CLI to create and manage orgs, synchronize source to and from orgs, and create and install packages.
Test Strategy Made Simple	Test Strategy	This resource includes a video that covers the reasons why a test strategy is an imperative part of the agile delivery lifecycle, especially with regression testing. This resource serves to introduce the concepts and provide some best practices from industry professionals.
Salesforce Test Automation	Test Automation	The resource covers many of the test disciplines that we attribute to Salesforce, including the concept of regression testing, which is the test cycle that ensures that existing code deployed into your environment is not adversely impacted when new code is deployed to your org. Review this resource to understand why manual testing and automated testing are important and the reasons why we must do it.

(*continued*)

Table 20-1. (*continued*)

Artifact	GitHub Ref	Description
Best Practices of Salesforce Change management	Salesforce Change Management	This resource covers the nine best practices of change management and how they relate to Salesforce. Having a robust process to manage change in your organization could dictate how successful your change implementations are and therefore should be reviewed and applied in the context of your overall process.
Salesforce DX Developer Guide: Continuous Integration Guide	Salesforce Continuous Integration	Continuous integration (CI) is a development practice in which developers regularly integrate their code changes into a source code repository. This resource describes some of the common tools that are used to complete this integration.

Phase I Standards

Throughout this resource base we have provided numerous resources that will help you to successfully navigate the governance process that your organization employs. And hopefully along the way, you have been able to improve your knowledge and understanding of the nine architectural disciplines that have been covered in this book. We would like to emphasize that when all the disciplines in this book are put together, the resulting outcome is a well-structured approach to governance and ultimately a successful Salesforce implementation.

For this chapter, "Development Lifecycle and Deployment," the emphasis is on the methodology you adopt for deployment. The subject of development is important and has been covered in numerous chapters in the book; however, deployment is equally as important, as how you deploy your artifacts into production, the process you employ, will dictate the success of your project overall. Let's just think about that for a second. The project overall could easily be successful if the technical output works as developed. But how do you know if the outcome meets the expectations of the consumer? This is one of the major benefits of using agile. As you go throughout the iterative process you will be eliciting feedback from your sponsors and therefore be able to react to any change in requirements or solutions dynamically as part of the delivery process.

So, what else do we need to have in place to deliver the right outcome for our customers? In the method, the deployment pipeline, environments, source code repository, and roles required to execute the steps in the process were discussed in detail. However, in the resource base we want to provide additional insight into the tools that can be used to facilitate some aspects of the deployment process.

Let's review some of the tooling options available, starting with some of the popular automated testing tools that are used with Salesforce. Automated testing tools are used for several reasons, the main ones being as follows:

- Automating tests saves time and expense. Apart from the initial investment for the tool, and the time it takes to configure your test process, repeating tests using an automated tool will save time for the testing team and therefore is a cheaper service to operate.

- Automating the test process makes the process more reliable and accurate than tests completed by human testers.

- With automated testing it is possible to simulate a specific user journey and other aspects like performance; for example, how the application performs under load.

- Testing can be scheduled or event based. It can run to a defined schedule or execute when code is checked in by a developer. This can speed up the development process and ensure that any failed tests are recorded, and the development team can be notified of the test result.

- There are several types of test processes that can be automated, regression testing being the most popular; unit and integration testing are also valid test automation use cases.

Table 20-2 provides a list of the supported features for some of the common tools used for the purposes of automated testing.

Table 20-2. *Automated Test Tooling*

Feature	PROVAR	Tricentis Tosca	ACCELQ	Selenium
Source control enabled / traceability	YES	YES		YES
Point-and-click interface and admin-friendly	YES	YES	YES	Record Button (using XREF)
Point-and-click interface identifies elements with Salesforce Dynamic IDs (and not XREF)	YES	YES	YES	No. Uses XREF
Point-and-click interface supports Salesforce components Embedded tables and tabs Visualforce pages Service Cloud console	YES	YES	YES	No. Uses XREF
Point-and-click integration to receive and read email for E2E validation	YES	YES	YES	Custom development required
Lightning ready	YES	YES	YES	Custom development required
CI Integration – Run as step on CICD pipeline	YES	YES	YES	YES
Widely used in Salesforce ecosystem	YES	YES	YES	YES

Then there are the tools that are used to push changes through the deployment pipeline to production. A point to note here is that deployment and release are really two different things. When we talk about deployment, we are referring to the process of deploying the code or change element to each environment, terminating in the production environment. However, with release, this is where the code or change element is deployed to its final destination and is therefore ready to be released for customers to use.

There are many tools in the marketplace that can be used to facilitate your deployment requirements, but Table 20-3 highlights some of the more popular options used within the Salesforce ecosystem.

Table 20-3. *Deployment Tooling*

Feature	Change Sets	Copado	GearSet	SFDX
Tool Overview	This is the default Salesforce process for moving change from one org to another.	Provides complete deployment and release management. Supports static code analysis, data masking, and data deployment.	Provides complete deployment and release management. Supports static code analysis, data masking, and data deployment.	Salesforce Developer Experience tool, incorporating a command-line interface for development and environment management.
Maturity	Standard Platform Feature	Industry leader, excellent features and support.	Industry leader, excellent features and support.	Reaching critical mass, widely adopted and used, Salesforce invested
Architecture	Standard Platform Feature	Salesforce Managed Package, with Heroku processing engine	SaaS-based application running on AWS	Predominately command line
Deployment Tools	Via Salesforce UI	Fully UI based, full-featured metadata deployment support	Fully UI based, full-featured metadata deployment support	Use CLI or by using VSCode
Org Comparison	NO	Provides org to org and Git commits to org-level comparison	Provides org to org and Git commits to org-level comparison	Provides DIFF capability to compare metadata between local projects and your org
Change Capture	YES	YES	YES	YES, via CLI
Source Control Integration	NO	YES	YES	YES

(continued)

Table 20-3. (*continued*)

Feature	Change Sets	Copado	GearSet	SFDX
Branching and Merging Support	NO	YES	YES	NO
Environment Management	Not native to the platform	YES	YES	YES, dev hub and scratch orgs
UI Testing	NO	YES	YES	NO
Customization	NO	YES	YES	YES
API Integration	NO	YES	YES	NO

In conclusion, the tools that you employ to assist in the deployment of your code, metadata, and tests will be pivotal in how efficient your development and deployment process will be; however, it also depends on the size of your organization and the level of expertise available to operate the process. In all cases, however, source control is an essential shift from change sets, and agile a complete change in mindset from waterfall. The tools you select to assist in the delivery of your products to your customers should enable you to govern delivery and ensure a successful outcome.

Checklists

The phase checklist simply tracks that each step and sub-step within the phase are governed correctly and completely. Each sub-step may have several subject areas via which to achieve complete coverage from a governance perspective.

Governance Step	
Development Lifecycle	**Pass / Fail**
Govern the development and release of applications on the Salesforce platform	
Govern the testing strategies and test plan	
Development Techniques & Considerations	**Pass/Fail**
Govern the deployment strategy and the platform tools, use cases, limitations, and best practices for environment management and data migration strategy	
Govern the tools (source control and continuous integration for release management)	

Index

A

Apex, 141, 146

Apex/visualforce/lightning
    GitHub account, 336
    phase checklist, 350
    phase F standards, 346, 347, 349, 350
    programmatic resources, 336, 345, 346

API documentation, 329

API Interface Specification, 330

Application architecture
    advantage, 33
    areas, 13, 28
    complexity, 33
    definition, 12
    developers/app builders, 12
    files/social, 27, 28
    formal method, 28
    formulas, 25–27
    general architecture, 13
        apex batch element, 14
        AppExchange components, 20
        coexistence, 16
        context, 14
        customization, 14
        data access, 19
        data models, 17, 19
        data ownership, 21
        data types/sizes, 18
        discrepancies, 21
        duplicating existing
            functionality, 16
        goal, 14
        integration, 20
        key points, 14
        licensing, 16
        maintenance, 14
        objects, 17
        platform limits, 18
        programmatic functionality, 15
        project's longevity, 16
        record types, 18
        relationships, 18
        reporting strategy, 19
        resources, 15
        testing, 18
        URL field type, 18
    governance level, 13
    governance team, 33, 34
    inputs, 29, 30
    integration architecture, 32, 33
    localization/global deployments, 21, 22
    Salesforce platform, 34
    scenario, 32
    steps
        files/social, 31
        formulas, 31
        general architecture, 30, 31
        localization/global deployments, 31
        outputs, 32
        workflow/process, 31
    stock control system, 33
    technical options, 12
    whitelist approach, 28, 29
    workflow/processes, 23–25

L. Harding and L. Bayliss, *Salesforce Platform Governance Method*,
https://doi.org/10.1007/978-1-4842-7404-0

Printed in the United States
by Baker & Taylor Publisher Services